THE
Biotech
INVESTOR

THE
Biotech
INVESTOR

*How to Profit from the
Coming Boom in Biotechnology*

TOM ABATE

TIMES BOOKS

Henry Holt and Company   New York

Times Books
Henry Holt and Company, LLC
Publishers since 1866
115 West 18th Street
New York, New York 10011

Henry Holt® is a registered trademark of
Henry Holt and Company, LLC.

Library of Congress Cataloging-in-Publication Data
Abate, Tom.
    The biotech investor : how to profit from the coming boom
in biotechnology / Tom Abate.—1st ed.
       p.   cm.
    Includes index.
    ISBN: 0-8050-7069-9
    1. Biotechnology industries—Finance.   2. Pharmaceutical
industry—Finance.   3. Investments.   4. Stocks.   I. Title.
HD9999.B442 A2 2003
332.63'22—dc21   2002028765

First Edition 2003

Designed by Paula Russell Szafranski

Printed in the United States of America

1   3   5   7   9   10   8   6   4   2

Contents

Preface: *The Biotech Wave*

In sitting down to write this book, several times I neared the point of despair. How could I ever hope to see far enough into the future to craft a biotechnology investment book that would still be useful two, three, even five years hence? After all, biotechnology is a cutting-edge field. Even its practitioners cannot guess how quickly scientific theories will develop into marketable products—if they ever succeed. And then there's the stock market, the poster child of unpredictability. Stock picking, says Lissa Morgenthaler, one of many professional investors who advised me in this project, isn't just figuring out which are the best biotech firms. It's about figuring out what the herd *thinks* are the best companies.

During one of many such doubt attacks, I took a break from writing to indulge my favorite hobby, gardening. I was down on my knees, rearranging paving stones on a bed of sand, when it struck me that my task was very much like writing this book. I was trying to build something on a foundation of sand. Every time I tapped a brick here to level the walkway, other bricks jumped up and out of place. The entire bed of sand kept slipping and sloshing beneath me in slow motion.

Still, I persevered, and the reward came before I'd finished my walkway. The very thing that appeared to be my problem, this notion of shifting sands, really offered the metaphor to put this book into perspective. We all know that markets are cyclical, that they follow a wave pattern up and down. But biotechnology's wave is not a quick, wet slap of water on the shore. The biotech wave moves at the speed of sand, a speed consistent with the nature of the industry. Biotechnology is an experimental field. Only a handful of biotech companies currently have products on the market. The vast majority of biotech firms run at a loss during long development cycles aimed at proving their founding thesis. Experiments take time, and they often fail. Even when experiments have been done, and their results analyzed and presented at scientific meetings, biotech medicines undergo an excruciating process of regulatory review that can lead to approval, rejection, or demands for more testing. People used to joke about Internet time, the notion that everything in high tech moves at an accelerated pace. Biotech investing is governed by the opposite notion. In biotech time, development horizons stretch for years, even decades.

But like a sand dune, this slow-moving biotech wave can suddenly and treacherously collapse, crushing its followers. Anyone who's ever built a sand castle knows what I mean. You scoop a little sand away from the base, and nothing happens. Take another scrape, and still the edifice stands. Then you touch the wrong grain, and the whole structure tumbles down. Sudden, unpredictable collapses in stock price are the bane of biotech investors. A stock will be building in value, growing slowly over time. And you're patient. You aren't worried. You've learned to buy and hold. Then a report crosses the wire. A clinical trial failed to meet its primary endpoint. A government panel says it needs more safety data to make up its mind. Before you can react, that nice share price that took so long to build up has dropped 30 or 50 percent. As biotech hedge fund manager Kurt von Emster explains, it's not that investors aren't clever enough to choose a portfolio that includes several winners. The problem is that the slow gains of these winning stocks can be completely wiped out by an unforeseen setback on a single pick. "What kills you in this business are the bombs," von Emster says.

Yet once you understand that you're dealing with a slow-moving sand wave, you can begin to detect the patterns of a stock that's near its trough, and another that's cresting so strong that any bit of bad news could send it toppling. The professional investors and money managers whom I interviewed in writing this book have learned to surf this slow-motion wave. They've learned how to profit from the movement of the wave itself. I don't simply mean the slow accumulation of grains over time, which is the classic buy and hold strategy. Many savvy investors realize they must play the ebbs and flows of the wave itself, accumulating stocks when they think they detect a trough, and cutting back their positions and harvesting profit when they fear the wave could topple. If this sounds like a trading strategy, it is. One of the important lessons in this book is that you will have to learn to sell the very stocks you love—because your analysis of the wave suggests that you'll be able to buy them back cheaper at a later date.

Obviously, I can't look out ahead and see where the wave will be on a given day, which stocks will be ascending or toppling. But with the help of the many experts who've shared their experiences with me, along with my own years as a financial reporter covering the biotech industry, I can paint a landscape that will look very much like the scenes you'll encounter as you build your portfolio. I'll show you where to stand to get the best view of a wave, and how to detect the signals that have, in the past, pushed it one way or another. I will also give you an overview of the many specialized niches within biotechnology. The creation of novel medicines is the main thrust of the industry and the predominant focus of this book. But biotechnology is also being used to modify crops and breed animals with desired traits. Biotech tools are being applied toward the development of new industrial enzymes. One day we may walk down the aisles of grocery stores and see detergents with the words BIOTECH POWERED emblazoned on their labels. Biotechnology is an industry with an ambitious agenda. It aims to understand and change living things, whether this means reprogramming bacteria to produce protein medicines, or genetically altering goats so their milk produces a protein that can be spun into fibers as supple as silk yet as strong as steel.

Each chapter in this book will cover a different niche or investment area. The first part of each chapter will generally be devoted to scientific and business developments affecting that niche. The last section of each chapter will have a different purpose: it will focus on investing tips or strategies—for instance, how to chart the ebb and flow of stock prices around key scientific meetings. These end-of-chapter tips won't apply just to that niche. They'll be general tools to help you invest in the coming biotech booms. At the end of the book I'll review the tools in one place, and make some suggestions aimed at different types of investors based on age, risk tolerance, knowledge of the underlying science, and familiarity with stock trading.

At that point, as you begin to investigate investments, you'll have to add something no book or author can possibly supply—your own focus and motivation. Of course, you want to make money. But if that's your only goal, there are easier ways. Biotechnology isn't rocket science; in fact, biotechnology makes rocket science look easy. Achieving your goals as a biotech investor will demand extraordinary study and research. I can show you how to sort the stocks and pick out the most promising disease areas and technologies. But you'll have to do the hard work and make the tough decisions. The motivation for that sort of roll-up-the-sleeves investing will probably spring from something deeper than a simple desire to cash in on a hot industry. Perhaps your motivation will come from some special medical knowledge, or from a fascination with biology left over from courses you've taken in school. Or perhaps you've beaten a disease or know someone who has, and you've become curious about the industry that seems bent on tackling the root causes of illnesses. Dennis Purcell, a leading biotech analyst and money manager, switched over from high tech and began following biotech stocks after he was treated for a tumor.

Wherever you find the motivation to follow this complex field, take comfort in the knowledge that biotech is not a passing fad that will blow over like the dot.com mania. Biotechnology is the industrial expression of a powerful movement in the history of science, a movement that has already been fifty years in the making. Just as our command of chemistry and physics transformed the twentieth century, leading to profound innovations like televisions and transistors, so, too, molecular biology—the science behind the biotech boom—will reshape the twenty-first century. This powerful scientific current has arisen at exactly the same time as a rapidly aging population, both in the United States and abroad, has increased the demand for new medicines and diagnostic procedures. The convergence of these two trends—the maturation of biotech science and the aging of the population—are the forces that make biotech such a promising area of investment. There's one more reason many people invest in biotech. The companies in this industry are attacking the root causes of cancer, heart attack, Parkinson's disease, and other modern scourges. The careful biotech investor can do well—and also do good.

I

The Foundations of
Biotech Investing

In 1953, two young scientists made an obscure discovery that would profoundly affect the way we diagnose disease, discover medicines, raise crops and animals, and make every chemical from detergents to clean-burning fuels. Along the way this discovery spawned a new industry—biotechnology. But creating an industry was the last thing on the minds of James Watson and Francis Crick, the junior researchers at Cambridge University in England who published a scientific paper in 1953 describing the structure of the DNA molecule. They were focused on one goal, being the first scientists to unravel the mechanics of life, an insight that eventually won them the Nobel Prize.

Even then, more than a half century ago, scientists had a strong suspicion that whether the subject was peas or people, it was the DNA molecule, found in the nucleus of every cell, that transmitted inherited traits from one generation to the next. But how did DNA accomplish this trick? That became clear only after Watson and Crick deduced that DNA was made of four basic chemicals strung together billions of times in a shape that resembled a ladder that had been twisted around like a rubber band. In time other scientists advanced this basic discovery and cracked the chemical code locked up in the DNA molecule. They showed that DNA created RNA, and that RNA in turn created proteins, the chemical agents that perform virtually every task in the body, from the contraction of heart muscles to the firing of brain synapses. Watson and Crick were leaders of a new branch of science called molecular biology. This science developed the notion that living things were complex machines, in which DNA played the role of the master software. RNA served as its messenger to make the proteins that are the gears and levers of living cells—and the targets for new medicines.

This mechanistic view of life is the foundation of biotechnology, which has grown from a scientific curiosity into a fertile ground for investment. Headlines bear this out. Every day seems to bring reports of breakthroughs in understanding the human body and the promise of new medicines and treatments. Genes, stem cells, proteins: these were words rarely heard outside research centers just a few years ago, yet now they leap out from news broadcasts. Investment dollars have followed the headlines.

But publicity is only part of the reason for the surge in interest in biotech investing. The search for novel medicines is driven in large part by the demographics of the developed world. The baby boomers are creeping toward retirement; with advancing age they're beginning to confront arthritis, cancer, Alzheimer's, and other diseases. This phenomenon is not confined to the United States; Japan is fast becoming the world's most aged nation, and European countries are on a similar trajectory. The growth in the aged population in the developed world is creating a huge new market for medicines. The confluence of these two trends—the promise of revolutionary new treatments and the prospect of a growing need—represents the core rationale for investing in biotechnology.

Just what is biotechnology? The main thrust of the field is finding new ways to treat disease, and most of this book will be devoted to showing you how professional investors segment biotech firms into niches by the types of diseases they attack. There are the cancer companies, the heart disease players, and so on. Obviously there's overlap. Some of the more established firms may compete in several disease markets. But when comparing potential investments, the pros look at all the competitors in a given therapeutic market. This book will adopt that proven organizing principle.

But the biotech industry involves more than making new medicines. Biotech firms are constantly inventing new instruments and software for diagnosing illness and studying life at its most fundamental levels. In chapter 3 we'll explore the field of genomics (gin-OH-mix)—the study of how genes influence health and disease—and in chapter 4 we'll turn to proteomics (pro-tee-OH-mix)—a new niche that looks at the structure and purposes of the proteins that make the body work. Chapter 5 will look at the toolmaking sectors of the industry. If biotech is like a gold rush, the toolmakers are selling the picks and shovels of drug discovery. I'll show you how to evaluate toolmakers as potential investments and explain why their stocks cycle in and out of favor on Wall Street.

Of course, human beings are hardly the only living creatures on the planet, and providing medicines for their care is not the only goal of the biotech industry. Chapter 6 will explore how biotech firms have applied their science to redesign grains, fruits, fish, and animals to meet a variety of human needs—from creating rice with extra vitamins to cattle with leaner meat. Biotechnology is also beginning to create new materials and new processes, such as extracting ethanol fuel from agricultural wastes. In chapter 7, I'll help you understand the investment opportunities in industrial biotechnology. Chapter 8 will look at the newest niches, such as stem cell research. Chapter 9 will shift gears and look at the biotech industry as a series of regional and global centers of innovation. In chapter 10, I'll wrap up all the investment advice and get you started on building your own stock or mutual fund portfolio.

Biotech is a risky field. What else would you expect from an industry bent on exploring the frontiers of knowledge? The goal of this book is to help you minimize the risks of investing without discouraging you from jumping into a field that will boom in the decades to come. Unfortunately, there are many ways to lose money by investing in biotechnology—chasing momentum stocks, for instance, or buying into the hype that often accompanies initial public offerings (IPOs). Novice biotech investors make a basic error. They allow themselves to get dazzled by some company experimenting with a promising development, and fail to appreciate that it can take five or ten or fifteen years to prove whether the idea works . . . or fails.

My goal is to show you the mistakes that veteran biotech investors have already made so you won't have to repeat them, and to teach you the tricks that professional money managers use so you can make them part of your investing toolkit. It isn't possible to boil an entire book down to a few paragraphs, but you should start with at least a sense of what the savvy investor needs to know. The fundamental lesson is this—biotech is a marathon and not a sprint. If friends or brokers offer you tips about brand-new developments, pat them on the head very gently as you would a child and advise them to come back to you in two years or, better yet, four. Because the dirty little secret in the biotech world is that of roughly five hundred public firms worldwide, only a few dozen have achieved profitability—the benchmark that allows their worth to be assessed by standard metrics. The vast majority are early-stage development companies, whose stocks bounce up and down for years on obscure news events that filter out of scientific journals or meetings. Thus the risk in biotech investing isn't that you'll miss the next big thing or get in too late. Rather it's that you'll jump in far too early.

Once you realize this, much of the complexity that frightens investors away from biotechnology begins to recede. You needn't worry about keeping up with every new development. Most biotech firms have to clear a series of regulatory hurdles. Let the system weed out the losers for you. I'll show you where the pros position themselves in order to pick the companies most likely to achieve sustained growth and profitability. That's not to say you should never invest in a biotech firm before it achieves a profit. Opportunities arise in the middle stages of a company's evolution, when it doesn't yet have products or profits but it does have enough candidate drugs in development that the potential for reward outweighs the risks of failure. I'll show you how the pros decide when to hop on such stocks by evaluating factors such as burn rate, cash position, partnerships, management, and sales expertise. Finally, I'll show you how successful money managers combine two different invest-ing styles—long-term holding and short-term selling—in order to hedge their bets and improve returns, given the volatility that is inherent in the biotech sector.

To improve your odds, you must base your investments on some knowledge or insight that allows you to buy or sell ahead of the herd. I'll show you how the pros gain these insights by scouring the abstracts of scientific meetings for clues about the results of experi-mental medicines. If all this sounds like a lot of work, it is. Only rarely, during bubbles like the one that occurred in 2000, do biotech stocks shoot up on their own and make stock picking as easy as throwing darts at a board. If, after finishing this book, you decide you don't have the time or discipline to build your own portfolio, I'll suggest how investing in mutual funds can allow you to profit from biotech's potential with a minimum of work or worry.

Who should invest in biotechnology, and how big a share of their portfolio should they devote to the sector? The *who* is easy. Virtu-ally anyone with an investment horizon over five years and some appetite for risk is a candidate. If you're already retired, and looking for a place to park your nest egg while you live off the interest and appreciation, biotech isn't the place. But if you're in your forties or fifties and looking ahead to your own retirement or your kids' col-lege education, you should have some exposure to the sector. *How much* depends on your means and risk tolerance; 5 to 10 to 20 per-cent of your overall portfolio would be reasonable. People in their twenties or thirties might be a little more bullish about the sector because time is on their side. Time is the key. Only now, after decades of experimentation, are the early biotech companies generating sus-tainable profits. The new biotech firms that spun out of the Human Genome Project or those working on stem cell therapies are a decade or more away from becoming companies with products. But we know some of them will succeed because our aging population needs the new medicines that biotech firms are working to provide.

San Francisco financier Steve Burrill, who has been involved in biotech for over twenty years and today heads his own banking and investment firm, makes an observation that goes to the heart of what you should expect to accomplish by reading this book and taking its lessons to heart. Biotech, Burrill says, is one of the most inefficient capital markets in the world. A relative handful of analysts cover the sector's five hundred public companies. As a consequence, he believes many biotech stocks are either undervalued or overvalued because their worth is so poorly understood. In contrast, hundreds of analysts pore over every detail of the operations of the world's dwindling number of airline companies. This coverage makes for an efficient capital market. The individual investor is hard put to gain any insight that might provide a competitive edge in trading airline stocks.

Ironically, the fact that biotech is so poorly understood creates opportunities for the disciplined investor. This book will teach you the factors that move biotech stocks and show you how to act on opportunities. Even if you don't have degrees in science, medicine, or finance, like the professional fund managers, you'll be far more savvy than the herd investor who buys stocks only when they're in the headlines. In time, you'll come to realize that when the herd charges in, that will be your signal to trim or unload your position.

But I've jumped the gun. I've said where we're going before explaining how biotech got here in the first place. It's time to introduce you to Genentech, Amgen, and some of the other "blue chip" names you need to know as a biotech investor. Looking back at their stories is one of the best ways for investors to understand the industry today.

From Science to Market

The biotech industry was born in northern California in the mid-1970s. There, at the University of California San Francisco, and Stanford University, in Palo Alto, scientists Herbert Boyer and Stanley Cohen discovered the property that would turn DNA from Watson and Crick's scientific curiosity into the foundation of an industry. Starting in 1953, scientists around the world had been expanding their basic understanding of how DNA's four chemicals—A, T, G, and

C—carried the code for making living things. Scientists invented techniques for cutting the long, double-stranded DNA molecule into lengths like sausage links. Other scientists showed how to separate the two strands of DNA lengthwise, as if opening a zipper. Researchers learned how to isolate genes, the short stretches of DNA that carry the codes for creating specific proteins. In the 1950s, 1960s, and 1970s, scientists demonstrated with increasing precision how genes made proteins, and how proteins were the body's working units, the gears, motors, levers, and transporters that came together like mechanized Legos—at a molecular level.

All of that was interesting science. But it was a series of experiments done by Boyer and Cohen in the early 1970s that showed how to make products by manipulating DNA. The two scientists discovered that a gene snipped out of one species could be inserted into the DNA of another species, and once there the transplanted gene would still produce whatever protein it was originally programmed to make. This suggested that human genes could be spliced into the DNA of fast-growing organisms like bacteria. As the bacteria multiplied they would produce medicinal proteins, such as insulin, as a by-product. This radical notion caught the attention of Robert Swanson, then a junior associate at Kleiner Perkins, the venture capital firm that was already famous for helping found some of the great companies of Silicon Valley. In 1976, Swanson and Boyer started a company to use this genetic engineering technique to make medicines and other products. They named the firm Genentech, short for "genetic engineering technology."

It took Genentech scientists several years to prove that medicinal proteins like insulin could actually be made in bacteria. Once they had done so, the company was ready for the next challenge— convincing Wall Street to buy into this new way of making medicines. In 1980 Genentech floated the first initial public offering by a biotech firm. The next year, another northern California biotech company, Cetus Corp., filed a second IPO. Others soon followed, including Chiron Corp., the northern California company that eventually absorbed Cetus. Southern California's future biotech giant, Amgen, also took advantage of Wall Street's fascination with this

50 Years of Biotechnology

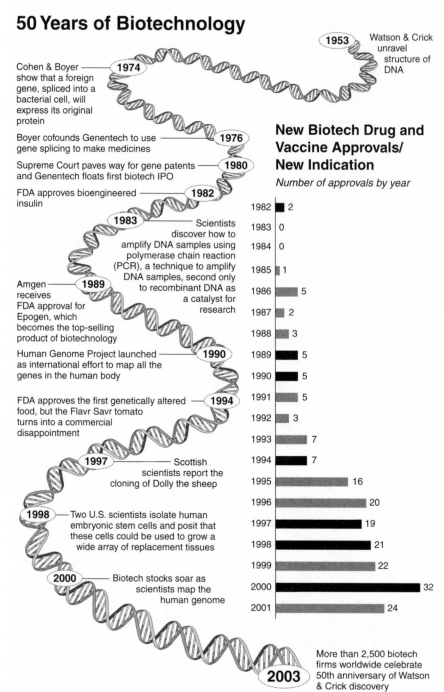

1953 — Watson & Crick unravel structure of DNA

1974 — Cohen & Boyer show that a foreign gene, spliced into a bacterial cell, will express its original protein

1976 — Boyer cofounds Genentech to use gene splicing to make medicines

1980 — Supreme Court paves way for gene patents and Genentech floats first biotech IPO

1982 — FDA approves bioengineered insulin

1983 — Scientists discover how to amplify DNA samples using polymerase chain reaction (PCR), a technique to amplify DNA samples, second only to recombinant DNA as a catalyst for research

1989 — Amgen receives FDA approval for Epogen, which becomes the top-selling product of biotechnology

1990 — Human Genome Project launched as international effort to map all the genes in the human body

1994 — FDA approves the first genetically altered food, but the Flavr Savr tomato turns into a commercial disappointment

1997 — Scottish scientists report the cloning of Dolly the sheep

1998 — Two U.S. scientists isolate human embryonic stem cells and posit that these cells could be used to grow a wide array of replacement tissues

2000 — Biotech stocks soar as scientists map the human genome

2003 — More than 2,500 biotech firms worldwide celebrate 50th anniversary of Watson & Crick discovery

New Biotech Drug and Vaccine Approvals/ New Indication

Number of approvals by year

Year	Number of approvals
1982	2
1983	0
1984	0
1985	1
1986	5
1987	2
1988	3
1989	5
1990	5
1991	5
1992	3
1993	7
1994	7
1995	16
1996	20
1997	19
1998	21
1999	22
2000	32
2001	24

Source: BIO

new frontier to go public during this period. California had no monopoly on biotech fever. Massachusetts, which had its own electronics corridor and venture capital network to rival Silicon Valley, gave birth to Biogen Corp. during the early 1980s.

Biotechnology excited investors because it offered a radically different way of discovering medicines. For nearly a hundred years, medicines had been pills. The most famous was aspirin, first sold by Bayer in 1899. Pill making was based on chemistry. Scientists found a leaf, twig, or mold that seemed to have some effect on an illness. They isolated the key ingredient in this natural substance and pressed it into a pill. Before biotechnology came along, drug discovery relied heavily on serendipity. Penicillin, for instance, was discovered in 1928 when a chemist noted that a mold, which had accidentally landed on a dish of bacteria, proved deadly to the microbes. Chemical drug discovery was a powerful tool in its time. Penicillin was mass-produced in World War II in time to treat soldiers wounded during the Normandy invasion. In contrast to the serendipity of the chemical drug discovery process, biotechnology, and its underlying science, molecular biology, were based on thinking about the body as a machine. Disease was seen as something that occurred when the mechanism got out of whack. To the new biotech scientists, curing disease seemed like a straightforward task of figuring out where the breakdown had occurred and devising some repair or replacement part.

What gets lost in the fog of time is just how little early biotech investors knew about the companies they were supporting, and how unprepared they were for how long it would take for these companies to deliver products and profits. The euphoria of the early '80s biotech revolution is summed up in an anecdote related by Andy Protter, a scientist who worked at a company then called California Biotechnology. Today it is Scios, and it got its first medicine approved in 2001, almost twenty years after its founding! Protter recalled one Saturday in 1982, when one of the company's early investors burst into the laboratory where he was working. The investor apologized for the intrusion, and said he didn't have much time to talk; he had to catch a flight to Singapore. But he had just invested $250,000 in the company and he had to know before he flew off—what did California Biotechnology do? Such euphoria is not just a thing of the past. It creeps up again and again, as it did during the human genome race in 2000. Biotechnology does not work quick miracles in science or the marketplace. The intelligent investor has to resist the impulse to follow the herd.

Throughout the 1980s biotech firms vied to use genetic engineering techniques to create proteins that could be sold as medicines. It was a challenging process that began with isolating a useful gene and then splicing it into some growth medium. (The industry started with bacteria but today companies produce therapeutic proteins in every vector from mammalian cells to goat's milk.) Genentech won the race to produce insulin for diabetics and human growth hormone for children with clinical growth deficiency. Amgen ultimately grabbed what turned out to be the biggest prize of all by isolating erythropoietin, the protein that prompts the body to produce red blood cells. In 2000 Amgen and its development partners booked about $6 billion in revenues on what is called Epo, which has long been the best-selling product ever to emerge from biotechnology. The success of Epo has, in turn, made Amgen by far the most valuable biotech firm as measured by market capitalization, the value of all the company's shares.

Science + Patents + Capital = Biotechnology

The technical achievements of the early biotech firms might have come to naught, however, without patent protections for the new biotech medicines. Patent laws had long recognized and protected the chemical pills developed by drug companies. But when Genentech was founded in 1976, it was by no means obvious that the courts would extend similar protections to the by-products of living organisms, namely the genetically engineered bacteria that produced medicinal proteins. The U.S. Supreme Court laid the groundwork for biotech patents in a 5–4 decision in 1980. That case revolved around Ananda Chakrabarty, a scientist who had altered a bacterium so that it would digest oil. His intention was to use it to combat oil spills. Though his invention never made a big difference in oil spill clean-up, the Chakrabarty decision set a precedent that genetically engineered organisms could be patented. The U.S. Patent & Trademark Office interpreted the decision as authorizing patents on genes and proteins discovered by biotech scientists. Just a few months after the Supreme Court announced the Chakrabarty decision, Genentech filed the first biotech IPO. The timing was no coincidence. Wall Street had been waiting for proof that biotech companies would be able to patent their inventions and protect their medical discoveries. Today, patents form the foundation of value for most biotech firms. Understanding the strengths and weaknesses of a firm's patent protections is an important, though difficult, aspect of smart investing.

While the Chakrabarty decision paved the way for the patenting of biotech innovations, other policy changes were encouraging the industrial formula that Genentech invented—partnering academic science with venture capital as a prelude to taking companies public on Wall Street. In 1976, when Boyer, the scientist, teamed up with Swanson, the financier, it was unusual for an academic to start a company. Academic culture looked down at industrial science. Those were the waning days of the Ivory Tower. All that began to change in the 1980s, however, when policy makers in Washington, D.C., grew concerned that factory closures at home and competition from abroad were eroding America's industrial base. Against this backdrop, lawmakers passed two statutes that, over time, have changed the nature of university-industry relationships in ways that continue to benefit the biotech industry.

The first was the Bayh-Dole Act of 1980, which allowed universities to patent inventions made by professors whose research was supported by federal funds. Most universities have rules that allow individual professors to share in any royalties that the university might derive from a patented discovery on which the professor is listed as an inventor. In retrospect, this policy change gave academic scientists an incentive to find practical uses for their intellectual achievements. In 1986, lawmakers followed the Bayh-Dole Act with a companion measure, the Technology Transfer and Advancement

Act. The tech transfer act spelled out how academics could take an innovation that began with federal funds, push it through the patent process, and hunt for venture capital to form a company around the invention. In retrospect these two laws, Bayh-Dole and tech transfer, have turned academics into entrepreneurs and have helped create hundreds of companies, not just in biotech but also in high-tech, telecommunications, software, and other knowledge-intensive fields. Some of the biggest firms in Silicon Valley, including Sun Microsystems and Cisco Systems, were spawned by developments that began at Stanford University. University of California scientists have founded dozens of biotech companies, beginning with Genentech and Chiron. Today, virtually every university has a technology transfer office that actively promotes inventions patented by its professors.

The biotech industry has been a chief beneficiary of tech transfer because of the nature of biomedical research. Medical experiments take time. Academic scientists have the luxury to explore new approaches because they enjoy extraordinary federal support from the National Institutes of Health. Over the last five years, Congress has doubled the NIH budget to an estimated $27 billion in 2003. The NIH supported the Human Genome Project, the program that fueled the popular excitement that caused the biotech bull market of 2000. In every way, from supporting basic research to promoting big projects like the genome effort, NIH support helps create a steady flow of academic discoveries, many of which become biotech products.

As all these policy changes fell into place in the mid-1980s, investors became intrigued with biotechnology and began to provide the capital needed to turn scientific theories into tested and approved medicines. The early biotech entrepreneurs were able to tap into the venture capital networks that built Silicon Valley and Boston's Route 128 corridor. Venture capitalists, or VCs, were comfortable with the notion of raising millions of dollars to fund risky ventures—with the hopes of making tens or hundreds of millions of dollars when they floated initial public offerings on Wall Street. Floating an IPO was the VC's "exit strategy," a way to extract a payoff by turning a private company into a public company. To this day, northern California and New England boast the greatest concentration of biotech firms, although other regions in the United States and Europe are emerging as strong competitors. I'll review these competing clusters in chapter 9, with an eye toward identifying interesting investment opportunities.

With ready access to capital, the first wave of biotech companies spent the 1980s trying to create novel medicines based on genetic engineering techniques. But as we'll see, this wave moved far more slowly than the hype around the industry would ever have led investors to believe.

Moving in Slow Motion

Although biotech entrepreneurs raised billions in venture and Wall Street capital during the 1980s, by the end of the decade the industry as a whole had just eighteen approved medicines on the market. A survey published in 2000 by the Pharmaceutical Research and Manufacturers of America (PhRMA), the drug industry's trade association, tallied the winning products. They included genetically engineered human insulin, based on Genentech's research but commercialized by Eli Lilly; two different forms of human growth hormone; and Amgen's home-run product, Epogen. Chiron developed the technology to create a vaccine against hepatitis B, and turned to Merck, the pharmaceutical giant, to get the product tested and approved for sale. There were several other products approved, but the real lesson was how long it took to go from concept to commercial product.

What the new biotech firms quickly encountered—and what investors must realize even today—are the two overarching realities of developing medicines. First, the U.S. Food and Drug Administration (FDA), along with comparable bodies in European and Asian nations, impose strict testing requirements before an experimental medicine is allowed to be sold. Second, even when approved, medicines rarely sell themselves. The large and rapidly consolidating drug companies have created huge specialty sales forces. These

13

sales specialists call on prescribing physicians in order to persuade them to use new medications. These twin barriers of winning approval for an experimental medicine, and then mounting a national or in some cases international sales effort, are the two barriers that bedeviled the biotech industry in the 1980s, and slowed progress in the field. During the 1990s, the biotech industry learned some lessons and picked up the development pace, getting another 125 medicines on the market. But to this day, an investor considering a bet on a new biotech firm must consider whether the company has the management depth and financial resources to run clinical trials and assemble a sales force. When the answer is no, small biotech firms end up licensing their best discoveries to one of the established drug or biotech companies—often accepting single-digit royalties instead of the big profits that shareholders might have expected.

I'll go into greater detail on the unequal partnering relationships between drug and biotech firms in chapter 7. Right now it's important to have a firm understanding of the FDA's clinical trials process. Clinical trials are the *main* hurdle facing biotech firms. But they can be your best friend as an investor, once you learn how to make the process work in your favor.

Despite the hype in news headlines and press releases, the odds of a particular discovery becoming an approved medicine are exceedingly small. The first serious step toward drug approval is the preclinical trial. Companies must test experimental remedies on animals to determine whether there are any toxic side effects that might make the medicine unsafe for human consumption. Although companies often tout the healing effects they observe in preclinical studies, the FDA doesn't care whether an experimental remedy work wonders in rodents—and neither should you. A successful preclinical trial proves only one thing: that an experimental treatment is safe for humans to try.

According to the Center for the Study of Drug Development at Tufts University, for every 250 compounds that undergo preclinical tests, only 5 go into human clinical trials. (Remember those odds— 2 percent—next time you're tempted to jump on a stock based on interesting animal data!) Those five lucky compounds get to "enter

Drug Discovery Timetable

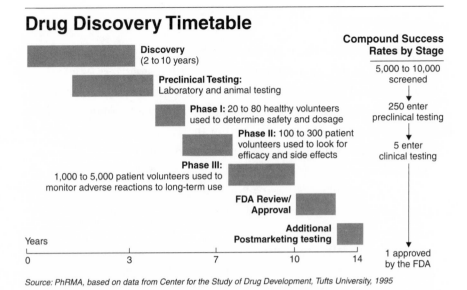

Discovery
(2 to 10 years)

Preclinical Testing:
Laboratory and animal testing

Phase I: 20 to 80 healthy volunteers used to determine safety and dosage

Phase II: 100 to 300 patient volunteers used to look for efficacy and side effects

Phase III:
1,000 to 5,000 patient volunteers used to monitor adverse reactions to long-term use

FDA Review/ Approval

Additional Postmarketing testing

Years

| 0 | 3 | 7 | 10 | 14 |

Compound Success Rates by Stage

5,000 to 10,000 screened
↓
250 enter preclinical testing
↓
5 enter clinical testing
↓
1 approved by the FDA

Source: PhRMA, based on data from Center for the Study of Drug Development, Tufts University, 1995

the clinic"—industry jargon for beginning the three phases of human trials that are prerequisites for getting a medicine approved. Getting into the clinic is an important milestone for a biotech company, but it's hardly a guarantee of success. Only one out of five experimental medicines that begins clinical trials is ever approved for sale by the FDA.

The three phases of studies get progressively more demanding and expensive. In Phase I studies, companies test medicines on a few dozen healthy volunteers to establish at what dose the treatment can be safely tolerated. In Phase II trials the number of patients can jump to several hundred—the exact size of the sample is negotiated between the company and the FDA on a case-by-case basis. Here the objective is to set the dose with more precision and to look more closely for any side effects. In a well-designed experiment, Phase II results can also provide the first suggestions of efficacy. Seasoned money managers often wait to see Phase II results before considering investments in young biotech companies. Phase III studies, often called pivotal trials, are the most critical and expensive stage of the test process. Thousands of patients can be involved, and the expenses of running the experiment can soar to tens of millions of dollars. The objective in Phase III is to show whether (and, if so, how

15

well) the experimental medicine works and to probe for any side effects that might not have appeared in earlier, smaller studies.

In a typical Phase III study, a company compares its experimental medicine against a placebo. It assembles two sets of patient volunteers with a disease. Typically, neither the volunteers nor the physicians who run the experiments know which patients get the treatment and which patients get the placebo. Trials of this nature are called double-blinded, placebo-controlled experiments. It's big news when a company "unblinds" Phase III data, and determines whether the patients who got the medicine responded better than patients in the placebo group. After unblinding Phase III data, companies generally issue a news release stating whether the trial has "met its endpoints," that is, proven whatever it was designed to prove. When a company admits that a Phase III trial has failed to meet its endpoints, the stock generally plummets.

But even when a company announces that a Phase III study has had "positive results" or "has met its endpoints," investors really can't relax. Companies routinely keep the details of clinical trials secret to deny their competitors any clues about how to design similar experiments. The FDA offers investors no help. The agency is legally obliged to respect the company's secrets. Therefore, it is up to the company to decide how much information to release about its Phase III data—and investors must decide based on management's track record whether this is an outfit that tends to hype results or provides the straight scoop. A terse release is not necessarily a sign of a management that is trying to hide something. Clinical trials are complex, and analyzing the data can take months. Savvy companies also try to present the details of Phase III studies at annual or semiannual scientific conferences, even if that means maintaining an air of mystery about the data, so that prescribing physicians can get the first look at the findings.

Setting aside the issue of what the data actually reveal, a company that announces positive Phase III results still faces two more FDA hurdles—an advisory panel hearing and a final decision by the FDA. The FDA often asks advisory panels of distinguished scientists to recommend for or against approval of a new medicine. Smart investors track advisory panel meetings, because companies are required to put their data into the public record on the day these committees meet. Investors can read the company's presentation on the FDA website and see what FDA staff scientists had to say about the results. (To learn more about the role of advisory panels and to obtain meeting schedules, visit www.fda.gov/oc/advisory/ default.htm.) A negative panel vote will usually send a company's stock plunging dramatically, but a positive recommendation generally merits a small rise. Smart investors know that the FDA usually follows the advice of its panels, but surprises do occur, and so there is always a risk of rejection until the FDA makes a final decision that a new remedy is safe and effective. It ain't a medicine until the FDA says it's a medicine.

Investing Tools: The Basics

Several years ago, Richard van den Broek, then an analyst with Hambrecht & Quist, an investment bank that specialized in tech and biotech ventures, prepared an analysis of what points in the development cycle offered investors the best risk-to-reward ratio. His conclusion was that when it came to picking individual stocks, waiting was the safest and most profitable course over time. He suggested that overall returns were best when investors waited until after a positive advisory committee vote or even until after the company had won FDA approval and started to demonstrate real earnings. Positive Phase III data is good but not necessarily good enough, van den Broek found. "The announcement of Phase III results is almost invariably done via a company press release and usually presents the data in the most favorable light. In contrast, at a[n advisory] panel meeting, the company presents a detailed review of all its data in great detail. More importantly, the FDA presents its own analysis of the Phase III trial data provided by the company. Often the data looks significantly worse under the scrutiny of the FDA. . . .

By waiting until after the outcome, investors can avoid the potential for significant losses that have brought the biotech sector infamy."

These were strong words, delivered by a respected analyst to the firm's institutional clients, including pension and mutual fund managers. All too often the record shows what happens when a biotech company gets hit by negative news late in the development cycle. In the summer of 2001, for instance, California-based Aviron (AVIR) sought FDA approval for an ouchless flu vaccine. Instead of being injected by a needle, the Aviron vaccine was designed to be inhaled through the nostrils as a fine mist. The company was hoping to launch the product in time for the 2001 flu season. But an FDA advisory panel raised safety questions and recommended against approving the novel vaccine. Aviron shares had stood at $40.80 before the advisory panel setback. On the next trading day the stock plunged 33 percent. In December 2001, as it became plain that the new flu vaccine faced significant delays, at best, Aviron agreed to be acquired by the Maryland biotech firm MedImmune (MEDI) in a stock swap that valued Aviron at $47.41 a share. Aviron had managed to get a premium for investors who bought the stock before the advisory panel meeting. But it certainly took them on a roller-coaster ride.

Trading versus Holding

Waiting for FDA approval isn't the only strategy for picking stocks—though it is the safest. Professional money manager Lissa Morgenthaler sometimes takes a riskier approach. She buys early-stage biotech stocks knowing full well that they could fluctuate 50 percent or more from high to low inside of a year. She makes money by moving in and out of these stocks. "People have been trained to think that high turnover is bad," Morgenthaler says. "But my turnover is an effort to reduce risk. I'm trying to make volatility work for me."

Beginners would be ill-advised to try timing the market. Eventually, however, successful biotech investors learn that selling is more important than buying. Smart investors recognize when hype has inflated the value of a good biotech stock, and they trim their holdings and harvest some profits—because they know they can often buy back the same company, at a lower price, after the herd has moved on. This seems to run contrary to the common advice to buy and hold. But with early-stage biotech stocks, the buy-and-hold strategy just isn't enough.

To see how buy and hold would have played over the 1980s and 1990s, I asked analysts at Nasdaq to calculate the share prices of some leading biotech stocks over time. If you had been lucky enough to have invested $100 in Amgen in the summer of 1983, your holding would have been worth $23,226 in the summer of 2001. That's a phenomenal return, almost on par with the performance of high-tech star Microsoft Corp. According to the Nasdaq analysts, a $100 investment in Microsoft in March 1986 would have been worth more than $34,837 in the summer of 2001.

But other leading biotech firms haven't delivered such astronomical returns. Genentech was wholly acquired by Roche, the Swiss drug firm, in May 1999. Roche then spun out part of Genentech to give it a new ticker symbol. But the first phase of the company's history ended with the Roche takeover. A $100 investment in Genentech in the fall of 1981 would have been worth $1,781 in May 1999. Biogen and Chiron are two other biotech pioneers. A $100 stake in Biogen back in March 1983 would have been worth about $1,001 in mid-2001. A $100 invested in Chiron in August 1983 would have been worth about $1,527.

These returns are nothing to sneer at. They represent annual percentage yields in excess of 13 percent. In recent years stock investors have come to expect 12 percent. So the biotech pioneers have exceeded that measure over time, in Amgen's case by a huge margin. But would you have bought and held only the four best biotech stocks, and ignored the larger universe of flops? Of course not. You probably would have picked some of the turkeys and ridden them right into the ground—and felt lucky if your Amgen returns brought your portfolio to break even. In chapter 10 you'll hear experienced retail investors tell you what I've just said. In fact I got the idea from them. For now, let me simply suggest that if you are a buy-and-hold investor, then focus on the handful of biotech companies that are already profitable. Their stocks move on earnings, and they behave very much like other companies you may already own. But if you plan to invest in the early-stage firms that compose the vast majority of the biotech industry, you'll have to learn, as Morgenthaler suggests, that trading can make volatility your friend.

Networks versus Niches

Many new biotech investors are refugees from the high-tech sector, and there are some lessons these newcomers must unlearn. High-tech investors are trained to look for companies like Microsoft, Intel, and Cisco that dominate their industries. Amgen is really the only giant in the biotech. Why aren't there more? The answer has to do with the difference between high tech and biotech. The high-tech world is all about networks. In the case of Cisco, this is easy to see: it sells the gear that runs the Internet. Microsoft has built a different network—a network of software developers who tailor their programs to run on Windows. Intel created a network of hardware manufacturers whose devices rely on Intel microprocessors. Ultimately, Microsoft, Intel, and Cisco have built the most important network of all—a network of customers so attuned to their style of doing business that competitors are virtually excluded.

In contrast, biotechnology is an industry of niches. It has to be this way because the body is so complex. Developing a new treatment takes years. When pioneers identify new areas, competitors have time to test different approaches to the same treatment. Consider the damage caused by stroke. No fewer than seventeen biotech companies are "in the clinic" with experimental treatments for stroke. The odds suggest three or four of these will eventually make it through the FDA review process and become medicines. But it's unlikely any single remedy will "cure" all patients and become the "Windows" of the stroke market. Medicines rarely work that way. Biotech companies often have to share.

Amgen is a singular case because it patented Epo, a protein medicine that is both widely prescribed and not easy to copy. Exclusive blockbusters of this sort have been rare in biotech, and trends suggest they could become even less common in the future. For

Biotech versus Nasdaq

After the collapse of 2000 bubble, biotech retains more of its gains.

American Stock Exchange Biotech Index

Nasdaq Composite Index

Source: Yahoo! Finance, April 2002

instance, cancer researchers now understand that there is not a single form of breast cancer or lung cancer. Instead, there are different tumor types within each cancer. A medicine effective against one type of breast cancer may not work on other variants. Genentech's Herceptin is a case in point. Breast cancer patients must take a test to see whether they have the type of breast cancer against which Herceptin is effective. This is an example of an emerging phenomenon called personalized medicine. The upside of personalized medicine will be more effective medicines with fewer side effects, and new diagnostic tests that should provide quicker paybacks for companies and investors. But the downside is likely to mean a further division of the market and even less chance for biotech firms to achieve the sort of dominance that Microsoft, Cisco, and Intel exert within the high-tech sphere. So biotech is likely to remain a market of niches. But don't be discouraged from investing. Just realize that the art consists of picking the biggest fish in some smaller ponds.

For more than two decades biotech has lived in high tech's shadow, but a comparison of two key stock indexes suggests that biotech may be rising in Wall Street's esteem. If you put the Nasdaq Composite, which is heavily weighted with high-tech firms, alongside the American Stock Exchange Biotech Index, it's clear that high tech led biotech through the '90s right up to the peak of the bubble of 2000. But, then, after the dot.com collapse and the market correction, something happened. Biotech retained more of its gains while high tech had a steeper crash. It's only been a couple of years since the market peaked, and there's no guarantee biotech will hold its position. But the sector seems to have emerged from the bubble onto a trading plateau that is much higher than where the sector stood just a few years ago. And there are many good reasons why growth investors are placing higher values on companies that invent medicines. In fact, if you're getting older, you may be one of the reasons why biotech is coming into its own.

2

The Age Wave and the Market for New Medicines

S o why would anyone put money into an industry in which products can take a decade or more to develop, hidden problems can erupt in the middle of costly experiments, and government regulators can decide at the end of the line that the medicine isn't up to FDA standards? The answer is easy. Winning makes the risk worthwhile. For decades, drug companies have been among the world's most profitable companies in rankings done by *Fortune* magazine. Part of the reason for this is margins that can reach 90 percent. Medicines are among the highest-margin products ever made. That only makes sense. The costs of making drugs are largely front-loaded into the research and development stages. By the time the medicine is approved, the cost of manufacture, sales, and distribution are often negligible by comparison to the risks and expenses already undertaken.

These profits have not escaped the notice of critics, and investors should be aware that, periodically, political pressure will rise to control drug prices. So far industry lobbyists have persuaded lawmakers that the current profits are necessary to offset the risks of drug development, and that any form of government-imposed price controls would wreck the U.S. capital markets that underwrite drug and biotech development. The *2001 Pharmaceutical Industry Profile*, published by the industry's main lobby group, states: "Standard

23

accounting measures of profitability, such as those quoted in *Fortune* magazine, are not an accurate reflection of the profitability of research-based pharmaceutical companies" because those rankings don't take into account up-front research costs. Any change in the status quo, and most particularly any action that suggests government price setting, would greatly upset the investment landscape, at least in the short term. For the foreseeable future, however, drugs—and by extension biologics—should retain their current and quite attractive profit profile.

But premium pricing is not the prime attraction to biotechnology. The most important reason by far for taking a strong investment position in biotechnology is the conviction that the market for medicines will greatly expand over the next twenty years as the people in the demographic bulge known as the baby boom reach their sixties, seventies, eighties, and beyond. Dan Perry, executive director of the Alliance for Aging Research, a not-for-profit think tank in Washington, D.C., sketches out the shape of things to come: "We know what the size of the baby boom is now and we know that it will reach its peak in 2029." Today there are about 35 million people over age sixty-five. In 2029, when the last baby boomers reach age sixty-five, there will be 60 to 75 million people in the retirement bracket. Half of these future seniors will be age seventy-five or over. In past decades this post-seventy-five age group has experienced the greatest surge in medical spending, according to Perry.

Ironically, although we have an excellent idea of when the age wave will hit and how large it will be, hard numbers don't exist on where drug spending will be twenty years from now, Perry says. Part of the reason for this is political. Congress continues to work on adding a prescription drug benefit to the Medicare program, and long-term estimates of drug expenditures will depend on the unforeseeable details of future federal spending. It's an open secret in Washington, D.C., that Congress doesn't particularly want to look too far into the future, because costs will loom so large once the boomers begin to retire that lawmakers cannot envision how to balance a budget that includes Medicare payments for drugs.

But there are also sensible reasons for not projecting too far

The Aging of the U.S. Population

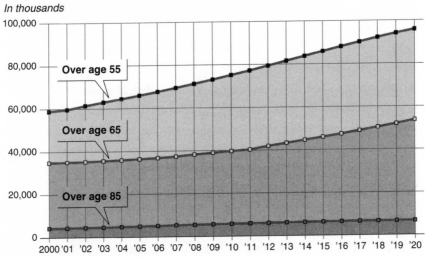

In thousands

Over age 55

Over age 65

Over age 85

Source: Census Bureau, Population Projections

Aging: A Worldwide Phenomenon

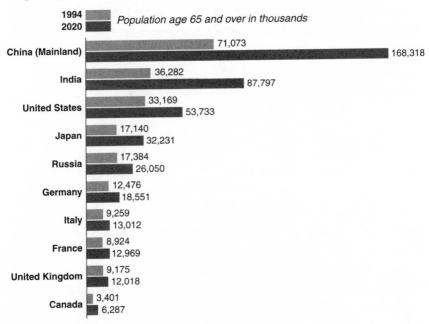

1994
2020

Population age 65 and over in thousands

	1994	2020
China (Mainland)	71,073	168,318
India	36,282	87,797
United States	33,169	53,733
Japan	17,140	32,231
Russia	17,384	26,050
Germany	12,476	18,551
Italy	9,259	13,012
France	8,924	12,969
United Kingdom	9,175	12,018
Canada	3,401	6,287

Source: Census Bureau, International Data Base

ahead. New medicines may not add to the current overall cost of medical care. Therapies on the horizon may replace institutional or surgical care—at lower expense to the health system. Richard van den Broek, the former biotech analyst who now helps manage a biotech hedge fund, gives this example: There are about 4 million people with Alzheimer's in the United States and about half of these have severe dementia that requires some form of institutionalization; the average cost of custodial care is about $40,000 a year. "If someone were to charge $10,000 a year for an Alzheimer's drug that kept people at home and improved their quality of life, it would be one of the biggest drugs of all times and a huge cost savings for the whole system," he says. In 2002 there were twenty-three medicines in clinical trials for Alzheimer's, and roughly half were in Phase III. At least a handful of these Alzheimer's hopefuls will survive the FDA's hurdles and make their way onto a market that currently has few means short of institutionalization to deal with severe memory loss. "There is no more valuable commodity in the health care sector than a new drug that meets an unmet medical need," says van den Broek.

Here in a nutshell is the central rationale for biotech investment. You'll need to memorize and repeat it when short-term market fluctuations make you question your sanity. *An aging population has arisen at just the time when an increasingly sophisticated biotech industry has aimed itself at unmet medical needs.* Although we can't look too far ahead with any certainty, recent history corroborates the notion that prescription medicines are on an age-driven, long-term climb. In 2000, the Henry J. Kaiser Family Foundation, a nonprofit health research institute in California, looked back at forty years of prescription drug expenditures. Between 1960, when national spending for prescription drugs totaled $3 billion, and 1998, the last year for which full figures were available, spending for doctor-issued medicines rose thirtyfold to $91 billion. The study projected that by 2008, national prescription drug spending would reach $243 billion. Demographics clearly play a driving role in the Kaiser analysis, which says increased use of medicines doesn't simply begin at retirement. "The population aged 45 and older is of particular interest, because at age 45 chronic conditions tend to surface and the potential for treatment with prescribed medications increases. Between the age of 45 and 75 prescription use nearly triples (from an overall average of 4.3 to 11.4 prescriptions per person annually)."

One phrase in the Kaiser assessment bears repeating: "the potential for treatment with prescribed medications increases." Age isn't the only factor driving this "potential for treatment." Biotech firms are working hard at devising remedies for maladies that could never before have been treated medicinally. Perry, with the Alliance for Aging Research, puts it this way: "Health care is increasingly being delivered in something that looks like a drug and moving away from physician's services and hospitalization. New drugs open up new treatments." Every aspect of health, from high cholesterol to obesity to depression, is now either being treated with medicines or is a target for experimental remedies.

In this chapter we'll look at treatments for cancer, heart disease, and central nervous system disorders. In the next several sections I'll show you how to pick investment targets by looking at disease areas. Specialization by disease is one way that professional money managers improve the quality of their research and thereby reduce some of the risks inherent in biotech investing. The human body, and our attempts to cure its many ills, is far too complex for any one person to comprehend. This is especially true for part-time investors who lack the resources and training of the professionals. To improve your odds of success, you'll have to narrow the universe of stocks you're willing to consider. Becoming a disease specialist is probably the best strategy for the novice. In each therapeutic area you'll find several companies in late-stage clinical trials, which makes them more predictable and therefore more attractive as potential investments.

When we discuss the various biotech niches, whether it's cancer in this chapter, or genomics or proteomics in later chapters, we can touch on only a few companies that represent the trends in each specialty. For a more complete look at the competing firms in each specialty, please consult Appendix II. It lays out the niches that are generally recognized by the investment community and lists the companies in each. This breakdown was created by the *BioCentury* trade newsletter, which updates the listings on a regular basis as companies redefine themselves. So be prepared for new competitors to appear over time, and for current competitors to disappear. Appendix II provides only the names of the companies in each niche. Use it in conjunction with Appendix I, which is an alphabetical list of biotech firms also compiled by *BioCentury*. Appendix I lists each company's stock ticker symbol and a few other details to help get you started in doing further investment research.

The Cancer Market

The single largest category of biotech medicines are those directed against various forms of cancer. In an analysis done in 2001, the Pharmaceutical Research and Manufacturers of America analyzed this key market and found that 170 companies had 402 experimental anticancer medicines in development. Of these, 68 were aimed at lung cancer, which is the leading cause of cancer death. Another 59 were aimed at breast cancer, which affects one in every ten women. There were 55 experimental remedies targeting colon cancer, and 52 others directed at prostate cancer, two conditions with a high prevalence among men.

More than thirty years after America first declared war on cancer, a cure still remains elusive. According to the American Cancer Society, about 1.2 million Americans were diagnosed with cancer in 1999, and more than five hundred thousand people died from cancers. These unfortunate facts have fueled sales of anticancer medicines. Jason Zhang, an analyst with the Stephens Inc. investment bank, has estimated the 2002 worldwide anticancer market at $14.6 billion. Zhang believes several factors make the cancer market particularly attractive for biotech investors. The first is the aging of the population in the United States and the rest of the developed world. That will almost assuredly result in more cases of cancer. New screening methods and diagnostic techniques are also catching cancer earlier. This means patients are likely to use medications over longer periods. Finally, new biotech remedies under development promise to have fewer side effects than treatments such as chemotherapy, so patients will be able to tolerate these longer stints on medication. "Therefore," Zhang wrote in a 2002 report, "we foresee the U.S. and global anticancer drug market growing at an average per annum growth rate larger than 15 percent going into the next decade, with the biological anticancer drug market growing at a rate larger than 20 percent."

With more than one hundred publicly traded biotech companies developing drugs for cancer, it helps to break this huge market into several smaller niches based on the strategy used to fight the cancer. Let's look at three cancer fighting strategies—antibodies, vaccines, and anti-angiogenesis—then follow with a few other tips about becoming a cancer investment specialist.

Investing in Antibodies

Antibodies are the natural disease-fighting agents of our immune systems. Antibodies have been described as guided missiles because they bind to specific targets on the surfaces of diseased cells. Investors got excited during the 1980s when biotech firms first proposed designing so-called monoclonal antibodies to unerringly seek out and destroy cancers and other diseases. But this was a lot easier said than done. The first antibody finally reached the market in 1998, when IDEC Pharmaceuticals (IDPH) and Genentech (DNA) won FDA approval for the anticancer antibody Rituxan. Genentech followed that success in 1999 by winning FDA approval for Herceptin, the antibody designed to fight a certain form of breast cancer. If investors ever needed a reminder of the time lag between the promise and the product in biotechnology, antibodies are the case in point.

Now, however, antibody technology is a mature field. Biotech scientists know how to make therapeutic antibodies. FDA officials know how to evaluate their safety and efficacy. Today when you come across an interesting company with an antibody medicine— whether it's for cancer or anything else—you can't simply assume it's a winner. But you have at least some assurance that it's a proven

29

technology with a shot at success. At present, about fifty therapies in clinical trials against cancer use some form of antibody therapy. If you decided to specialize in cancer antibody companies you'd have a large universe of late-stage investment options.

The long delay in winning FDA approval for antibody therapies stemmed from the fact that at first biotech companies took antibodies from mice and tried to use them to fight human diseases. The human immune system saw these mice antibodies as foreign invaders, and attacked the very things that were supposed to be medicines. In recent years, Protein Design Labs (PDLI), Abgenix (ABGX), and Medarex (MEDX) have found ways to make antibodies that were either humanized (they still contain a few mouse parts but not enough to trigger an immune reaction) or fully human. These human or humanized antibodies minimize immune system side effects, raise fewer safety concerns, and speed up the FDA review process. Protein Design, Abgenix, and Medarex are developing their own antibody medicines and have also licensed their technology for making antibodies to other biotech firms. Protein Design, Abgenix, Medarex, Genentech, and IDEC are all candidates for inclusion in a portfolio of cancer-fighting biotech firms.

IDEC Pharmaceuticals broke new ground in February 2002 when the FDA approved Zevalin, an antibody with a novel approach to treating low-grade, non-Hodgkin's lymphoma (a class of cancers that develop in the lymph nodes). IDEC took a mouse antibody and armed it with a dose of the radioisotope Yttrium-90. The antibody zeroes in on the cancer cell and delivers the radioactive charge designed to kill the cancer. IDEC deliberately chose mouse antibodies to deliver the payload because it wanted the patient's immune system to flush out Zevalin antibodies after a few days, to minimize any unwanted damage that might be caused by residual radioactivity.

Other companies are trying to follow in IDEC's footsteps, by creating antibodies armed with radioactive or chemotherapeutic payloads. So far, however, they have been rebuffed by the FDA, giving investors another reminder that novel therapies face extraordinary regulatory scrutiny. A case in point is Corixa (CRXA), a Seattle biotech firm that has been trying to win approval for Bexxar, a monoclonal antibody armed with a radioactive charge and designed to treat low-grade, non-Hodgkin's lymphoma. In March 2002, the FDA told Corixa that it had not presented enough evidence to warrant an FDA review of Bexxar, but in June the FDA reversed itself and said it would take another look at the therapy. Meanwhile, Corixa has had legal troubles with Bexxar. Its medicine sounds a lot like IDEC's Zevalin, and the two firms have been embroiled in a patent dispute. Patents allow inventors to control the use of inventions. Unless they settle out of court, Corixa and IDEC will have to go to trial to decide which company controls the technology for arming an antibody with a cancer-killing payload.

Finally, no discussion of cancer antibody companies would be complete without mentioning ImClone Systems, a New York biotech firm whose saga offers many lessons for investors. ImClone's most promising development has been an antibody therapy called Erbitux, which has been in clinical trials to treat a variety of tumor types. In February 2001 the FDA promised ImClone a speedy review of its bid to sell Erbitux to treat colorectal cancer. This is the sort of regulatory milestone that moves a stock. At the time, ImClone had been trading around $40 a share, and its price rose in the ensuing months as ImClone released encouraging data from late-stage clinical trials of Erbitux. In September 2001, when ImClone was trading in the mid-$50s, the New York drug firm Bristol-Myers Squibb paid $1 billion for a 20 percent stake in ImClone. The deal was a huge validation for Erbitux, the sort of insider endorsement that catches the attention of investors.

In early December 2001 ImClone shares peaked around $70—just before the Erbitux story began to unravel. On December 28, ImClone announced that the FDA had decided not to accept its application to sell Erbitux. In January and February 2002, its shares plunged as low as $15 when ImClone became the center of allegations that then–chief executive Samuel D. Waksal engaged in insider trading. Questions were also raised about Martha Stewart, a friend of Waksal who sold her ImClone shares just before the bad news broke. The stock has recovered somewhat since then, and Erbitux could still end up being approved as a cancer treatment. But ImClone is almost a parable for the riskiness of biotech investing. The company seemed to have everything going for it in 2001. The FDA had agreed to a speedy review of Erbitux. A big drug company had sanctioned the deal. And yet it all fell apart, and investors still don't know exactly what happened or how this whole affair will end. If there's a lesson here, it's that nothing is certain until after the FDA has approved a medicine.

Investing in Cancer Vaccines

Most people think of vaccines as preventing diseases, but in the cancer setting, biotech firms are developing vaccines designed to "teach" the immune system how to fight tumors. The body has mechanisms to destroy wayward cells. Cancers occur when cells evade these regulatory processes and run amok. In order to grow, tumors develop stealth techniques to evade the immune system, which normally helps detect and destroy cells that behave inappropriately. Cancer vaccines attempt to make these stealthy tumor cells visible to the immune system once again so the body's self-defense system can attack them.

Cancer vaccines are a promising but unproven therapy. The pioneering firms won't find it easy to win FDA approval for what remains an experimental approach to fighting cancer. Still, the potential is so huge that investors should pay attention. Coupled with early detection, cancer vaccines hold the promise of creating powerful therapies without the debilitating side effects of surgery and chemotherapy. For conditions such as pancreatic cancer, where few alternatives currently exist, vaccines would serve an unmet need. The trick for investors is not to get so blinded by the promise as to lose sight of the hurdles. Again the sensible approach is to focus on the companies in later-stage clinical trials:

- Avi BioPharma (AVII) is developing an experimental vaccine called Avicine. A Phase III clinical trial is under way to test Avicine against colorectal cancer. The company has also undertaken Phase II studies to test Avicine against pancreatic and prostate cancers. Avicine is designed to teach the immune system to recognize human chorionic gonadotropin (hGC), a hormone present on the surface of many types of cancer cells. Scientists believe that hGC helps cancer cells invade surrounding tissues. Avicine consists of a portion of the hGC molecule joined to a bit of diphtheria vaccine. By joining these two molecules, Avi BioPharma hopes the immune system will recognize the hGC present on cancer cells and attack them.

- Cell Genesys (CEGE) is testing its GVAX compound against a variety of cancers. The company is poised for Phase III trials against lung cancer. It has also undertaken Phase II studies testing GVAX on prostate and pancreatic cancers, as well as leukemia and myeloma (cancers of the blood). GVAX consists of tumor cells that have been genetically engineered to express a hormone known to stimulate the immune system. These bioengineered tumor cells are then irradiated to prevent them from replicating, and injected into the patient. In theory, these irradiated cells will cause the immune system to attack anything that looks like them, i.e., the cancer cells.

- Corixa (CRXA) won Canadian government approval in 2001 for Melacine, a vaccine to treat melanoma (skin cancer). Corixa has said it hopes to win FDA approval to sell Melacine in the United States, but as of mid-2002 the company and the FDA were still in discussions over what Corixa calls "the future regulatory path of Melacine."

- Titan Pharmaceuticals (TTP) has attracted support from the National Cancer Institute to conduct Phase III studies of CeaVac, a vaccine aimed at colorectal cancer. The vaccine, which targets a feature on the surface of certain types of tumor cells, is also in Phase II tests against lung cancer.

- Progenics Pharmaceuticals (PGNX) is in Phase III tests of GMK, an experimental vaccine that targets melanoma.

Investing in Anti-Angiogenesis

In order to grow, solid tumors need access to a supply of blood. The process by which the body develops new blood vessels is called angiogenesis. The notion of fighting cancers by choking off their blood supply is known as anti-angiogenesis. This term burst into the public consciousness several years ago after an unduly optimistic *New York Times* report about how noted cancer researcher Dr. Judah Folkman had choked off tumor growth in mice using experimental compounds that interfered with angiogenesis. Folkman's experimental agents, endostatin and angiostatin, were licensed to the biotech firm EntreMed (ENMD). In a lesson about the power of news to drive stock prices, shares of EntreMed soared from $12 to $50 immediately after the *Times* report. But the stock didn't stay there, and ever since EntreMed's share price has bounced around on positive or negative news.

A number of firms in addition to EntreMed are pursuing anti-angiogenesis strategies against cancer:

- Aeterna Laboratories (AELA) is a Canadian company testing whether Neovastat, a compound derived from shark cartilage, can cut off blood flow to a variety of cancers. Results from a Phase III clinical trial on kidney cancer and a Phase II trial on myeloma are scheduled to be announced in 2003. Final results from a Phase III clinical trial on lung cancer are slated for a 2005 announcement.

- Celgene Corp. (CELG) is trying to prove that Thalidomide, the drug that became infamous for causing birth defects during the 1960s, can halt tumor growth. The company's compound, called Thalomid, received FDA approval in 1998 to treat leprosy. Phase II clinical trials are now under way to see whether Thalomid can treat kidney, lung, liver, prostate, and skin cancers, as well as multiple myeloma, leukemia, and glioblastoma (brain cancer). As might be imagined, FDA safety scrutiny will be intense, but wouldn't it be amazing (not to mention lucrative) if this pharmaceutical pariah proves to be a cancer killer!

- Genentech (DNA) is in the late stages of testing an anti-angiogenic agent called Avastin. Investors should know by early 2003 whether Avastin is revealed to be safe and effective in Phase III tests against metastatic breast cancer. Says cancer analyst Jason Zhang: "If it works, it will validate the whole field. If it doesn't, we'll have to rethink anti-angiogenesis."

Investing in Other Cancer-Fighting Strategies

As must be apparent by now, biotech firms follow a myriad of paths to promote health and fight disease. One interesting and unusual experiment is being pursued by Onyx Pharmaceuticals (ONXX). It is trying to explode cancer cells from the inside out by stuffing them with a bioengineered virus. This virus only replicates in cells where cancer has disabled the cell's natural defenses against the virus. Think of a balloon being filled with water. The Onyx virus takes the place of water. Onyx is conducting Phase III trials of its compound, ONYX-015, on head and neck cancer. It is in Phase II studies of colorectal, pancreatic, and lung cancers.

Onyx offers only one example of the offbeat strategies biotech firms are using to combat cancer. Here are some suggestions for staying abreast of developments in the field:

- The American Cancer Society (www.cancer.org) is a good starting point for information about the various forms of cancer and experimental treatments for them.

- The National Cancer Institute (www.nci.nih.gov), the federal agency that funds basic cancer research, provides a wealth of information about research, including details of current clinical trials.

- The American Society of Clinical Oncology (ASCO) (www.asco.org) holds a prestigious research conference each spring. Companies compete for invitations to present clinical trial data before thousands of cancer clinicians and researchers. About a month before the conference, ASCO announces which companies have been invited to present data and publishes abstracts of these presentations on its website. Stocks of cancer companies often rise or fall depending on what the abstracts reveal. But only ASCO members get this early look at the conference abstracts. To join ASCO, one must be a credentialed cancer specialist. This is no obstacle to professional money managers who have the proper credentials and can afford the $120 to $370 membership fees. But this policy puts retail investors at a disadvantage because *they* can't read the abstracts until *after* the annual meeting—weeks behind the market bigshots.

Central Nervous System Disorders

Setting cancer aside, one of the most exciting areas of biotech innovation involves disorders of the central nervous system. The CNS category includes a wide variety of conditions that will probably be further segmented as new genetic discovery tools increase our understanding of these complex disorders. At present, CNS describes at least three broad groups of disorders. First there are the ailments that have long been recognized as having a physiological basis including cerebral palsy, epilepsy, chronic pain, migraines, multiple sclerosis, Huntington's and Parkinson's diseases, and stroke. A second group of conditions once went under the heading of mental illness, and are now being treated at their biochemical roots; these include depression, anxiety, Alzheimer's disease, schizophrenia, and bipolar disorder. Finally, CNS includes conditions like obesity and autism that were not thought to be treatable with medicines in the past.

In a 2001 report, analysts at the UBS Warburg investment bank made the case for investment in the CNS niche. They observed that on a worldwide basis, sales of CNS drugs have been growing 16 percent per annum. Three of the world's best-selling drugs—Prozac, Zoloft, and Paxil—are used to treat depression. "We conservatively estimate that in the U.S. over 23 million individuals, or 8 percent of the total population, suffers from a CNS disease or disorder. Globally that figure stands at 368 million," according to the UBS report that adds that "treatment for many CNS disorders has not changed during the past decade."

Given this perception of a large, unmet medical need, money has been flooding into the CNS sector. The flow of venture capital into CNS start-ups has doubled in the last three years. By definition, venture-backed start-ups are usually just beginning their development process and are therefore extremely speculative as investments. In fact, your first exposure to the new CNS companies could come during a wave of IPOs (I'll discuss the wisdom—or folly—of jumping into IPOs in chapter 4). Still, the smart investor should have at least a sense of what's going on in one of biotech's biggest growth areas, and there are some CNS companies that fit the criteria for near-term investments, because they have products on the market or in late-stage clinical trials. If you decide to specialize in this area, start by looking at the following:

- Cephalon Inc. (CEPH) won approval in 1999 to market a drug called Provigil for what is called "excessive daytime sleepiness," one manifestation of the sleep disorder known as narcolepsy. The company is now engaged in clinical trials aimed at broadening the approved use of Provigil to include sleep disorders associated with a wide variety of fatigues stemming from depression, Alzheimer's, Parkinson's, and multiple sclerosis. UBS Warbug estimates that the potential worldwide market for Provigil could reach $750 million, but Cephalon's drug will face competition from medicines such as Ritalin. (In addition to growing its Provigil franchise, Cephalon is testing several different compounds in earlier-stage trials against various cancers. The combination of a marketable drug with potential for expansion, coupled with potential in the anticancer market, makes Cephalon worth noting.)

- Titan Pharmaceuticals (TTP), which we touched on earlier in the cancer section, also has candidates in the CNS category. Its experimental compound Iloperidone is in Phase III clinical trials to treat schizophrenia. Titan has licensed Iloperidone to the Swiss drug firm Novartis, which will pay Titan an 8 to 10 percent royalty if the drug is approved. Novartis is running additional Phase III studies before deciding whether to ask the FDA to license the medicine, which would be aimed at a U.S. population of roughly 2.5 million schizophrenics. Titan also has a compound called Spheramine in Phase II trials to treat Parkinson's disease. Titan has partnered with the German drug firm Schering AG to develop Spheramine. Royalty arrangements have not been disclosed. (I'll explain more about partnerships in the Investor Tools section at the end of this chapter, and return to the topic in even greater detail in chapter 7.)

- Pain Therapeutics (PTIE), as the name implies, is embarked on the quest to develop more effective pain relievers by creating proprietary combinations of existing drugs. The company has four such pain-killing cocktails in late-stage clinical trials to treat pain associated with cancer, arthritis, and trauma. Although the underlying cocktails are based on known drugs such as morphine and naltrexone, the precise technology behind the formulations was developed by the Albert Einstein College of Medicine and is protected by several patents (the first expires in 2012) to which Pain Therapeutics has exclusive worldwide license. Although success in clinical trials can never be assured, the fact that the company is combining drugs with known safety profiles narrows the risk, since the trials will be focused on proving that the new mixtures are efficacious. Pain relief has become a new medical mantra, and the company anticipates that it could enter a $2 billion market if the drugs are approved.

Cardiovascular Disease

Heart attacks, strokes, high blood pressure, clogged arteries, and other ailments of the circulatory system remain a leading cause of death in the developed world. In the United States alone, some 61 million people suffer from some form of cardiovascular illness and nearly a million Americans each year die of heart disease, creating a large target for drug development. There are about 122 experimental medicines in human clinical trials to treat the various forms of heart disease, and many biotech medicines have already been approved by the FDA. The prevalence of heart disease and the plethora of novel treatments make the cardiovascular arena a prime area of investor interest.

Several companies in the cardiovascular niche have approved medicines on the market and clinical trials under way designed to prove that these medicines can be used in related conditions. Smart companies follow this strategy of "expanding the label" for approved medicines—and smart investors want to latch on to such companies. For instance, after the former California biotech firm Cor Therapeutics won FDA approval to sell Integrilin for acute cardiovascular disease, it worked on broadening its market. Cor shareholders reaped the reward when Millennium Pharmaceuticals (MLNM) offered a 77 percent premium in December 2001 to acquire Cor and its growing Integrilin franchise.

Biotech leaders like Genentech (DNA) add a more sophisticated wrinkle to this strategy of expanding the label, by creating improved versions of approved medicines. Take the famous clot-busting medicine Activase, originally approved for the treatment of heart attacks caused by blocked arteries. Genentech later pursued additional clinical trials to show that Activase was effective in treating stroke. But Genentech didn't stop there. It improved its basic technology to create a faster-acting clot-buster called TNKase that can be administered as a single dose in five seconds—in contrast to Activase, which is administered over thirty to ninety minutes. When Genentech won FDA approval for TNKase, it was good business and good medicine. The company protected its clot-buster franchise and improved the outcome for patients by creating a medicine that acts more quickly to limit the damage caused by arterial blockages.

New treatments—and new investment plays—are coming over the horizon. One company to watch is CV Therapeutics (CVTX). The California biotech firm should seek FDA approval in 2003 for Ranolazine, an experimental compound to treat angina. Some 6 million Americans suffer from this condition, in which clogged arteries limit blood flow to the heart and deprive that muscle of the oxygen it needs to create energy. Heart muscles can derive power by burning fats or sugars. Since fats require more oxygen per unit of energy, Ranolazine encourages heart cells to burn sugars. In theory, this shift to a sugar fuel should help weak hearts work more effectively and relieve the pain and shortness of breath associated with angina. Ranolazine is likely to go through an advisory panel hearing before the FDA makes a final decision—and investors discover whether CV Therapeutics is the next wonder in the heart niche or the latest biotech disappointment.

Investor Tools: Doing Research

As I have done with cancer, central nervous system disorders, and heart disease, investors should look at companies as competitors inside a disease category and then focus on those firms in the later stages of clinical trials. Don't let my suggestions narrow your search, however. In Appendix II you can browse a list of therapeutic areas, and the companies in each area, that professional biotech investors use to segment the market. (Not all the breakdowns are by disease type, and in subsequent chapters I'll look at investments in companies that provide tools or techniques for research.) But the obvious question at this point is: How do I come up with an investment focus, and how do I research it?

Start with what you know or what interests you. Let's say, for instance, a relative or friend has just been diagnosed with diabetes. That's a shock but not a death sentence, and as you think about it, you get the hunch that this person may be part of a trend that could form the basis for a biotech investment. Fire up the Web and visit your favorite search engine. (At this point I'll assume you have a computer with Internet access, or are willing to use the facilities at your public library.) By typing words like *diabetes* and *prevalence* I quickly found the home page of the American Diabetes Association (ADA) (www.diabetes.org), "the nation's leading nonprofit health organization providing diabetes research, information, and advocacy." You'll find that for almost any disease or condition of interest, there will be an advocacy group that will serve as a clearinghouse for both consumer and technical information. Often, the association will be affiliated with scientific organizations whose annual meetings are a focal point for the release of new clinical trial data. Disease associations are great starting points for novices.

Finding an Unmet Medical Need

Facts and figures on the ADA website reinforce your hunch that diabetes is a growing national and worldwide problem. Being a careful investor, however, you'd like corroboration. After all, a diabetes association is bound to see the disease as a huge problem. Fortunately there is a neutral public source for medical information. The Centers for Disease Control, in Atlanta, is the federal government's central source for information about health trends affecting U.S. citizens. On the CDC website (www.cdc.gov) locate the Health Topics A–Z directory on the left and click on the entry for "diabetes." According to the CDC: "Diabetes is a serious, costly, and increasingly common chronic disease that affects nearly 16 million Americans and contributes to almost 200,000 deaths a year. An estimated 10.3 million Americans have diagnosed diabetes, and another 5.4 million have undiagnosed diabetes. Among adults, the prevalence of diagnosed diabetes . . . increased 33% from 1990 to 1998."

Convinced that you've tapped into a trend, you continue your research and learn that there are two types of diabetes. Type I diabetes, which generally occurs in young people, accounts for 5 to 10 percent of all cases. Type II diabetes, often called adult onset diabetes, is the overwhelming problem. Moreover, Type II diabetes is associated with advancing age, fat-rich diets, and obesity. In the absence of a complete revolution in diet and lifestyle, the incidence of Type II diabetes seems destined to grow as the baby boomers get older. You've hit upon a solid investment thesis—provided you can find companies that have approved products or late-stage clinical trials for new ways to diagnose or treat diabetes.

Finding Products and Trials

A good place to start hunting is the website of the Pharmaceutical Research and Manufacturers of America (www.phrma.org), the trade association of the drug industry. The association maintains a free list of medicines on the market and in clinical trials, which is searchable by a number of criteria including type of disease. A few minutes of playing around with the search parameters reveals that biotech and drug firms have not been asleep to the potential of the diabetes market. There are literally dozens of firms in various stages of clinical trials for diabetes. I simplified my search by ignoring the companies still doing preclinical (animal testing) or Phase I trials (the first introduction to human subjects). That narrowed the field but not enough. I eliminated treatments for Type I diabetes (which is the smaller part of the market) and focused on Phase II and Phase III trials aimed at the much larger Type II indication (get used to these buzzwords that describe exactly at which disease a medicine is aimed). That still left a couple of dozen entries, all of which had confusing names. To further narrow the field, I returned to the imaginary friend whose plight launched this avenue of research. Our friend was dreading the prospect of having to take insulin shots. Wouldn't it be great if there were some way to avoid the need for that needle stick?

Pills versus Proteins

At this point I have to fill in some background. Biotech medicines, such as proteins and monoclonal antibodies, can't be ingested like

Investment Research 101

*The "New Medicines in Development" database compiled by the Pharmaceutical Research and Manufacturers of America (PhRMA) is a great place to start doing research. This free website (**http://www.phrma.org/searchcures/newmeds/webdb/**) allows you to run searches by disease, indication, drug, or company. Use the database to find new investment prospects or learn more about companies of interest.*

New Medicines. New Hope.

| Who We Are | PhRMA International | Genomics | PhRMA Foundation |

New Medicines in Development

Search by Disease

Heart Disease ▼ Continue

Search the disease category to prospect for investment opportunities in areas like "heart disease." When you select that entry and press continue a list of "indications" pops up. (All drugs are tested and approved to treat specific indications, so get accustomed to using this FDA lingo.) If you click on one of the indications under heart disease, it will lead you to drugs in development and, ultimately, the companies behind them.

Search by Indication

Incontinence ▼ Continue

As you become more experienced you'll learn to bypass the disease heading and go straight to the indication list. The database will reveal which companies are testing what medicines and whether they are in Phase I, Phase II, or Phase III development, etc.

Search by Drug Name

natrecor Continue

If you're following a company with an approved drug and want to learn about its competitors, here's one place do it. Type in Natrecor (a drug made by Scios) and press continue. The first level of the search tells you Natrecor is indicated for congestive heart failure. If you click on "congestive heart failure" you'll find other medicines aimed at that indication.

Search by Company

Amgen ▼ Continue

In biotech you'll hear a lot about the "pipeline." This is the list of all the experimental medicines a company has under development. Since many experiments fail, the bigger the pipeline the better a company's chances. Type in "Amgen" or "Genentech" and you'll get a long list. Be wary, however. The database can understate the pipeline of the smaller companies. They often partner with larger firms to carry out clinical trials, and sometimes only the larger partner's name is listed.

Source: PhRMA

pills. If you were to swallow a protein medication, your digestive system would break it down just as if it were a piece of food. You can swallow pills because their active ingredients are molecules small enough to slip through the digestive tract into the bloodstream. Five or ten years ago, the difference between drug and biotech companies was based on this difference. Drug companies made small-molecule medicines—commonly called drugs—while biotech firms made protein-based therapies, called biologics or biopharmaceuticals. Nowadays, those distinctions have blurred. Big drug companies often make biologics and biotech start-ups develop drugs whenever possible. The term *biotechnology* now refers mainly to a way of approaching medical discovery, based on the principles of molecular biology we touched on in chapter 1. The takeaway message for an investor is that biopharmaceuticals must be injected or delivered intravenously. And while sick people will readily take these biologics, especially when there is no alternative pill, the need for injection or infusion always presents some barrier to consumer acceptance of biopharmaceuticals.

With this in mind, your research might lead you to two companies, Inhale Therapeutic Systems (INHL) and Aradigm (ARDM), both in advanced clinical trials of devices to deliver insulin through the lungs. Both companies are trying to eliminate the needles and replace them with inhalers that would make taking insulin as easy as taking a breath. This sounds like a smart investment thesis. Take the increased prevalence of age-related diabetes and couple it with an unmet medical need—in this case, the desire to avoid taking shots. Of course, you'd want to do a lot more research before deciding whether these companies would make wise investments, and we won't go through all those steps right now. Instead, let's use these two companies to note the investment implications of a trend I touched on earlier in this chapter, the tendency for biotech firms to form partnerships with drug companies.

Introduction to Partnerships

If you visited the Inhale or Aradigm website, you'd see that each firm has found partners to help them conduct clinical trials and market their versions of inhaled insulin, if the products are approved. Inhale is allied with Pfizer and Aventis Pharmaceuticals, while Aradigm has partnered with Novo Nordisk Pharmaceuticals. These are smart deals for all concerned. Pfizer, Novo Nordisk, and Aventis are among the world's leading suppliers of injected insulin. Alliances with these players gave Inhale and Aradigm access to the manufacturing capability to produce the product and the sales clout to win market acceptance. Without such relationships, young biotech companies might never be able to raise enough money to bring their technologies to market.

For the drug companies, a different logic prevails. In order to deliver the earnings growth that Wall Street expects, drug companies need to bring a steady stream of new products to market. Because their growth needs exceed their internal development capabilities, drug companies are constantly looking for biotech firms that have promising technologies but lack the resources to develop them. Given their long involvement in the insulin market, Pfizer and Aventis had every reason to team up with Inhale. Likewise, for Novo to protect its own insulin franchise, the Danish drug maker needed Aradigm's technology. These deals are examples of the symbiotic relationships that have evolved between drug and biotech companies.

But these alliances are rarely marriages of equals. The drug industry is a hundred years old. Drug companies have profits and revenues, global sales forces, manufacturing and regulatory expertise, and a backlog of approved products. The biotech industry is barely thirty years old. Few biotech firms have approved products and even fewer have profits. When biotech firms partner with drug companies, it can be a Faustian bargain. Young biotech companies are often forced to give up the rights to control their own technologies, in return for cash payments to keep them afloat and royalties of varying value, if and when the product is approved. In the Investor Tools section of chapter 7, we'll look closely at the devil in the details of these partnership arrangements, which can make or break the fortunes of a biotech firm.

Until then, one anecdote will drive home how partnerships can affect biotech investments. In June 2001, Inhale was trading in the high $20s to low $30s. Its program was in Phase III while Aradigm's project was in Phase II. Investors anticipated that Inhale's insulin was poised for FDA approval. But in July 2001, Pfizer chief executive Henry McKinnell told a CNBC interviewer that he was considering a delay in seeking FDA approval to conduct more safety tests. The Pfizer statement came at the time when the FDA was being particularly zealous about safety, after having been forced to recall several drug because of side effects discovered after the agency had approved them. So it seemed only prudent for the company to extend its own safety reviews rather than trying to rush toward FDA approval.

But the announcement had a catastrophic effect on Inhale, whose share price was predicated on the assumption that its inhaled insulin was close to market. Within weeks Inhale shares had lost half their value, and the stock has been weak ever since. Of course, our thesis about replacing needles with inhalers could still be correct and Inhale's version of insulin may yet be approved. But if you bought Inhale at $30 a share, it would be tough to keep the faith when it sank below $10. Biotech stocks are prone to such setbacks because decisions critical to their future may be made by others. Pfizer's shares actually went up after it revealed the inhaled insulin delay. It has so many programs in the works that its investors were unfazed by the delay. Not so for Inhale, whose hopes were riding on that project. The lesson for biotech investors is that the value of their companies may be determined by the actions of drug partners with agendas all their own.

(Author's note: Inhale was in the process of changing its name as this book went to press, but had not yet revealed its new corporate identity.)

3

The Genomics Wave: The Drug Discovery Marathon

The completion of the first rough-draft map of the human genome in the summer of 2000 was the pivotal event in a yearlong public and financial euphoria. Although the dominant market trend of 2000 was the ill-fated dot.com boom, a gene frenzy of almost equal magnitude briefly sent biotech stocks soaring to unsustainable highs that year. A chart created by Ernst & Young shows how public fascination with the Human Genome Project propelled the biotech boom. From July 1999, when the media began to notice the genome project, through May 2000, when E&Y concluded its comparison, mentions of the word *genome* in major media correspond with the movement of a leading biotech stock index. Investment bankers took advantage of the public fascination with genomics to float more than sixty initial public offerings of biotech firms in 2000. Never in more than two decades of biotech history had the industry seen such a boom. Burrill & Co., a San Francisco merchant bank specializing in biotech finance, calculated that between IPOs, secondary stock offerings, venture capital investments, debt offerings, and other equity instruments, biotech firms raised in excess of $32 billion in 2000. That was roughly three times as much as the industry raised in 1999. In fact, biotech firms raised more in 2000 than they had in the four previous years combined.

By the first quarter of 2001, Wall Street had returned to its senses,

Media Attention on Genomics Mirrors the Biotech Index

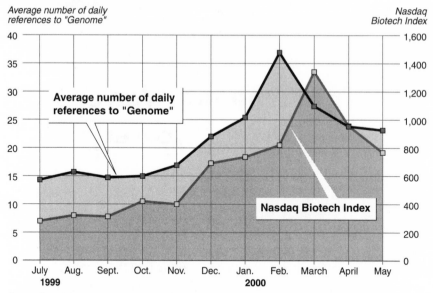

Average number of daily references to "Genome"

Nasdaq Biotech Index

Average number of daily references to "Genome"

Nasdaq Biotech Index

July 1999 — Aug. — Sept. — Oct. — Nov. — Dec. — Jan. 2000 — Feb. — March — April — May

Source: Ernst & Young, LLP

U.S. Biotech Industry Financings

In millions

	1996	1997	1998	1999	2000	2001
PUBLIC						
IPO	1,465	688	369	670	6,490	440
Follow-on	2,414	1,601	521	5,805	12,651	2,539
PIPEs	537	1,283	977	1,433	4,061	1,714
Debt/Other	352	1,288	1,262	1,520	5,728	4,848
PRIVATE						
VC	449	56	800	1,084	2,872	2,397
Other	103	184	84	184	203	9
TOTAL	**5,320**	**5,613**	**4,013**	**10,696**	**32,005**	**11,974**

IPO: initial public offering; **Follow-on:** additional shares offered by a public company; **PIPE:** block purchases of stock at discount; **VC:** venture capital

Source: Burrill & Company

and the air began to come out of the biotech bubble. Unlike the dot.com bust, however, the biotech correction still left the industry as a whole valued at higher levels than it had enjoyed in the period before the boom. Wall Street had briefly overstated biotech's value. But the correction created a new floor for biotech valuations. The boom also created a handful of new biotech giants including Human Genome Sciences (HGSI), Celera Genomics (CRA), and Millennium Pharmaceuticals (MLNM), companies whose strength is derived from the enormous amounts they were able to raise in follow-on offerings. Now these companies are using their war chests to become full-scale drug development companies.

The net result of the genomics boom was far different than its genesis. The public euphoria was triggered by the mistaken belief that mapping the human genome would quickly point the way to cures. That led to an early and incorrect investment thesis that gene information was so valuable that small gene-discovery companies could make a business out of selling their knowledge to large biotech or drug discovery firms. In the correction that followed the initial boom, Wall Street laid down a new dictum—selling knowledge about genes wasn't a business model. Companies that went public in 2000 on the premise of simple gene discovery have since that time been busy reinventing themselves with an eye toward turning their own gene discoveries into drugs or diagnostics.

In this chapter we'll look at how the genomics revolution arose, why the publication of the gene map was such an extraordinary achievement, and how biotech companies are attempting to transform that scientific success into commercial opportunities. In essence, the human genome frenzy helped to create a new wave of biotech companies that took a somewhat more sophisticated approach to understanding disease than the first two waves of biotech start-ups in the 1980s and 1990s. Yet these new genomics companies have only begun the drug discovery marathon. They must now create business development teams and clinical trial programs, and learn all the other nuts-and-bolts skills that bedeviled their biotech predecessors. Investors must therefore approach this new wave of gene discovery companies with realism and skepticism. The science of mapping the genome was the easy part. The tougher task ahead will be converting this raw knowledge into products and profits.

Genomics in a Nutshell

Genomics is the effort to understand how human DNA governs health and disease. The birth of genomics can be traced back to 1990 when the National Institutes of Health launched the Human Genome Project. It was originally envisioned as a fifteen-year effort, by hundreds of academic scientists around the world, to decode the entire length of DNA. The first stage of the project was completed ahead of schedule in 2000, in part thanks to instruments invented by biotech firms and competition from the private gene-mapping firm Celera Genomics.

The genome is the sum total of the DNA found in our twenty-three pairs of chromosomes. At conception, when sperm fertilizes egg, the genome directs the division, multiplication, and specialization of cells that turn an embryo into a fetus and ultimately a child. It is the genome that directs the formation of the heart, liver, nerves, and other essential organs. The genome molds our fingers and toes and plants our heads with hair. After birth, the genome takes on a different, more modest role. The entire genome is copied and preserved each time the body manufactures a new cell. (That's why cloning is possible. The nucleus of an adult cell can be scooped out and planted into an egg whose nucleus has been removed. There, the inserted nucleus takes charge and its genome directs the development of an embryo and fetus, doing away with the need for fertilization by a sperm cell.) Under ordinary circumstances, however, only portions of the genome become active in any given adult cell. That's why skin cells are different from nerve cells or muscle cells or liver cells. Yet each of these different cells has the same glob of DNA in its nucleus. In other words, each cell has a complete copy of the genome. Somehow this string of chemicals is regulated in such a fashion that only the functions appropriate to nerve cells are turned on in nervous tissues, while skin cells activate a different portion of the genome, and so on.

Even with the knowledge gained from the Human Genome Project, scientists are far from comprehending how, at the embryonic stage, the genome is capable of creating a human child out of proteins harvested from the mother's body or, once that child is developed, how portions of the genome selectively go into "retirement." But ever since scientists first deduced the structure of DNA in 1953, they've been trying to crack the code that is spelled out in the four chemicals, represented by the letters A, T, G, and C, that are strung together 3 billion times to make up the sequence of the DNA molecule.

Two surprising facts were driven home by the first stage of the Human Genome Project in 2000. First, the vast majority of the genome sequence serves no obvious purpose, composing what scientists call junk DNA. If junk DNA does have a purpose, it remains beyond our current understanding. Perhaps that's because scientists have devoted most of their energy to studying the short stretches of the genome that do seem to play active roles in growing and sustaining cells. We call these active regions genes. Scientists currently believe there are about thirty-five thousand genes in the human genome (the number is continually being revised), and that these genes account for only about 1.5 percent of the sequence of ATGCs.

Scientists eventually hope to understand the purpose of all 3 billion chemical letters in the genome, including the junk DNA. From the point of view of drug discovery, however, interest remains focused on the roughly thirty-five thousand genes and the processes they set in motion. Scientists know that genes create intermediary agents called RNA molecules. These RNA molecules, in turn, create the proteins that are the working components of every cell and tissue in the body. Illness occurs when some part of this gene-RNA-protein mechanism goes awry. The point of failure is called a "target" in biotech lingo. A target is some process that can be set right by a chemical intervention, i.e., a medicine. The reason genomics has excited the investor community is that having a comprehensive list of genes promised to greatly expand the universe of targets for new medicines.

"From 1898 to 2000, scientists have discovered 412 drug targets," analysts from Thomas Weisel Partners wrote in one report on genomics. "Nearly all marketed drugs act on one or more of these targets." The publication of the gene map in 2000 gave drug researchers a huge new set of potential targets. Right now the business of genomics is sifting through the thirty-five thousand genes, in hopes of discovering those that play important roles in mediating between health and sickness. The Weisel report suggested, "5,000 to 10,000 new targets will be identified in the next decade."

Caught up in the genome fever of 2000, however, investors got overly excited by this sudden rush of targets and forgot that targets are only clues. Even when clues prove fruitful, it takes years of preclinical studies, followed by human clinical trials to get a drug on the market. None of these cautions mattered in February 2000, when Celera hit $296 a share on the eve of a 2-for-1 stock split. Celera was the poster child for genomics. It was founded in 1998 on the premise that it could use machines to find human genes faster than the NIH-sponsored Human Genome Project. Celera's initial business model was to sell drug and biotech companies subscriptions to its gene database, to give them first crack at the new drug targets. Days after its stock split, Celera roared back to $235 a share. But then, in March 2000, a series of factors began to let the air out of the genomics stocks and the biotech sector in general.

Some have blamed the biotech slide on President Bill Clinton and British prime minister Tony Blair, who made a joint statement on March 14, 2000, that was misinterpreted as signaling their official hostility to gene patents. In fact, Celera's stock had started falling before their political gaffe. Wall Street had already begun looking for more rational valuations for the genomics companies and indeed for the entire biotech sector, which had been carried to lofty levels by the gene-mapping craze. Looking back on that period, Mark Simon, biotech investment banker for Robertson Stephens, used the term *soufflé rally* to describe the biotech surge in the first quarter of 2000. "What causes a soufflé to rise? Hot air," Simon said.

Fortunately, biotech did not fall as flat as a soufflé, and Wall Street did not entirely lose its appetite for the genomics companies because they do represent a powerful new wave of innovation in medical discovery. What the market has signaled, however, is that genomics is not an end in itself but rather the means to an end—the creation of novel medicines, diagnostic tests, or other products with broad markets. Several dozen firms have carved out a variety of niches within the broad umbrella of genomics. We'll look at these niches in turn and show the many ways that genomics companies are trying to turn the science of gene discovery into a profitable industry.

The New Age Drug Discovery Firms

The most visible companies in the genomics space are a handful of players that began as gene discovery firms but are in varying stages of becoming full-fledged drug development companies. In short, they have heeded Wall Street's dictum that selling information about drug targets is not nearly as good a business as developing these targets into medicines. These firms also have significant numbers of patents on human genes and still derive revenues by selling subscriptions to their database of gene discoveries. Future valuations, however, will depend on their success taking experimental medicines through the clinical trials process. In this category the key names to know are:

- Human Genome Sciences (HGSI)
- Millennium Pharmaceuticals (MLNM)
- Celera Genomics (CRA)
- Incyte Genomics (INCY)
- Hyseq Inc. (HYSQ)

- Human Genome Sciences (HGSI) was founded in 1992 by Dr. William Haseltine, who was one of the first biotech executives to recognize that new instruments were making it possible to read DNA sequences and extract whole or partial genes. The deal that put the company on the map was a 1993 agreement under which drug maker SmithKline Beecham agreed to pay $125 million for access to HGSI's gene database. Human Genome Sciences has already been awarded more than 160 patents on full- and partial-length human genes. The company has hundreds more applications pending and expects to win many additional patents on human genes and proteins. Royalties or other income from this patent database should provide a revenue stream to bolster the company's stock price. However, the most important factor in the company's valuation is that HGSI recognized earlier than some of its genomics peers that Wall Street was more interested in drugs than patents. Under Haseltine's leadership the company has developed the skills to do the preclinical and clinical studies associated with bringing new drugs to market. HGSI has already put several experimental medicines into human clinical trials. It has preclinical studies under way on other potential compounds and is building a manufacturing plant to enable it to produce therapeutic proteins that might win FDA approval. In short, it is conducting itself as a fully integrated drug discovery firm along the lines of an Amgen or Genentech, with the advantage of a growing patent portfolio that represents the potential for significant royalties. Provided the company continues to enjoy good management, it should remain one of the bellwethers of the genomics sector.

- Millennium Pharmaceuticals (MLNM) was founded in 1993 by a team that included Eric Lander, a Massachusetts Institute of Technology professor and one of the scientific leaders of the Human Genome Project. From its inception the company conceived of itself as a pioneer in a new style of drug discovery based on the use of high-speed equipment and novel techniques. Its goal is to automate every possible step in the process of turning gene discoveries into targets and then developing drugs to act on these targets. Chairman and chief executive Marc Levin is a Genentech veteran who went on to become a venture capitalist with the May-field Fund, where he played a role in founding such biotech firms as Tularik and Cell Genesys. Like Human Genome Sciences, Millennium caught the attention of investors with big deals to sell its gene discoveries. In 1997, Millennium signed a $343 million deal to sell agricultural genomics leads to Monsanto. In 1998, Millennium signed a $465 million agreement with Bayer. Millennium has also moved to develop and market its own medicines and diagnostic tests. In 2001, it won FDA approval for Campath, a treatment for chronic lymphocytic leukemia. Millennium also acquired the heart medicine Integrilin when it completed its takeover of Cor Therapeutics in 2002. Sales of these approved medicines give Millennium a revenue stream while it develops new medicines and diagnostic tests arising from its own gene discovery efforts. The company has seven experimental compounds in Phase I or Phase II clinical trials to treat heart disease, cancer, inflammation, and metabolic disorders. Millennium is also a pioneer in commercializing screening tests based on its gene discoveries. Whereas it takes many years to develop, test, and win approval for a new drug, there's a shorter cycle for commercializing diagnostic tests that can detect a gene or protein abnormality in order to provide an early warning of disease. The company's most advanced diagnostic effort, a test for malignant melanoma, is in the process of being commercialized.

- Celera Genomics Group (CRA) and its charismatic leader, J. Craig Venter, played a central role in establishing genomics as a science and an industry. But under Venter the company lagged behind its rivals in making the transition from information vendor to drug developer, and in 2002 he was eased out of his operating role and replaced by veteran diagnostic industry executive Kathy Ordonez. Celera has an odd corporate genesis. It is an independently traded business

unit of Applera Corp., which also controls Applied Biosystems (ABI). CRA and ABI trade independently, but their des-
tinies are entwined. Applied Bio was founded in 1981. It is
one of the first companies to commercialize instruments for
rapid DNA analysis. In 1998, ABI president Mike Hunkapiller
recruited Venter to form Celera. In the incestuous world of
genomics, Venter was the maverick scientist who had long
advocated a speedier approach to gene mapping through
the use of instruments. In 1992, he had established a nonprofit gene-mapping effort called The Institute for Genomics
Research (TIGR). But Venter became disenchanted after
Haseltine's Human Genome Sciences acquired key commercial rights to TIGR's data. When Hunkapiller broached the
idea of forming Celera in 1998, Venter seized the chance to
use ABI's newest and fastest DNA instruments to map the
genome before the NIH-sponsored Human Genome Project.
As it turned out, however, NIH scientists led by Lander (a
Millennium cofounder!) established their own DNA sequenc-
ing factories to rival the Celera operation, and the public
and private gene-mappers finished in a dead heat. Celera
has built a large business selling subscriptions to its database, which contains data about human, mouse, and fly
genes. But data from the NIH project, which is in the public
domain, has somewhat undercut the value of Celera's
proprietary database. In 2001, Celera, which is based in
Maryland, acquired California biotech company Axys Pharmaceuticals, which had expertise in designing chemical
drugs. Investors are waiting for that merger to bear fruit.

- Incyte Genomics (INCY) was founded in 1991 and is arguably
  the first company to undertake a systematic study of human
  genes and proteins. It has amassed an enormous database
  that links gene and protein abnormalities with human diseases. Nineteen of the world's twenty largest drug companies subscribe to the Incyte database. The company has

been awarded hundreds of patents on genes and proteins of potential medical interest, and was profitable for eight consecutive quarters in 1997 and 1998. But since then Incyte has slipped into the red, and now the company's database sales are shrinking. In 2001, Incyte had annual revenues of $219.2 million. But the company expects 2002 revenues in the range of $130 million to $150 million. The company underwent a substantial layoff in 2001 and brought in a new executive team to help turn it into a drug discovery firm, along the lines of Millennium and Human Genome Sciences. Chief executive Paul A. Friedman and chief scientific officer Robert Stein previously headed drug discovery at DuPont Pharmaceuticals Research Laboratories. Friedman and Stein have opened a drug research laboratory for Incyte inside DuPont's Stine-Haskell Research Center in Newark, Delaware. Only time will tell whether the former DuPont duo will succeed in adding a drug development capability to Incyte's information business, or transform the company through a merger or spin-off.

- Hyseq Inc. (HYSQ) was founded in 1993, at roughly the same time as the other early gene discovery firms, but never achieved the traction of its rivals. But Hyseq got a new lease on life in 2000 when biotech legend George Rathmann took over as chairman. Rathmann earned his stripes in biotech by leading Amgen in its early years. In the 1990s, he repeated his success as the head of ICOS Corp. (ICOS), the Seattle biotech firm that is helping develop an experimental drug called Cialis as a possible competitor to Viagra. At Hyseq, Rathmann has brought in a new executive team focused on drug development, but it is unclear whether the entrepreneur can work his magic yet again—or whether he's the champ who stepped back into the ring one time too many.

Beyond this handful of genomics firms that aspire to be full-fledged drug discovery companies, there is a larger universe of niche players. Some may be fortunate enough to latch on to a promising discovery, and retain financial control of that discovery through the long clinical trials process, ending up with the sort of blockbuster product that can turn a niche player into a fully integrated drug discovery company. But for the time being, most genomics firms are niche companies. Let's look at the niches and the stocks in turn.

Supplies and Reagents

A modest and easily overlooked niche within genomics is composed of companies that sell consumable supplies used in experiments. Bypassing the genomic supply market would be a mistake, however, because unlike firms in early-stage drug development, several of the supply vendors are already profitable.

It makes sense that if genomics is a new gold rush, at least some suppliers will be making money meeting the demand for the raw materials of experimentation. In many instances getting a small sample of a unique gene sequence, a certain RNA fragment, or a bit of purified protein is a prerequisite for starting an experiment. Then, with this sample in hand, the researcher will need other chemical agents, called enzymes or probes, in order to manipulate and study the material that is the subject of the experiment. It might take an advanced degree in molecular biology or organic chemistry to understand these experimental processes in any detail. But the concept is relatively simple. Biological materials are chains of chemicals. Think of paper clips strung together. Scientists generally want to isolate a small portion of the chain, and since all of this activity is happening at a molecular level, they can't simply use tweezers to get the job done. Instead, they use one set of chemicals to manipulate another set of chemicals. Some of the chemical supplies consumed in experiments are commodities, but many of these reagents—the substances that initiate the experiment—are novel, patented chemicals that are priced accordingly. In fact, as we'll see later in chapter 5, drug and biotech companies run so many experiments, consuming such quantities of chemicals in the process, that instrument vendors are looking for ways to reduce the consumption of reagents in order to put a lid on the overall cost of research. Will instrumentation ever become so efficient that chemical consumption will be a diminishing business? Well, it's hard to say since we're on a new frontier, but remember how computers were supposed to usher in the era of the paperless office? Didn't happen.

Keep the paper supply analogy in mind, however. To some extent the companies listed below are warehouse operations. Yes, they're distributing some gee-whiz supplies, but if you decide to invest in this niche, be alert for issues that would affect any warehouse operation, such as gross margins, sole-source versus competitive supply, and the efficiency of order processing.

- Charles River Laboratories International (CRL) is a fifty-year-old supplier of research animals used in designing new drugs, medical devices, and other therapies. The company operates at a profit, a pleasant surprise when surveying biotech investments. Revenues in 2000 grew nearly 40 percent to $306 million. In 2001, net sales rose 52 percent to $465.6 million, a pace that will be challenging to maintain.

- Techne Corp. (TECH) is a profitable distributor of instruments, purified proteins, antibodies, and experimental supplies used in clinical and experimental medicine. Fiscal 2001 revenues totaled $115 million. Over a five-year period the company has achieved a 29 percent growth in earnings per share (EPS) on a 16 percent growth in sales. For the nine months ended March 31, 2002, sales rose 13 percent to $95.3 million while net income rose 11 percent to $27.4 million.

- Harvard Bioscience Inc. (HBIO) focuses on protein purification and ADMET screening. (ADMET is an acronym for absorption, distribution, metabolism, elimination, and toxicology, a process designed to measure how well drugs

59

circulate through the body.) The company has been intermittently profitable. Sales in 2000 totaled $30.5 million, up 16.8 percent over the previous year. Revenues rose 34 percent to $40.9 million for 2001, but the company still ran in the red.

- Invitrogen Corp. (IVGN) manufactures or distributes over ten thousand products aimed at biotech, drug industry, and academic scientists. In recent years it has rapidly expanded its product offerings, in part by acquisition, in a bid to become the one-stop shop of the biomedical industry. As a result, sales have grown more than elevenfold from $53.7 million in 1998 to $629.3 million in 2001. But acquisition-related expenses depressed earnings between 1999 and 2001. Looking ahead, investors will track net income to make sure the company profits from its rapid growth.

- BioSource International (BIOI) distributes experimental kits, antibodies, proteins, peptides, and other research chemicals. As of the third quarter of 2001, BioSource had a five-year sales growth rate of 30 percent. Revenues totaled $32.2 million in 2000. Profits have been uneven. The company reported a loss of 47 cents a share in 2000. In 2001, net sales rose 9 percent to $35.2 million, with earnings of 7 cents per share.

- Qiagen N.V. (QGENF) is a Dutch firm that trades on Nasdaq as well as on Germany's Neuer Markt exchange. Qiagen has created a profitable business out of supplying the instruments and chemicals needed to prepare and purify DNA and RNA for use in experiments. In 2001, it enjoyed a five-year sales rate of 40.7 percent. Its five-year EPS growth rate was 43.3 percent. For all of 2001, revenues increased 37 percent to $295.9 million, while net income rose 81 percent to $38.6 million.

- Other companies in this sector can be found in Appendix II, under the ADMET and Supply/Service niche lists.

Functional Genomics

Knowing the sequence of a gene is not, by itself, enough information to begin drug development. It is first necessary to identify what
the gene does, what protein or proteins it makes, and how much of
these protein products is normal or abnormal. In short, it's important to know the function of the gene, and here we'll look at four
companies that follow different approaches to functional genomics.
All of these niche companies face the same basic challenge: making
short-term revenues by taking on what amounts to contract research
from large drug or biotech companies, while simultaneously looking
for that breakthrough discovery that they can own and leverage into
a hit product.

- Exelixis (EXEL) was founded on the premise that nature
  does not reinvent the wheel—it simply adds spokes, tubes,
  or other features in the course of evolution. Science has
  shown that the genes most important in human development—the ones that sculpt the heart and wire the nerves—
  are similar to genes that perform the same functions in flies
  and fish. Scientists can tinker with the genes of these experimental creatures to see whether a heart or nerve abnormality results, and this in turn provides clues about the
  function—or in some cases the malfunction—of correspond-
  ing genes in humans. Exelixis has announced more than a
  dozen partnerships, including cancer development deals
  with Bristol-Myers Squibb and Protein Design Labs worth
  about $60 million in investment and research capital. The
  company also has multiyear relationships, worth approximately $100 million, to help Aventis and Bayer discover new
  crops, pesticides, and insecticides. (We'll visit Exelixis again
  in chapter 6 when we discuss agricultural genomics.)

- Lexicon Genetics (LEXG) and Deltagen (DGEN) both use
  mice to ascertain the function of human genes. Mice are a

superb choice for several reasons. Humans have only a few hundred genes that are not found in the mouse genome. So the chances are that any gene important in the mouse plays a similar role in humans. Scientists also know how to create a mouse with extra copies of a given gene or, conversely, to subtract a certain gene from the animal's genome. These are powerful techniques for determining gene function. Both firms have industrialized this process of creating and observing altered mice. They settled a patent dispute in 2001 allowing them to focus on competing in the field rather than in the courts. Both have an array of corporate partnerships; check their websites to stay abreast. Looking ahead, Lexicon and Deltagen are trying to transform themselves into full-scale drug discovery companies. Like Celera and Millennium, Lexicon and Deltagen hope to develop drugs based on their own research, in addition to winning income through contract relationships. Of the two companies, Lexicon has the higher market capitalization. (Market cap is the total value of all outstanding shares. We'll talk more about market cap comparisons at the end of this chapter and also in chapter 5.)

- Sangamo Biosciences (SGMO) has created a technology that seems to control gene expression. Remember that every cell has a full copy of the genome. But most of those genes are silent or inactivated. Sangamo is developing the ability to turn genes on and off. In the short term, this could help reveal the function of unknown genes. In the long term, finding a reliable way to switch genes on and off could have many applications in medicine and agricultural biotechnology. Sangamo lists many corporate alliances, but revenue from these deals has been thin. In 2001, the company reported a $25.2 million loss on revenues of $4.9 million.

Clinical Diagnostics

One of the earliest practical applications of genomics will be the creation of tests to detect protein or gene abnormalities that might signal disease. As mentioned earlier, some of the larger genomics companies like Millennium already have their eyes on this opportunity. Applera, the parent of Celera and Applied Biosystems, has also created a diagnostics division. The Swiss giant Roche has traditionally been strong in diagnostics and should be expected to continue that trend with a new generation of gene-based tests. Other drug makers will probably get into the act. Several new and more specialized genomics companies have already begun to create markets for diagnostic tests. How large these markets will be is an issue yet to be determined. The size of the test market will in turn determine whether genomic-based testing becomes a sustainable industry. It could be that companies specializing in genetic diagnostics won't be able to achieve critical mass, and either they or their tests will end up being acquired by outfits like Quest Diagnostics (DGX) or Laboratory Corporation of America (LH), two multibillion-dollar firms that have already developed nationwide networks of clinical test sites.

Whether genomic companies create a new test niche or get absorbed into larger entities will probably depend on whether their tests can be coupled with effective treatment. Patients, physicians, and insurers may be unwilling to pay for gene-based tests unless this knowledge can lead to a therapy that would improve the person's prognosis. Testing could raise policy or political issues if insurance companies use genetic test results to issue—or deny—policies and set premiums. The diagnostics industry is likely to find that the path to profitability leads through some social quagmires. I don't mean to frighten investors away from the diagnostics niche, but simply to inoculate them against the tendency toward hype that seems to hover around new technologies.

With that caveat in mind there are pure plays in the diagnostics niche. As you evaluate these potential investments, remember: *The most useful, and therefore most valuable, tests will be those aimed at large patient populations, where the diagnostic procedure is clearly coupled with some drug or surgical therapy that will improve the patient's outcome.*

- Biosite (BSTE) has developed a series of kits to screen for drug abuse, pathogen and parasite infections, heart failure, and heart attack. It is profitable. In 2001 the company reported a net income of $6.7 million on revenues of $65.6 million. On a year-over-year basis, revenues grew 19 percent, while earnings increased 9 percent.

- Visible Genetics (VGIN) has an FDA-approved test that can disclose whether an AIDS patient is infected with certain disease-resistant strains of HIV, a determination that could prompt physicians to change medications. It uses a technology called genotyping to test the genetic material of the virus, and is developing similar tests for hepatitis B, hepatitis C, tuberculosis, and cancer. The company is not profitable.

- ViroLogic Inc. (VLGC) also tests HIV-infected blood to determine what drugs would be most effective at fighting the virus, but it uses a different technology, called phenotyping. It is trying to extend this technology to other viral infections, but so far is still unprofitable.

- Cepheid Inc. (CPHD) has developed fast, portable genetic-screening systems that can detect a variety of pathogens. The company got a boost after its system was touted as a fast test for anthrax and other bioterror agents, but it is more likely to find sustaining markets in small medical centers and environmental test settings. Cepheid continues to operate in the red.

- Diagnostics is one of the most heavily populated biotech niches and Appendix II lists fifty-one firms pursuing Diagnostic/Imaging technologies.

Pharmacogenetics and SNP Analysis

One of the important puzzles drug and biotech firms must solve is why people react differently to medicines. Every medicine has side effects. But in some people, a drug can cause a variety of unwanted symptoms even to the point of death. Some of these differences are thought to have a genetic basis. Pharmacogenetics is the attempt to correlate genetic profiles and side effects, and to create screening tests to predict which patients might react poorly to a given medicine, or, conversely, to identify the ideal patients for the drug.

Pharmacogenetics is sometimes referred to as personalized medicine, although that is very likely an overstatement. Still, we are already seeing the beginnings of this trend. Breast cancer patients are tested to see if they manifest the particular mutation that can be treated by Genentech's Herceptin.

A related field of endeavor is the effort to identify what are called SNPs. SNP is an acronym for single nucleotide polymorphism. A nucleotide is one of the four chemicals that spell out the genetic code. A polymorphism is a variation. An SNP is a change in a single letter of the genome that might make one person more or less susceptible to a disease. Of course there are differences between the genomes of any two individuals. That's one of the reasons we don't all look alike. SNPs are a different category of difference. They are troublesome variations in important genes, where a single misplaced chemical—an A where there should be a T, or a G where most people have a C—that could cause the gene to make the wrong protein, or alter the quantity of protein created by the gene. At this point researchers don't know how many SNPs are common in the human population. Nor do we have reliable maps or tests that would enable a physician to determine whether an individual has a genetic tendency toward a given ailment. Obviously this is an area of great commercial and social interest. What will we do with SNP information? On the positive side we'll use it to forecast disease. I'll leave it to science fiction to warn about the possible abuses of our increasing ability to link genetic variations with physical or behavioral differences.

The effort to commercialize pharmacogenetic and/or SNP technologies is in its early days. If you're tempted to explore investments in this niche, you are heading into some of the most complex and varied terrain in biotechnology. Here is a partial list of companies in this space:

- Luminex Corp. (LMNX) uses a DNA analysis system based on the use of microscopic polystyrene beads.
- Illumina Inc. (ILMN) employs beads and fiber optics to perform many DNA tests simultaneously.
- Sequenom Inc. (SQNM) has developed a MassARRAY technology to screen large numbers of genes in large populations in an attempt to correlate with disease.
- Genaissance Pharmaceuticals Inc. (GNSC) and Variagenics Inc. (VGNX) are looking for SNPs that could affect drug development.
- Appendix II lists several additional firms under Pharmacogenetics.

The overarching challenge facing this niche is conceptually simple. The identification of genetic differences that affect medical outcomes is so important that all large drug and biotech firms will have to develop pharmacogenetic skills. If you consider investing in this niche, be sure you understand the company's game plan. Is it aiming to develop some proprietary technology so powerful that it will be able broadly to license its approach, on its own terms, and thus remain independent of the drug and biotech giants that will be its customers? Or is it more likely to remain a small firm for which success would mean being acquired, presumably by one of the large companies that has adopted its technology? Be mindful of these questions as you explore this area.

Investor Tools: Welcome to the Neighborhood

Picking stocks in the genomics sector presents the same basic challenge that confronts most potential investments in biotechnology—the companies are fascinating, their work may lead to the development of marvelous new medicines, but most are losing money now and many seem destined to continue operating in the red for years to come. How are investors supposed to decide when the price and time are right to make a purchase? Without meaning to sound glib, the fact is that the valuations of early-stage biotech companies are all relative—and somewhat arbitrary to boot. "Biotech is always a moving target," says former money manager Lissa Morgenthaler, mentioning some of the "metrics" that have been used to gauge—or perhaps justify—the stock prices of public companies that didn't have earnings. At one point, analysts counted the number of Ph.D.s on staff. "That was the original metric," she says. "You were trying to figure out whether they were wasting money on administration or putting it where it should be, into the brains of the operation." At other points analysts counted the number of experimental compounds that a young company had under development. In biotech lingo, this is called the product pipeline. It is indeed useful to have a deep pipeline. The deeper the pipeline, the more fallback possibilities exist in case the company's lead experiment fails in human clinical trials. But assigning a value-per-experiment is still just a way to rationalize a stock price until a company is profitable. At one financial conference I heard veteran venture capitalist Sam Colella quip that biotech stocks are valued on the "price-to-dreams" ratio.

Witticisms aside, most biotech companies are research firms that don't have earnings (this is especially true in newer segments like genomics). Thus, whatever numerical support analysts offer in their written recommendations, the most consistent, honest, and reliable yardstick for comparing stock prices is that biotech companies are measured against their peers. Or, as I said before, when it comes to valuation, it's all relative. "It's all in the comps," says Tom Dietz, senior managing director at the Pacific Growth Equities investment bank. "Valuation is based on what other companies are in the space and what people are willing to pay for them." This may seem like a nebulous, even cynical, way to assess biotech stocks, but if you think for a moment, it's obvious that we make similar judgments on many other investments, notably real estate. We don't expect to pay the same amount for a two-thousand-square-foot house in downtown Omaha and in downtown Manhattan. We accept the fact that property value depends on the neighborhood, as well as the mood of the market at any given time. The same concept applies when buying or selling biotech stocks. That's why I've organized this book as much as possible to keep like companies together, to segment them into their niches, and to place them alongside their competitors—because that's the framework within which professional money managers and analysts make purchases or issue recommendations.

In a sense, to become a successful biotech investor you'll have to learn to recognize the neighborhoods (i.e., niches) of biotechnology, as well as the factors that make some firms in each niche prime properties while others are fixer-uppers. In short, you have to become an expert on the relative values of the properties in your neighborhood. Specialization is the first step. No one can be expert on the nuances of every niche in biotechnology. The analysts who cover biotech at the big brokerage firms generally divide the sector by specialties and limit their research to a handful of companies. Follow their example. Focus your research and make your investments based on a sound understanding of the relative values of the stocks in the niche or niches that become your targets.

The first step in developing this expertise is to track all the stocks in the niche that interest you. I've exposed you to several niches already and future chapters will cover more. Appendix II provides a comprehensive breakdown of niches and lists the companies in each niche. Free services like Yahoo! Finance or Bigcharts.com offer tools to track stock prices over time. *Be aware of the fifty-two-week high and low of the stocks in your niche. You'll want to know when they're trading near the top of their fifty-two-week high, and when they're trading at the bottom.* And, just as important, you'll try to figure out why the stock is up or down. It's also a good idea to track your stocks against the two biotech indexes, the American Stock Exchange Biotech Index (ticker symbol ^BTK) and the Nasdaq Biotech Stock Index (^NBI). The Amex Biotech Index tracks the aggregate value of seventeen of the largest biotech stocks. The Nasdaq Biotech Index represents a larger basket of stocks. These indexes gauge the market's overall sentiment regarding biotechnology. This will help you notice when your stocks are moving with the general sentiment, and when they're bucking the trend. Whenever you see an unusual movement, you'll have to figure out why. For instance, in the spring of 2002, Genentech's stock chart shows a sudden sharp drop. It's not hard to figure out why. The April 11 leak of lukewarm preliminary results in the Phase III clinical trial of a cancer treatment reminded investors of other recent setbacks in Genentech's development efforts, including delays in experimental asthma and psoriasis medicines.

In later chapters, I'll show you how this research affects buy/sell decisions, but at this point I'm still laying the groundwork by showing how you can get to know your companies. For the purposes of this analysis, let's assume the companies you're tracking are still operating in the red. In addition to following their stock prices, you'll want to follow other variables, including:

- Cash position. This is one of the most important bits of quantitative information about a money-losing company. You can find it on the balance sheet when the company reports its quarterly earnings. It's generally entitled "Cash and Cash Equivalents." I'll show you how to use that number in a moment.

- Quarterly expenses. Track the patterns and be sure you understand management's explanation of any trend. Rising expenses can be good news, provided a company is spending for the right reasons, such as putting an experimental treatment into human clinical trials—and has the cash to fund the expense. Read quarterly and annual SEC filings on the company website, not just the press releases.

- Income. Even companies that lose money have some income. It is common for small biotech companies to earn money by doing contract research for larger companies. Be sure you understand when and how the money will be paid. Companies often tout the total amount they could earn but downplay the fact that most of the income is contingent on meeting performance milestones. Check quarterly reports. When companies earn money, they put it on their balance sheets. If it isn't on the balance sheet, then it hasn't been earned.

- Net Income (Loss). You'll find this plainly stated on the quarterly report.

- Years of cash. Calculate this figure by dividing the cash position by the net loss for the last four quarters. The more cash a company has, the more operating flexibility it enjoys. Any company with less than two years of cash has to start worrying about where it's going to get its next jolt of capital. Any company with under a year's cash has got its back up against a wall. It may have to license off its most valuable experimental compound at unfavorable terms just to stay in business. (We'll talk more about licensing later.)

- Product pipeline. This is the sum of all the products a company has under development. Don't just count numbers; look at where these potential products are in the development process. One product in Phase III clinical trials could be worth a dozen products that are still being tested in rodents.

- Management. Proven leaders inspire confidence. As you read the management biographies on the company websites, look for managers who have track records in biotech. Make sure the management team has the skills appropriate to the company's current challenges. If it is putting experimental medicines into clinical trials, does it have leaders who have managed that process before? If it is on the verge of launching a product, does it have manufacturing and sales expertise?

■ Market capitalization. This is the stock price multiplied by the total number of outstanding shares. You can find it by calling up a stock quote on Yahoo! Finance or Excite's Money section. Market capitalization represents the investment community's collective judgment about a company's worth. If you're looking at several companies in the same niche, those with the highest market caps are the ones Wall Street has designated sector leaders. Consider the genomics firms. On the same day in spring 2002, Millennium Pharmaceuticals had a market cap of about $5 billion; Human Genome Sciences was worth $2 billion; the market valued Celera shares at $1 billion; Incyte was worth half that; Hyseq had a market cap of less than $70 million. Having looked at all the factors that go into a company's worth, investors have established the pecking order in this niche. This is not to say you should only invest in leaders and shun laggards. The art of investing is detecting or predicting changes, whether it's a sector leader headed for a crash or a laggard gaining ground. Helping you detect these opportunities is the purpose of this book. For now, however, just be sure you know where your companies stand relative to their peers. In chapter 4 we'll explore how market caps stratify companies into yet another type of neighborhood.

4

The Proteomics Wave: Proteins and the Next Medicines

Biotechnology is an industry of endless frontiers. In the previous chapter we looked at the relative conquest of the genetic landscape. I say conquest because it was an astonishing achievement when public and private scientists read the entire sequence of the DNA molecule. After all, it was only fifty years ago that scientists first deduced the structure of DNA and began to explore how the regular arrangement of chemicals in that molecule might encode inherited traits. The genome is the result of hundreds of millions of years of evolution. Yet human science unraveled much of its meaning in a few decades! This scientific achievement is all the more remarkable considering that virtually all of the genetic sequence was derived between 1998 and 2000, when Applied Biosystems (ABI) and Amersham Biosciences (a division of Amersham plc, ticker AHM) shipped a new generation of instruments that could pull apart and read DNA's chemical letters at speeds hitherto unimaginable.

Yet despite our pride in having sequenced the genome, the fact remains: What scientists don't know about the genome vastly exceeds what they do know. We have only a rough estimate of the number of human genes. Current estimates were made by computer programs designed to spot unknown genes by looking for patterns in the genome's 3 billion letters. Scientists will revise the gene count many times in coming years, just as they'll puzzle over the function of the vast majority of genetic letters—the so-called junk DNA—whose purpose remains a mystery. Of course, we needn't have all the scientific arguments settled in order to make use of genome data. Drug and biotech companies are already trying to pick out those genes that relate to disease in order to speed the search for new medicines.

But a heavy dose of humility is in order before we journey into the next biotech frontier—the systematic study of the role that proteins play in maintaining health and causing disease. In financial lingo, this field is called proteomics (pro-tee-OH-mix), a term derived from the better-known moniker, genomics. In part the choice of a name involves clever marketing by the biotech firms that specialize in protein studies. The investing public has at least some rough sense of what genomics is about, and even if that understanding is vague, the term has a positive connotation. But the name is not simply a marketing ploy. Proteomics companies are attempting to do what genomic companies have already accomplished—invent high-speed instruments and techniques to industrialize the study of proteins, and find new drug targets in less time than is presently possible.

However, proteomics is at an infant stage of development compared to genomics. Many of the interesting companies in this niche are still privately held and thus awaiting an opportunity to go public. If historical patterns hold true, the proteomics firms will go public as a group, at a time when popular enthusiasm for biotechnology generates a buying frenzy. At such times investors will tend to forget that proteomics is an early and complex field, populated by companies that are losing money and will in all likelihood continue to lose money for many years. Instead, the market will dwell on the hype—which contains the grain of truth—that proteomics will zero in on disease at an even more fundamental level than genomics, because proteins are more closely related to disease than genes.

But just because proteomics is important doesn't mean it will make a fruitful investment in a one-, two-, or five-year time horizon. *In fact, biotech history suggests that retail investors get clobbered in the stampede for the next frontier: they tend to get in too late to cash in on the initial momentum, then hang on until after the market has come to its senses.* To the extent that investing is like a game of musical chairs, it's the small investor who gets left standing when the music ends. So if I lay on the caution rather thickly, it's not from a lack of appreciation of the potential of proteomics. Instead, I'm trying to inoculate you against the inevitable hype that will minimize the difficulties inherent in making a business out of cutting-edge science.

Proteomics 101

For more than 150 years, biologists have operated on the principle that the cell is the fundamental unit of all living things. There are more than two hundred different types of cells in the human body. The interior of these cells is the province of molecular biology, the science underlying biotechnology. Over the last quarter-century, biotech scientists have used the tools of molecular biology to examine the inner workings of cells. At this intracellular level, the basic working parts are DNA, RNA, and proteins. We already know that DNA makes RNA and that RNA makes proteins. Scientists also know that proteins are made up of smaller building blocks, the amino acids, that are strung together like pearls in a necklace. In humans and other mammals twenty different types of amino acids can be strung together to make proteins. If only life were that simple! But even at the cellular level, life is exceedingly complex. Scientists have come to understand that there is not a one-to-one relationship between genes and proteins. For reasons not completely understood, many genes make multiple proteins. Moreover, the proteins routinely interact with one another, adding or subtracting chemical groups that change the function of a protein—in essence, creating a novel protein for a different task. Scientists really haven't got a firm grasp of how many proteins there are in the human body. Figures like five hundred thousand to a million proteins get tossed about. Whatever their number, the point is that proteins do the body's work. If each cell were a mechanical watch, the proteins inside would be the whirring, winding, clicking parts. Although all this action takes place far below the level of sight, we have strong evidence that intra-cellular processes are governed by the shape and fit of proteins. I described the proteins as necklaces, strung together out of amino acids; that was correct, but only up to a point. After the amino acids in a protein are strung together, the protein chain must fold into a particular shape. That shape is crucial to determining how the protein works. The hemoglobin protein has four lobes, each with a hole in the center, to carry four oxygen molecules. Actin and myosin, two proteins critical in muscle contraction, ratchet past each other. Inside our cells, proteins are constantly jostling one another, looking for a fit. In a simple sense, therefore, proteomics is the study of the composition, the structure, the function, and the interactions of proteins.

Given our understanding of how the body works, it's easy to see why proteomics is the next logical step in drug discovery. Diseases occur in tissue types, that is, specific groups of cells. Say a person suffers from an inflammation in the lungs, or an enlargement of the prostate. Whatever the condition, the underlying cause is usually some protein mechanism inside the cells that has gone awry. The theory behind proteomics is that the systematic study of proteins will help us understand entire new classes of protein defects associated with diseases. Armed with this information, drug researchers could then go to work designing chemical remedies, having the particular shape that is needed, to correct the structural defect responsible for the malady.

In a sense, therefore, proteomics is an extension of what biotech scientists have been doing for years—using knowledge about the smallest building blocks of cells to design better medicines. In 2001, for instance, Amgen won FDA approval for Aranesp, a second-generation version of its best-selling protein medicine Epogen. Amgen scientists redesigned the natural protein. They added two sugar groups to the protein's structure and showed that this addition increased the length of time that the protein remained active in the bloodstream. By modifying the protein, Amgen also sidestepped an old revenue-sharing agreement with Johnson & Johnson that had covered the first-generation protein medicine. So Amgen pulled off both a great feat of protein science and a business coup in one fell swoop.

Amgen spent a decade studying and modifying this single protein. The new proteomics companies are betting that they can devise ways to rapidly determine the structures and functions of large numbers of proteins, including entire new classes of unknown proteins. The payoffs for success would be huge. But so are the obstacles.

The difficulties get back to the fact that proteins are far more complex than DNA. Proteins have twenty building blocks. DNA has four. DNA has a regular structure, which was figured out fifty years ago. Proteins do not; they fold in different ways. There's probably a Nobel Prize waiting for whoever figures out a general theory to predict protein folding. Meanwhile, scientists must work out the structure of each protein through a variety of processes, after isolating and purifying a sample of the protein. None of these steps is easy. In fact, protein analysis is so daunting that, to date, only a few thousand protein structures have been disclosed. A few thousand down, only half a million or more to go! Of course, the central aim of proteomics is to industrialize each step in the process of protein analysis so companies can pump out new protein structures in weeks instead of years.

But I'm not sure how quickly companies will be able to automate protein analysis and turn this automation toward profitable drug discovery. Every new biotech gold rush has taken longer to hit pay dirt than was initially supposed. For instance, monoclonal antibodies were first discovered in the mid-1970s, but it was twenty years before the FDA approved the first monoclonal medicine. Gene therapy experiments have been going on for more than a decade without yielding any big success or approved products. Bear that in mind as you explore the players who have already staked out niches in proteomics.

Subniches in Proteomics

I've broken the companies in the proteomics space into four groups based on a similarity of approach. First, I'll present those that make and sell instruments for doing protein analysis. Although they're not generally pure plays in proteomics, most of the instrument vendors are big-cap companies (which gives them a broader audience on Wall Street), and some are already profitable. Increasing the sales of proteomics instruments should drive their stock prices. The second group of companies is engaged more directly in proteomics. That is, they are using new instruments and techniques—sometimes of their own invention—to discover novel proteins and turn them into drug targets. Third, I'll introduce you to several private proteomics firms that would probably like to go public at the first opportunity. (In the Investor Tools section at the end of this chapter, I'll discuss whether retail investors should invest in newly minted public companies. This is an issue that transcends proteomics, but since proteomics is likely to be one of the rallying cries of future biotech bull markets, this is a good time to bring up the topic.) Finally, I'll introduce you to a set of companies that maintains chemical libraries or specializes in designing small-molecule drugs (which can be orally ingested) to hit specific drug targets—that is, disease-causing proteins. Small-molecule drug design is a natural complement to protein analysis. The kinship between understanding proteins and designing chemicals to interact with proteins makes this a good place to discuss the chemistry niche.

I've chosen these divisions because by and large that's how Wall Street will probably evaluate these companies. I say probably because this is such a new area that the proteomics companies are still experimenting with their business models, looking for the right formula to win sales and attract attention. This is particularly true of the small-cap companies that must struggle to get attention on Wall Street. If you decide to evaluate any of the companies in this chapter as potential investments, pay particular attention to their business models and partnerships. Are they tool vendors? If so, look for validating deals and partnerships. In other words, are drug and biotech companies buying their technology, and, if so, under what terms? And what kind of tool vendors are they? Are these arm's-length equipment vendors who demand cash upon delivery? Or are they more like service partners whose income depends on using a set of tools or techniques to find new drug targets or qualify those targets for human clinical trials? Some companies would like to be both equipment vendors and development partners. In short, they would like to collect up-front payments for delivering some equipment or technique, and negotiate a share of royalties or additional payments if they help qualify drug targets. These companies espouse a hybrid business model, blending attributes of the equipment vendor and the development partner. None of these definitions is static. Companies redefine themselves all the time depending on the nature of the deals they're able to negotiate. Until these companies develop profits and can be rated on the basis of earnings per share, the most important numeric variables are likely to be:

- Cash position (years or months of cash remaining is a prime indicator of the health of money-losing R&D firms)
- Sales growth rate (reveals whether drug and/or biotech companies are buying the start-ups' tools or expertise)
- Market capitalization (tells you how Wall Street values the company in absolute and relative terms)

The Instrument Makers

The starting point in proteomics is often a glob of biological material containing many intermingled proteins. The first step in the process of analysis is to separate out these intermingled proteins, and to determine how many individual types of proteins are present in the sample. Two processes are commonly used to accomplish this separation or purification step. These processes are gel electrophoresis and high-pressure liquid chromatography. Both processes involve forcing proteins through a porous matrix—think of it as an obstacle course. The smaller the protein, the faster and farther it moves. Big proteins lag behind. Once the proteins in a sample have sorted themselves in this fashion, other instruments are used to help determine the sequence of amino acids in each protein. The instrument most commonly used for this process is the mass spectrometer. It allows scientists to measure the weight of proteins and protein fragments. These protein fragments are called peptides. A peptide is a short chain of amino acids. Knowing the weight of a fragment is a good clue as to the nature of the amino acids in the fragment. Other measures help to determine the precise order of these amino acids. Determining the sequence of amino acids in a protein or group of proteins is the starting point for further analysis. Sales of purification gels and spectrometry systems constitute the heart of the current market for proteomics instruments. A recent report by Frost & Sullivan, a noted market research firm, estimated that the proteomics instrument market was worth $1.37 billion in 2001 and projected a compound annual growth rate of 34 percent through 2006. The leading players in this space include:

- Applied Biosystems Group (ABI) is the corporate cousin of Celera Genomics. Although ABI is best known as one of the inventors of DNA-processing instruments, the company is also a leading vendor of the mass spectrometry systems used in proteomics. ABI has the revenues, profits, and market capitalization required to stay competitive as new tools are developed. Typically, innovation occurs at small biotech start-ups that often find they do not have the critical mass or the sales clout that it takes to drive a new tool into the marketplace. ABI will likely to be in a position to acquire interesting new tools even if it doesn't invent them. Frost & Sullivan estimated that proteomics systems would account for more than 12 percent of ABI's 2002 revenues, making this a sizable niche product essential to the company's stock valuation.

- Amersham Biosciences is ABI's chief rival in the gene instrumentation market and as a prime competitor in proteomics instruments as well. At this writing, Amersham Biosciences is a division of Amersham plc (AHM). In October 2000, a prospectus was filed in support of an initial public offering for the division, but the subsequent stock market slump foiled that attempt and the IPO was shelved. If Amersham plc ever renews its bid to float an IPO for its biotech division, it would create a company with more than a billion dollars in revenues, and a recent sales growth rate in the neighborhood of 15 percent. The company has also been profitable in the past. Frost & Sullivan estimate that proteomics accounted for 7 percent of Amersham Bioscience's sales in 2001, and rose to an estimated 8.6 percent of sales in 2002. The company's core proteomics offerings are in gel electrophoresis systems.

- Bio-Rad Laboratories (BIOA) was founded in 1957 to supply specialty chemicals to scientific and drug researchers and has grown over time to a billion-dollar company with a worldwide distribution network. The company has been profitable. Sales growth has been strong. According to Frost & Sullivan estimates, proteomics accounted for 11 percent of revenues in 2001 and 13 percent of sales in 2002, making this sector a key driver in the company's overall stock valuation. Bio-Rad is strong in protein separation and gel electrophoresis and has established alliances with start-ups such as Luminex Corp. (LMNX) in a bid to update its catalog of protein analysis tools.

- Waters Corp. (WAT) is an instrumentation company with sales in the neighborhood of a billion dollars, a history of profitability, and a strong market capitalization. Through two of its divisions, called Waters and Micromass Ltd., it sells two lines of instrumentation geared toward proteomics. The Waters division sells high-pressure liquid chromatography systems for protein separation. The Micromass division sells

sophisticated mass spectrometry equipment. Frost & Sullivan estimate that proteomics instruments accounted for 12.2
percent of 2001 sales and 14.7 percent of 2002 sales. Continued interested in proteomics thus plays directly to Waters's
strengths.

- Bruker Daltonics Inc. (BDAL) specializes in mass spectrometry instruments. In terms of sales it is a far smaller company than some of the previous instrument vendors. Frost
& Sullivan estimate its 2002 revenues in the vicinity of $119
million. But the company is profitable, and it supports a
large enough market capitalization to get noticed on Wall
Street. Proteomics is estimated to account for more than a
third of total revenues.

- Thermo Electron Corp. (TMO) is a large, well-regarded instrument maker that offers some technically advanced mass
spectrometry equipment through a division called Thermo
Finnigan. According to Frost & Young, however, proteomics
sales accounted for something under 4 percent of Thermo
Electron's overall revenues. Thus while Thermo Finnigan's
technology may be interesting to protein researchers, success as a proteomics vendor may not be enough to drive
TMO's stock.

- Ciphergen (CIPH) is a pioneer in creating and selling chips
to automate protein discovery. Its protein chips make it easier to analyze proteins drawn from tissue samples, and study
differential expression: that is, to figure out how much of
the protein is found in the diseased tissue as opposed to
healthy cells. Its early start in protein chip technology
enabled Ciphergen to go public during the 2000 IPO rush. It
is a pure play in proteomics. But Ciphergen's sales and market capitalization are far smaller than rival vendors of traditional protein analysis technologies, and the company is

losing money. Other privately held protein chip makers are waiting in the wings to go public. Ciphergen will face challenges from these rival protein chip players even as it attempts to convince drug discovery scientists that its chips are superior to standard protein analysis techniques.

Proteomics Discovery Firms

Many of the instrument suppliers are profitable, and thus offer investors a relatively low-risk way to participate in proteomics. However, the real promise in the field lies in using protein analysis tools to discover disease targets and then create new diagnostic tests or medicines to treat them. At some level all drug and biotech firms are engaged in proteomics. After all, drug discovery almost always involves finding and fixing some protein process that has gone awry. What sets the proteomics companies apart as a class, however, is their commitment toward wholesale protein discovery. Most drug and biotech firms specialize in disease areas. There are cardiovascular companies, infectious diseases companies, cancer companies, etc. In the course of their investigations these firms become expert in the protein interactions involved in their diseases. But their focus remains the disease.

In contrast, proteomics firms start with protein analysis and work backward toward a broader understanding of the disease. Proteomics companies would like to automate differential protein analysis so they can more readily compare the protein complements of diseased and healthy cells. Finding any anomalies—high or low concentrations of a given protein associated with some diseased state— would focus drug research. The strong inference would be that the aberrant protein was an accomplice to the disease (a diagnostic marker), if not the culprit (a drug target). The desire to automate the process of analysis carries through to determining the structure of the protein, learning how it folds and functions. This step is a prerequisite to designing a small molecule drug for that particular drug

83

target. Sometimes the proteomics companies buy tools. Sometimes they must invent tools. In other cases they integrate purchased and proprietary tools to create novel systems.

The companies in this niche are experimenting on many levels, not just on their techniques but also in their business models. In fact, one of their chief challenges is figuring out how to make a business out of proteomics. The recent lesson of the genomics gold rush was that Wall Street isn't fond of database companies. Setting up a company whose objective is to discover unknown proteins isn't considered a viable business model. So the proteomics companies have tended to come full circle and focus on looking for proteins implicated in diseases. In short, they're trying to become biotech companies with a particular strength in protein analysis.

How do proteomics companies compare to previous generations of biotech firms? Today they may have an edge in the techniques of protein analysis, but that advantage may not last long. If researchers decide that new protein analysis tools are becoming fundamental to drug discovery, these techniques will soon be purchased, invented, or otherwise adopted by everyone in the field—by Big Pharma, by big-cap biotech companies, and by every start-up that hopes to get a product on the market. *Thus, the current crop of proteomics companies could sort out into three types of companies:*

- Those that come up with a superior tool that becomes the foundation for an independent, sustaining tools business
- Those that use their edge in protein analysis to get a few drugs into clinical trials and become drug developers
- Those that get absorbed by some larger company that wants to buy a team of hot protein scientists

Although there are a couple of efforts under way to map the universe of proteins, as has already been done for human genes, many scientists consider such an undertaking premature. Too little is known about proteins at a theoretical level to warrant a wholesale effort on the scale of the Human Genome Project. The human proteome—the name given to the full complement of proteins in our body—is so vast that we'll have to be content for a while with chipping away at the edges of the unknown. As you evaluate the protein-discovery companies, remember that they're embarked on a long-haul project. Having strong cash and market-cap positions will be as essential to success as their breakthrough technology. Since the latter is obvious only in retrospect, let's start by looking at the larger companies in this niche:

- Myriad Genetics (MYGN) is a drug discovery and diagnostics company with a particular expertise in identifying novel protein-protein interactions. In 2001 Myriad Genetics formed a subsidiary called Myriad Proteomics, in which it holds a controlling stake. Myriad Proteomics' stated objective is to identify all the protein interactions in the human body by roughly 2004. Partners in the subsidiary include the Japanese computer giant Hitachi Ltd., the Swiss investment group Friedli Corporate Finance, and the database software vendor Oracle Corp. Rival proteomics firms say it is unrealistic to map all or most protein interactions given current technology. They also question what knowledge would be gained from mapping proteins at random. Myriad officials maintain that the random technique will turn up novel disease pathways, and that the process can detect proteins in lower concentrations than tests that use diseased tissue as a starting point. Meanwhile, Myriad Genetics remains focused on drugs and diagnostics. It has experimental compounds in human and preclinical trials. It is not profitable but is well capitalized, and it has strong support from institutional investors.

- Celera Genomics Group (CRA), one of the stars of the gene discovery rush, has a large proteomics program under development. In 2001, Celera acquired a chemistry firm to complement its other programs. Between its commanding position in gene discovery, its budding proteomics effort, and its new chemical expertise, Celera hopes to discover

85

drug targets at an accelerated rate and either partner them out to drug companies or turn them over to its in-house chemists to design small-molecule drugs. Interestingly, Celera chose the random method when it came to gene mapping, but it has rejected that approach in its protein discovery effort. Instead, Celera will focus on studying proteins that seem to be implicated in disease.

- CuraGen Corp. (CRGN) employs a broad array of gene and protein discovery techniques to find drug targets. It uses a proteomics technology called Pathcalling to identify protein interactions with an eye toward understanding how their interactions cause or aid disease. The company has identified numerous protein targets in many different disease areas. Some of these it has licensed to drug companies. Its partners include Biogen, Genentech, Roche, GlaxoSmithKline, and Bayer. CuraGen also intends to develop its own protein therapies in the areas of cancer, diabetes, inflammation, and nervous system disorders. The company has attracted strong support from institutional investors and a middle-tier market capitalization.

- Oxford GlycoSciences (OGSI) is a British biotech firm, spun out of Oxford University, which has improved and automated the commonly used process of gel electrophoresis. It has also made refinements in mass spectrometry and protein-protein interaction techniques. It is commercializing these advances in several ways: fee-for-service deals with companies including Pfizer and GlaxoSmithKline, collaborations with companies like Medarex (the antibody developer) that allow Oxford to retain some rights to discoveries, internal development of promising leads, and the creation of a pay-per-view protein database. Oxford has also acquired a late-stage experimental medicine (Vevesca), in hopes of creating a revenue stream by getting the drug approved. But in June 2002 the FDA rejected its application, which caused the company's shares to plummet as investors were forced to rethink their premise for taking a stake in this proteomics pioneer.

- Cytogen Corp. (CYTO) and Large Scale Biology Corp. (LSBC) are two small-cap proteomics firms. Cytogen has a subsidiary, AxCell Biosciences Corporation, that is developing a database of protein pathways to aid in drug development. Large Scale Biology has developed a high-throughput system for comparing protein expression in healthy and diseased cells, and is using its ProGEx technology to create databases, protein markers, and other proteomics products.

Emerging Proteomics Companies

Proteomics is such a cutting-edge field that many companies with novel technologies in this area are still private as of this writing. If history is any guide, most of these companies will go public at their earliest opportunity, and probably as a group. By highlighting some of these emerging proteomics players, I don't mean to suggest that they are superior investments to other companies that might pop up in the next round of public offerings. In fact, in the Investor Tools section at the end of this chapter I'll take a rather skeptical look at whether individual investors should jump on the IPO bandwagon. But I do want to spend a few pages exposing you to some of the proteomics technologies under development because they are clearly trying to address some of the bottlenecks in protein analysis. Even if you never invest a nickel in any of these firms, and avoid the entire proteomics niche because it's too early and speculative for your investing tastes, a firm understanding of protein analysis is essential.

With that in mind, one of the keys to understanding proteins is solving their structures. As you may recall, proteins are chains of amino acids. But the sequence of amino acids doesn't tell the entire story. Proteins must fold into specific shapes to do their job. In many cases the search for a drug involves finding or designing some man-made chemical that can fit into a given protein, in order to prompt or retard some activity. Thus, solving protein structures is often a prerequisite to drug discovery. This is such a laborious process—and yet one so obviously useful to drug development—that proteomics start-ups are trying to speed up the determination of protein structure by:

- Improving the process of X-ray crystallography
- Developing new structural analysis techniques, notably nuclear magnetic resonance (NMR) spectroscopy
- Inventing computer algorithms to predict protein folding patterns based on amino acid sequence information

X-ray crystallography is the incumbent science when it comes to determining the structure of biological molecules. It has been in use since the 1940s. Watson and Crick relied on X-ray data from British scientist Rosalind Franklin to solve the structure of DNA in 1953. The process begins with growing a crystal of the protein in question to freeze its shape. The crystal is bombarded with X rays to reveal a pattern that suggests the position of each atom in the protein. Although X-ray crystallography has been around for decades, each step in the process remains difficult and not easily automated. Nevertheless, start-up companies are trying to do just that. Structural GenomiX and Syrrx are two San Diego companies that have won venture capital backing to speed up structure determination through crystallography. Both firms have techniques to speed up the process of growing the crystals, which has often proved a bedeviling task. They have also secured access to high-quality X-ray sources at national laboratories. Protein structures are not revealed by your dentist's X-ray machine!

NMR spectroscopy is another technique for determining protein structure with advantages and disadvantages relative to crystallography. NMR can be used on proteins in solution, which avoids the difficult step of growing a crystal. Moreover, NMR allows scientists to determine the structures of proteins in their natural state, that is, capable of folding and unfolding, whereas crystallized proteins are frozen in one position. At present, however, NMR can be used only to determine the structures of relatively small proteins. Future advances may increase the size of the proteins that can be studied using NMR, but it is unlikely that this process will ever supplant crystallography, which works on proteins of any size. Some start-ups are already using NMR and crystallography together, sometimes in conjunction with computer modeling programs, in an effort to attack protein structures from several angles. For instance, Gene-Formatics Inc. is a San Diego start-up with programs in crystallography, NMR, and computer modeling. Affinium Pharmaceuticals of Toronto, Canada, combines an array of protein analysis techniques, including mass spectroscopy, NMR, crystallography, and protein-protein interaction screening.

Other private firms worth a mention include MDS Proteomics, a subsidiary of the Canadian medical supply firm MDS Inc. (MDZ). MDS Proteomics is using an array of proteomics techniques to identify drug targets. Caprion is another proteomics player from Canada. Hybrigenics is a French start-up active in proteomics and functional genomics. GeneProt is a Swiss company that is automating various steps in protein analysis. And, of course, there is no shortage of U.S. firms trying to become proteomics pioneers, including Zyomyx, a California biotech firm that is developing chip technologies to study proteins.

In the final analysis proteomics is about finding new drug targets before some other company can claim them. The technologies of proteomics are so complex, and are evolving so rapidly, that even the drug and biotech company scientists who are the consumers for proteomics systems and services take months to evaluate and adopt new technologies. If you are tempted to invest in these or other proteomics start-ups when they go public, be sure to look for proof that smart buyers are willing to pay for whatever it is the company is selling. I'll have more to say on IPOs shortly. Meanwhile, one of the reasons I took you through this section on protein structure is to get back to the point of drug research—finding chemicals that can be pressed into pills and used as medicines.

Chemistry Strikes Back

Biotechnology began a quarter century ago as something of a rebellion against the drug industry. As you may recall, biotech firms began by creating protein medicines, making insulin for diabetics or growth hormone for children who failed to develop. These were conditions that couldn't be treated by traditional drugs—that is, chemicals that were pressed into pills. But no advance comes without a downside. Proteins are large, complex molecules, and they are more costly to make than chemical drugs. Protein medicines are also more difficult to administer. They must be injected or taken intravenously, to avoid getting chopped up into amino acids by the digestive system. By contrast, once a pill is swallowed, its chemicals dissolve and make their way through the bloodstream. If a pill and a protein could both solve the same health problem, the pill—or, as it's called in the trade, the small-molecule drug—would win every time.

The preference for pills hasn't put biotech firms out of business, but it has changed the nature of biotech discovery. Nowadays biotech firms need not create a protein. Instead, they might identify a protein that causes a disease, deduce how the protein's function relates to its structure, and then—assuming the protein is out of whack—find a small-molecule drug to tweak it in the right spot. Several biotech firms specialize in this last step—designing small-molecule drugs to hit specific protein targets. These chemistry companies maintain libraries of chemical compounds, or design molecules, to fit specific protein targets. Their business models are all over the map. Sometimes they work on a fee-for-service basis. In other instances they sign partnering agreements in which fees are contingent upon performance, such as making sure the experimental chemical makes it into human trials. Many prospective drugs prove toxic in preclinical animal studies and never make it into the clinic.

Albany Molecular Research Inc. (AMRI) has the largest market capitalization of the companies in the chemistry niche. The company has also been profitable, an attribute that sets it apart from the vast majority of biotech firms, as well as its rivals in the chemistry niche. Four other chemistry firms traveled together in the same market-cap range. They are Array BioPharma (ARRY), Pharmacopeia Inc. (PCOP), ArQule Inc. (ARQL), and 3-Dimensional Pharmaceuticals (DDDP). Other smaller market cap players include Discovery Partners International (DPII) and Argonaut Technologies (AGNT).

Whatever their current pecking order, the chemistry companies seem to be a hot group because they supply expertise crucial in the final stages of drug discovery. Chemistry is essential to designing small-molecule drugs. Companies that have amassed terabytes of genome data have found that Wall Street wants them to become drug developers, and that means acquiring skills in pharmacological chemistry. When Celera Genomics acquired Axys Pharmaceuticals in a $177 million stock deal in 2001, former Celera president J. Craig Venter joked that he "needed a chemistry set." At roughly the same time, Lexicon Genetics, which uses mice genetics to find drug targets for human diseases, acquired Coelacanth Corp. because the latter had the chemistry skills to fashion drugs against those targets. In 2002 Lexicon's competitor, Deltagen, purchased a chemistry unit from Bristol-Myers Squibb for the same reason. As biotech firms are discovering: It's the chemistry, stupid!

Investor Tools: IPOs and Other Manias

You might infer from the foregoing discussion that chemistry firms make likely acquisition targets, and therefore even those companies that don't achieve independent success may still become a division inside some larger company. Being acquired is one way that small, struggling biotech firms can reward shareholders—at least those who bought the stock when it was cheaper than the acquisition price. But the real problem from the investor's point of view is that the biotech industry is too specialized. The industry is populated by far too many firms that excel at one piece of the drug discovery puzzle but can't develop blockbuster products and profits. Investors who buy into these specialized companies, which often flood into the market during periods of high IPO activity, are frequently disappointed with their returns.

In a way biotech specialization makes sense. Big companies are often poor innovators. Biotech and high-tech entrepreneurs have shown that the best way to drive an innovation into the marketplace is to build a company around the idea, recruit people who believe in the concept, and give them stock options for added incentive.

But great concepts don't necessarily build companies that can sustain themselves on sales and deliver profits to investors. Let's take an analogy from the high-tech world. Spreadsheets were a great advance when they first came out, and spreadsheet vendors were hot properties in the early days of personal computing. Ironically, however, spreadsheets proved so valuable that their basic functions were turned into an operating system accessory. Independent spreadsheet companies dwindled. What had once been a technical advance quickly became a routine feature, and while the analogy to drug discovery isn't perfect, experience suggests that biotech speciality firms—the chemistry companies, the proteomics pioneers, the gene-discovery outfits—will probably go the way of the spreadsheet vendors. When Celera acquired Axys it was doing more than buying a chemistry set. It was acknowledging that *Wall Street believes the true value in biotech lies in selling drugs, not services or information.* Celera was reinventing its business because Wall Street had deemed its original niche as a gene database as too narrow for sustained profitability.

Yet periodically Wall Street mints whole cohorts of new companies, including many specialized firms, through initial public offerings. During the genomics craze of 2000, a record number of biotech companies went public. The big technology fad then was gene discovery. In late May 2002, I looked at the stock prices of forty-nine of these companies from the 2000 IPO cohort. All had been public for more than a year, some longer than two years. My starting point was the opening price of the stock on the day it went public. (The IPO opening price is different from the offering price; some stocks were so "hot" at IPO that the investment banks handling the deal boosted the price on opening day, when the shares first became available to the general investor.)

Using prices provided by FactSet, a prominent financial database, I compared the opening price of each company to its value on a given day in 2002. Only five companies had stock prices above their IPO opening when I performed this exercise! The rest of the stocks were priced far below their IPO opening, and most of these had lost more than 40 percent since going public. In short, had you bought biotech IPOs when the sector was "hot" in 2000, you stood a 90 percent chance of losing money!

The performance of the IPOs floated during the 2000 stock bubble have been so abysmal that the Securities and Exchange Commission and other authorities have been investigating investment banks and brokerage firms to determine whether they violated any laws. Those investigations have centered on high-tech, telecom, and dot.com IPOs. Though these actions may not touch biotech directly, biotech investors still need to understand why bullish IPO markets are dangerous events that inexperienced investors should avoid.

Everything you need to know about IPO bull markets boils down to two key terms: *exit strategy* and *window*. Exit strategy is how venture capitalists make back the money they invest in early-stage companies. Venture capitalists bankroll start-ups. They like to get their money back, at a profit whenever possible, by selling the company within a few years' time. Some venture-backed start-ups sell themselves to one of the big drug or biotech firms. That's not your concern. The exit strategy that is most likely to affect the retail investor occurs when a venture-backed firm sells itself through an IPO.

IPOs often occur in flurries. From time to time, Wall Street gets into a bullish mood. Investors large and small start imagining that every stock—even those of young, money-losing companies—is bound to climb. During such exuberant periods investment pros say the "window is open." At a recent investment conference, biotech venture capitalist Sam Colella flashed a slide that biotech companies live and die by. It showed that over the last twenty years, the biotech windows have lasted between eight and fifteen months,

The Disappointing IPOs of 2000

A record number of biotech firms went public in 2000, but within months most of these stocks had crashed. In spring 2002, only five of the forty-nine stocks listed here had prices above their IPO opening price (the price at which they first appeared on the public markets). Check their opening prices against their most recent quotes to see where they stand today.

Ticker	Company	IPO Opening Price ($)	Ticker	Company	IPO Opening Price ($)
DDDP	3-DIMENSIONAL PHARMACEUTICAL	19.0	ILMN	ILLUMINA INC	29.9
ACLA	ACLARA BIOSCIENCES INC	30.5	INMX	INFORMAX INC	22.1
ADLR	ADOLOR CORP	15.0	ITMN	INTERMUNE INC	30.1
AGEN	ANTIGENICS INC	45.0	INGN	INTROGEN THERAPEUTICS INC	8.5
AMEV	APPLIED MOLECULAR EVOLUTION	25.0	ISTA	ISTA PHARMACEUTICALS INC	10.6
ARNA	ARENA PHARMACEUTICALS INC	18.0	KERX	KERYX BIOPHARMACEUTICALS INC	9.5
ARRY	ARRAY BIOPHARMA INC	8.2	KOSN	KOSAN BIOSCIENCES INC	14.0
BDAL	BRUKER DALTONICS INC	20.5	LSBC	LARGE SCALE BIOLOGY CORP	26.9
CPHD	CEPHEID INC	6.3	LEXG	LEXICON GENETICS INC	22.0
CRL	CHARLES RIVER LABS INTL INC	19.5	LMNX	LUMINEX CORP	19.5
CIPH	CIPHERGEN BIOSYSTEMS INC	34.0	MAXY	MAXYGEN INC	36.0
DCGN	DECODE GENETICS INC	29.5	MDCO	MEDICINES CO	7.9
DGEN	DELTAGEN INC	18.0	ORCH	ORCHID BIOSCIENCES INC	10.0
DNDN	DENDREON CORP	10.0	PDGM	PARADIGM GENETICS INC	7.1
DPII	DISCOVERY PARTNERS INTL INC	18.0	RTIX	REGENERATION TECH INC	16.3
DVSA	DIVERSA CORP	56.0	RIGL	RIGEL PHARMACEUTICALS INC	7.3
DRRX	DURECT CORP	17.5	SGMO	SANGAMO BIOSCIENCES INC	15.0
DYAX	DYAX CORP	19.6	SQNM	SEQUENOM INC	71.0
EXEL	EXELIXIS INC	18.0	SFCC	SFBC INTL INC	10.0
GNSC	GENAISSANCE PHARMACEUTICALS	15.0	TNOX	TANOX INC	28.5
GCOR	GENENCOR INTL INC	22.5	TELK	TELIK INC	7.0
GNSL	GENOMIC SOLUTIONS INC	8.1	TBIO	TRANSGENOMIC INC	30.0
GNVC	GENVEC INC	10.6	TLRK	TULARIK INC	20.5
HBIO	HARVARD BIOSCIENCE INC	8.5	VGNX	VARIAGENICS INC	22.8
			VLGC	VIROLOGIC INC	7.3

Source: FactSet

Biotech's Fickle Window

The biotech industry cycles between brief rallies and longer troughs. Privately held start-ups race to take advantage of these rallies to float initial public offerings (IPOs). In Wall Street parlance they say "the window is open," because once the drought begins and the window shuts, raising money to fund experiments become much tougher.

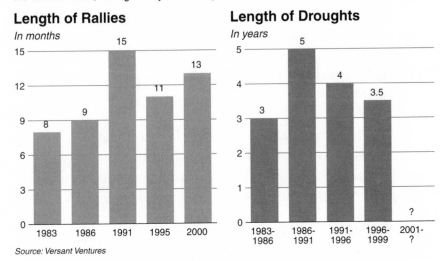

Length of Rallies

In months

15
13
11
9
8

1983   1986   1991   1995   2000

Length of Droughts

In years

5
4
3.5
3
?

1983-   1986-   1991-   1996-   2001-
1986   1991   1996   1999   ?

Source: Versant Ventures

while the down markets in between have run from three to five years. "The (IPO) window is only open for months while the droughts last for years," Colella said. Given this reality, if you are running a biotech firm when the window opens, every instinct in your body—not to mention the venture capitalists on your board—scream, "Take the company public, now!" If there are gaps in your business plan—like you can't figure out how the firm will make a profit given its current line of business—well this isn't the time to quibble over details. Get the company public first and tweak the "business model" later. Investors will understand.

Of course, most small investors don't understand. These IPO flurries occur during bull markets. Inexperienced investors only notice the momentum that drives IPOs higher during the initial frenzy and try to get in on the action. In fact, it's like a game of musical chairs that the retail investor is almost certain to lose. Initial public offerings are generally sold to institutional investors and high-net-worth individuals—Wall Street's high rollers. Some of these high rollers flip their shares immediately. The investment bankers who take companies public often get what's called a "green shoe" allotment. This is a block of shares they can sell after the IPO is fully subscribed at the opening price. The average investor buys these second-generation shares, those that get flipped by the high rollers or sold out of the green shoe. Eventually the madness fades. Buyers realize they're holding stock in companies whose technologies they can't fathom and whose profit prospects are, to put it kindly, rather distant. Once the sell-off begins, hot IPOs cool quickly. Inexperienced investors, who bought near the peak and didn't anticipate the collapse, get burned.

When I began research for this book, and was wondering how to help you make wise investments, or at least when to be wary of the foolish ones, I sat down with Tom Dietz, senior managing director at Pacific Growth Equities, an investment bank in San Francisco. We were talking about the risks of buying early-stage biotech companies, a description that certainly encompasses IPOs, though we weren't talking about public offerings in particular. "I know what I don't know when I buy early-stage companies, and it worries me," Dietz said. "What about a retail investor?"

With these caveats in mind, here are three rules for screening biotech IPOs. They're really no different from the rules for evaluating any biotech investment:

- The best candidates are companies with profits, or at least predictable revenues based on some product on the market.
- The next class of IPOs will be companies with at least one and preferably several drug candidates that have completed Phase II or Phase III clinical trials; you can almost see the light at the end of the tunnel.
- Companies that don't fit either of the two preceding categories are speculative plays, and while you might make money buying and flipping them during a bull market, you risk getting stuck when the music ends.

5

Picks and Shovels:
The Biotech Toolmakers

Biotechnology began as a new way to make medicines, by creating proteins that were delivered through injection. This was a revolution compared to the drug industry's previous practice of fashioning chemical remedies that could be swallowed in pill form. Over the last quarter century, however, biotechnology has caused an even more profound change in the way drugs are developed. In the early part of the twentieth century, medical discovery was based mainly on observation and serendipity. The discovery of penicillin is a classic example. A researcher noticed how a certain mold controlled the growth of bacterial cultures. It wasn't clear why it happened; the important point was that the observation led to the development of an important, lifesaving medicine. Such observations might be considered the low-hanging fruit of drug discovery. By the end of the century, as biotechnology came into prominence, most of these low-hanging fruit had already been plucked. To devise treatments for tough, untreated conditions such as cancer or Alzheimer's, medical researchers—whether they worked at drug companies, biotech firms, or universities—found that they needed to understand the inner workings of diseases. This meant peering inside living cells, to figure out what had gone awry at a molecular level, and then use this knowledge to devise a fix. In the process of exploring these new molecular frontiers, biotech scientists have invented a complete repertoire of tools to probe and analyze molecular processes. These tools have become the foundations for new companies and these companies have created new areas of potential investment.

The main categories of biotech tools are biochips and biocomputing. Both result from the convergence of high-tech and biotech skills. Many biotech instruments are powerful special-purpose computation or detection systems. In addition to taking advantage of the processing power of off-the-shelf microprocessors, biotech toolmakers have borrowed the manufacturing expertise that high-tech firms gained by making fast, cheap silicon chips. Biotech firms have used chip-making technologies to create devices that automate experiments involving DNA and proteins. Biochips don't work by conducting electricity; instead, they perform biochemical operations. Biochips allow drug-discovery scientists to perform more experiments in less time. Instead of analyzing a single tissue sample, biochips enable researchers to study thousands of samples simultaneously, comparing healthy cells with diseased cells to look for patterns.

Because these automated experiments generate huge volumes of data, it's no longer possible for researchers to make observations on pad and paper. In any case, many experiments track phenomena that take place far below the level of vision. The results of biotech experiments are often so subtle they can be discerned only by sensitive instruments. Generally speaking, these instruments aren't looking for a single result because it's beyond our current science to create experiments involving single molecules. Instead, biotech experiments look for patterns in large numbers of experiments. Researchers might compare a thousand samples of diseased tissue with a control group of healthy cells, hoping that instruments will detect differences in gene or protein activity. Biotech experiments therefore depend on automated detectors that feed data directly to computational systems. So much data is generated by such experiments that drug developers increasingly depend on sophisticated software to sift through results and highlight patterns. Other laboratory information management systems enable research directors to keep track of the hundreds of experiments that might be going on in their laboratories at any given time. These software systems have generated their own market niche called bioinformatics.

From an investment viewpoint the good news about biochip and bioinformatics vendors is that these tools seldom need FDA approval. Tools companies can sell their wares directly to researchers at drug, biotech, and university laboratories and thus begin generating revenues much sooner than early-stage drug development companies, whose products must survive the clinical trials gauntlet. Tool vendors were popular during the 2000 bubble. Investors decided that in our current gold rush to develop medicines, biotech tool vendors were selling picks and shovels to the miners. Many tool vendors went public in 2000.

Unfortunately, the pick-and-shovel premise seems to have been oversold, and the stocks of tool companies have been hard hit in the correction that followed the bubble. New public toolmakers such as Aclara Biosciences, Ciphergen Biosystems, InforMax, and Illumina have experienced stunning stock drops. Once the stock market turned bearish in 2001, Wall Street disavowed the idea that pick-and-shovel vendors would become profitable sooner, and returned to the more traditional notion that drug developers make the best investments, because even though it takes them longer to win FDA approval, blockbuster medicines generally create sustained profits.

Given Wall Street's fickle attitudes toward their niche, some tool vendors have tried to create a hybrid business model. They try to generate some income from sales of their devices or software, while simultaneously forming discovery partnerships with key customers who promise them a share of royalties from any drugs discovered using their proprietary techniques. No one can predict what the overall investment sentiment will be toward tool companies at any given time, or what business model is appropriate for a given company. The point is that when analyzing stocks in this sector, you must be mindful of Wall Street's changing attitudes toward the toolmakers. Be wary of buying tool stocks when they're considered "hot" because odds are they'll cool off at some point and leave you underwater. Conversely, if you buy tools when they're out of favor relative to drug-discovery companies, be sure you have some bit of knowledge that might improve stock prices in the sector, or at least the stock you're considering.

Gauging the market for biochip technologies is still more art than science. The field is so young and small that it lacks the sort of market reporting services that allow investors to track semiconductor shipments on a year-to-year basis. But a UBS Warburg research report has estimated the total market for biochips at $300 million in 2000, and projected growth of 40 percent, indicating a market worth of $1.2 billion in 2004. In a similar vein, the Frost & Sullivan market research group fixed shipments of bioinformatics software at $1.4 billion in 2000, and projected growth to $7 billion by 2007.

Most biochip and bioinformatics companies are young firms with relatively small market caps. It's not clear which will grow into middle- or top-tier companies and which will be acquired (most likely by a customer that has come to depend on its technology). Still, investors who have experience with high-tech stocks may feel comfortable taking positions in these companies that marry biotechnology with Silicon Valley.

Biochips Part I: Microarrays

One of the objectives in drug research is to find the genetic differences between healthy and sick patients. Often the goal of an experiment is to compare two sets of tissue samples, one drawn from a healthy patient or patients, and the other drawn from diseased individuals. The goal of such comparisons is to spot differences in gene activity. As you may recall, virtually every cell in the body carries a full copy of the genome in the DNA that makes up its nucleus. But only a certain percentage of genes are active—scientists say expressed—in any given cell at any given time. A basic premise of drug research is that differences in gene expression will provide clues about where to look for drugs. If a certain gene is overexpressed or underexpressed in diseased tissue samples, drug researchers target that gene and look for ways to bring the aberrant gene activity into the normal range. DNA microarrays, sometimes called DNA chips, are fundamental tools for doing such differential gene expression analysis.

DNA microarrays are slivers of glass, silicon, or some other material studded with thousands of DNA probes. Each probe is a short length of single-stranded DNA designed to fish out an active gene. In nature DNA is double-stranded. The two opposing strands match up in a precise pattern. In order to create a protein—that is, to perform some function—DNA forms a single-stranded molecule called a messenger RNA (mRNA). The presence of messenger RNAs in a tissue sample is therefore a proxy for gene expression. In a typical experiment, drug researchers will extract mRNA from a tissue sample, label this mRNA with fluorescent tags, and then pour the sample onto a DNA microarray. Over a period of several hours the mRNA molecules will bind to the matching single-stranded probes on the chip. These probes correspond to specific genes or regions of the genome. The microarrays are generally inserted into special instruments that detect the fluorescent tags. The detectors indicate where mRNAs have attached to probes, thus indicating which genes are active in the tissue sample. Researchers will typically compare many samples from healthy and diseased cells, looking for differences in gene activity that might be the cause or consequence of an illness—and therefore clues to further research. In a sense the DNA chip allows scientists to "see" what is happening inside cells at a genetic level.

Affymetrix (AFFX) is the technology pioneer and market leader in microarrays. Any discussion of this niche must begin and focus on Affymetrix, because the other players are so much smaller. The company began commercial shipments of its technology in 1996. Researchers are the main consumers for Affymetrix chips that sell for anywhere from $45 to $2,000, depending on the density of genetic probes on the device and the number of genes the chip is designed to spot. Affymetrix's technology for making microarrays is based on the same processes used to manufacture silicon chips. Over the years the company has increased the density of the probes it can pack into a microarray, making its chips a favored tool of commercial drug and biotech researchers. Between 1997 and 2000,

Affy's sales grew tenfold from $19.8 million in 1997 to $200.8 million in 2000. In 2001, however, revenue growth slowed as the company's microarray franchise came under pricing pressure from rivals. Affymetrix ended 2001 with revenues of $224.9 million, an increase of 12 percent over the prior year. The company was not profitable. In the first six months of 2002, Affymetrix posted a 33 percent increase in revenues to $138.8 million, and narrowed its loss by 74 percent to $5.2 million. Going forward, investors will be looking for Affymetrix to leverage its market leadership position to deliver sustained profits. Its stock chart shows its slow progress before the 2000 bubble, its quick rise and fall, and its current search for a proper valuation.

Late in 2001, one of Affymetrix's chief rivals, Incyte Genomics (INCY), quit manufacturing microarrays to focus on drug development. Rather than completely exit the business, however, Incyte licensed some of its technology and intellectual property to other high-tech firms including Agilent Technologies (A) and Motorola (MOT). Thus, it is unclear whether Affymetrix faces less pressure, or just a new set of competitors.

In addition to competition from other vendors, Affymetrix continues to suffer poaching from "home-brew" microarrays. Several academic centers publish complete how-to manuals for making microarrays, and many researchers prefer to make their own chips, either to save money or customize their experiments. Home-brew chips can't match the density of Affymetrix's offerings, but for many experiments that may not matter. In any event, home brews represent a form of guerrilla competition.

After Affymetrix the other microarray vendors include the following:

- Hyseq (HYSQ) is a genomics company intent on reinventing itself as a drug development company. Hyseq had been in litigation with Affymetrix over patent disputes involving their microarray technologies, but they settled their differences late in 2001. Hyseq subsequently created a subsidiary, Callida Genomics, to carry on its microarray business. The

Affymetrix: Tool Leader Searches for Value

Closing price

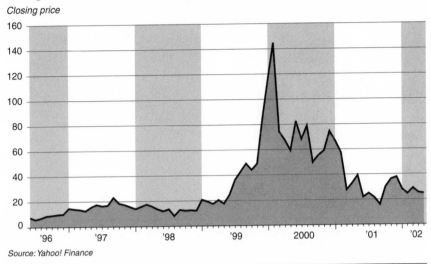

Source: Yahoo! Finance

settlement gave Affymetrix a minority stake in Callida, and the option to increase its control of future technology that might be spun out of Callida. Hyseq has a powerful and sensitive microarray technology but has not been able to drive this technology into the marketplace in any meaningful way. The settlement frees the parties from wasting energy on patent litigation, and gives both Affymetrix and Hyseq a way to benefit if Callida succeeds.

- Illumina (ILMN) creates microarrays by depositing gene probes on tiny fiber optic beads. The company was formed in 1998 to exploit this new technology. Illumina has allied itself with Applied Biosystems (ABI) to sell a line of microarrays designed to detect single-nucleotide polymorphisms or SNPs. SNPs are minute genetic differences between individuals that may make one person more prone to disease or manifest an adverse reaction to a drug. Illumina is a tiny, early-stage company. In 2001, the company reported a loss of $24.8 million that was almost precisely ten times its revenues of $2.5 million.

- Nanogen (NGEN) has pioneered a microarray technology that promises faster experimental results with greater sensitivity. Founded in 1993, the company has aimed itself at the diagnostic market rather than the research arena. In 2001, Nanogen hired a new chief executive, Randy White, a veteran of thirty years in the clinical diagnostics business. Nanogen intends to use its biochip technology to create tests aimed at diagnosing specific diseases by detecting gene or protein markers. In 2001, Nanogen reported a loss of $32.5 million on revenues of $11.2 million

Over the long term, all the players hope and expect that microarrays will find their way into routine clinical diagnostics, along the lines that Nanogen is pursuing. But this is not likely to be a quick migration from the laboratory to the clinic. In order to pursue the clinical market, microarrays will have to become foolproof. Think of the person who drew blood last time you had a cholesterol screening. To commercialize diagnostic microarrays, manufacturers will have to create test kits that produce flawless results every time when used by technicians with varying levels of skill. Health care providers are cautious about adopting new technologies. Technical challenges will compound the difficulty. It is very possible that microarray technology will have to be blended with microfluidics (which we'll read about in the next section) in order to create a truly easy-to-perform test. Above all, individual tests must clearly demonstrate a benefit and must win the approval of the physician community.

Here are some final investment tips in looking at the microarrray vendors:

- Affymetrix needs to turn the corner to profitability and prove that its market leadership can provide sustained earnings.
- The smaller players must demonstrate revenue growth; meanwhile, keep your eyes on their cash balances. If they get under two or one year's cash, that's a danger sign.

Biochips Part II: Microfluidics

The era of the test tube and flask in biology ended long ago. During the last decade, biotech scientists grew accustomed to performing experiments in what are called microtiter plates. These are trays, about the size of your hand, dotted with 96 tiny wells. (Some plates hold 384 wells.) Each of these 96 wells can hold a few drops of experimental liquid. That's all the volume needed to run most experiments. And in any case, it probably isn't possible to extract enough relevant biological material to fill an old-fashioned test tube.

Now, however, the microtiter plate is slowly being replaced by an even smaller experimental platform, the microfluidic chip. These chips are slices of quartz, glass, or plastic whose surfaces have been etched with canals far thinner than human hairs. An infinitesimal drop of experimental fluid, placed onto the chip, is conducted through a series of reaction chambers that have been cleverly arranged to automate the several steps usually required to perform an experiment. Because fluids in small volumes behave differently than in rivers or streams, a whole variety of tricks are needed to keep experimental liquids flowing through the devices, hence the name *microfluidics*. Like DNA arrays, microfluidic chips have evolved from the manufacturing techniques used to create silicon chips. One of the key principles driving the acceptance of microfluidic chips is the ability to put several steps of an experiment into one foolproof package that can allow researchers to do more experiments in less time, or allow senior scientists to delegate repetitive work to technicians. Hence these microfluidic devices are often called lab-on-chip technologies. But the basic idea is simple—these devices bring the high-tech mantra of smaller, faster, and cheaper to biology. This is a new field, and reliable measures of potential market size are elusive. Analysts for UBS Warburg have projected that the total biochip market will be worth $1.2 billion in 2004, but did not break down how much of that would be microarrays and how much would be microfluidic devices.

The immediate customers for microfluidics are biotech and drug-discovery firms trying to make their research operations more efficient. The scale of modern drug discovery is awesome. One example of a microfluidic application is high-throughput drug screening. Drug and biotech firms typically have access to libraries of chemical compounds, and they want to know whether any of these compounds might react with a target gene. To answer this question, they must systematically throw a dash of the compound into a tube with a sample derived from each potential target gene to look for any sign of a reaction. Given the number of genes of interest and the number of chemicals that have already been isolated for medical purposes, a large drug or biotech company might run tens of millions of screening experiments per year. The sheer cost of the materials needed to run these biological screening operations is daunting. Executives with Aclara Biosciences (ACLA), a leading microfluidics vendor, estimate that it costs about $1 per test for the enzymes and other consumables used in screening experiments. Because microfluidic chips require smaller volumes of materials, they can cut the cost-per-experiment in half.

More important than the savings derived from using smaller amounts of materials, however, is the potential for accelerating the pace of experimentation. Daniel Kisner, chairman of Caliper Technologies (CALP), a microfluidics pioneer, points out that most human genes have already been identified. The chemical libraries are also well established. Now the question is which drug discovery firms will be the first to match some chemical with a novel gene target— and thus be in position to patent a potential remedy. According to Kisner, Caliper chips are enabling some drug researchers to run forty thousand screening experiments a day. "These companies are in a race," he says. "There's a land grab out there to convert this gene information into targets for drugs."

Although drug and biotech researchers are currently the prime marker for microfluidic chips, UBS Warburg expects these devices to penetrate other sectors that need to perform routine chemical analysis. These markets include environmental testing, agricultural research, forensics, and bioterror detection. The nation's heightened sensitivity to the potential for chemical and biological attacks has put a premium on methods for detecting even tiny traces of harmful chemicals. Since 1997, the Defense Advanced Research Projects Agency (DARPA)—the Pentagon department that promoted the early development of the Internet—has supported biochip research at biotech firms and academic and government labs. During the anthrax scare of 2001, investors began to notice companies like Cepheid (CPHD), which has used its DARPA support to develop mobile test units for detecting a variety of hazards including anthrax, smallpox, and Ebola virus. Cepheid's system consists of two main parts. First, there is the consumable chip that contains all the chemistry needed to perform the test, once the field agent drops a sample of suspect fluid into place. The consumable chip is then fed into a portable instrument, not much larger than a personal computer, that can perform the analysis in as little as thirty minutes. A rugged version of the instrument, suitable for use in the field, can even be powered off a car battery!

One would hope bioterror detection will remain an exceedingly small market, but the ability to couple relatively foolproof test chips with small, reliable instruments points to the potential "killer app" for biochips—the ability to create precise genetic diagnostic tests for routine clinical application. These would include testing patients *before* issuing prescriptions to make sure they don't have the genetic traits associated with adverse reactions or using biochips to diagnose diseases based on gene or protein markers. In a special report on biochips issued by futurist George Gilder's publishing company, biotech specialist Scott Gottlieb wrote: "The big winners in the biochip market will be companies whose products suit the clinical, with its larger market and higher margins, rather than the research market. Biochip companies whose technology platform comes to dominate doctors' offices and hospital labs will see explosive growth."

But how long will it take for lab chips to find their way into routine clinical settings? Optimistic forecasts suggest hospitals could be using biochip systems in as little as a few years' time, with doctors getting into the chip-testing act within a decade. Technology often outpaces the marketplace, and the health care industry often resists technical advances—especially if they add costs without a clear benefit. Those will be battles fought later. In the meantime, lab-on-a-chip vendors face a daunting task in simply making their new technology hardy enough for everyday use. As Aclara chief executive Joe Limber says: "To make a (microfluidic) chip that performs flawlessly, does some necessary task, sells at a reasonable price, and delivers a decent margin is no small feat."

The publicly traded players in the microfluidics space include:

- Caliper (CALP) based its early lab-on-a-chip systems on quartz to take advantage of that material's superior optical characteristics. It is considered the microfluidics pioneer, and has maintained the largest market capitalization in its niche.

- Aclara (ACLA) has focused on plastics, which offer some advantages in ease and cost of manufacturing. Caliper and Aclara settled some early intellectual property battles after Aclara agreed to pay Caliper $32.5 million, and the two parties cross-licensed certain patents. But despite clearing this legal roadblock, Aclara signaled late in 2002 that it was de-emphasizing microfluidics.

- Cepheid (CPHD) initially targeted the research market but has also sought to promote itself as a bioterror play. It, like Aclara, is a very small cap company that trails Caliper in this key measure.

In addition to these public players, several private microfluidics firms wait in the wings for an opportunity to go public, even as they compete for sales in the research and diagnostics markets today. Private firms are always tougher to research. Start with their websites for basic information. In order to float an IPO they will have to file a prospectus that will then make their financial data public. The private players include:

- Fluidigm, a (South San Francisco) California company that makes its chips out of flexible silicone and uses microvalves and pumps to drive fluid through the systems
- Gyros AB, a Swedish firm that etches microfluidic channels onto CDs and uses centrifugal force to drive fluids through reaction chambers
- Micronics, a (Redmond) Washington firm based on microfluidics technology initially developed at the University of Washington and further refined with support from DARPA

Like the microarray vendors, the public and private microfluidics firms hope to develop clinical applications that would allow them to sell into the broad consumer market for diagnostic tests. Various analysts project that the clinical diagnostics could be a $20 billion market within a decade's time. But investors would be wise to ignore such distant projections and focus on a few numbers that will determine the fortunes of these companies:

- Revenues and revenue growth (the higher the better)
- Cash position (more than two years' cash preferred, less than one year a crisis)
- Market capitalization (Wall Street's pecking order)

Bioinformatics

Over the last several years, the biotech industry has evolved a niche called bioinformatics that is the intersection of computer science and biology. DNA is the most elaborate data storage system our science has ever encountered. Contained in the double strands of the DNA molecule are all the instructions needed to reproduce every living creature, from the fruit fly to you and me. And as we saw in the previous chapter, DNA is just the beginning of life's complexity. Beyond the genome exists an even larger and more complex universe of proteins whose forms and functions still largely defy our understanding. Even if we understood the shape and purpose of every protein, we would still have to understand how these proteins interact within the cells of the body, and then how these cells interoperate to give rise to complete organisms. The thrust of biotechnology is to understand how living systems function. Toward this end we have devised many tools and techniques for taking systems apart, including microarrays and microfluidics chips. As an industry, biotechnology is one giant exercise in reverse engineering. We're taking living systems apart to see how they work. But we can't store the pieces in a cup or label them to reassemble the mechanism at a later date. Biotech scientists are taking apart molecules. What they generate is not parts but data—terabytes of data, information that must be stored and analyzed and shared with other researchers. All of these tasks fall under the broad heading of bioinformatics: the acquisition, storage, archiving, retrieval, and analysis of data toward some desired end, generally the development of novel medicines.

Investors were infatuated with bioinformatics in 2000, reasoning that every biotech company needs to manage and share data, which implies a huge and growing market for vendors of bioinformatics software. A Frost & Sullivan market research report fixed the value of the U.S. bioinformatics market at $1.4 billion in 2000, with a projected growth to $7 billion by 2007. Behind those large numbers, however, looms the reality that bioinformatics is too huge, important, and complex to be dominated by any single vendor or even a handful of vendors. There is not yet a killer app that has swept the biotech world and created a Microsoft of biology. Instead, the bioinformatics area is populated mainly by small firms struggling for attention and profitability.

Some of the most successful bioinformatics firms are already trying to redefine themselves as drug discovery companies and downplaying their bioinformatics roots. In its marketplace analysis, Frost & Sullivan includes the market for data that has been extracted from experimental systems, the most notable example of which is gene sequence information. "The Database Content Providers portion of the bioinformatics market has grown at incredible rates," the report noted, citing how revenues jumped from $207.8 million in 1999 to

$338.1 million in 2001, a 62.7 percent increase. The report projected a slower but still robust 26 percent compound annual growth rate through 2007, when database revenues are projected to reach $1.7 billion. Yet Incyte Genomics and Celera Genomics—ranked number one and two in market share among the database vendors—have both signaled their intent to refocus their business away from data sales and toward using their data to discover new drugs. It could be that database revenues will continue to grow—but the two leading vendors can't seem to see how to make that a profitable business. *When market leaders deemphasize a niche, investors should see red flags.*

Wall Street was excited about bioinformatics during 2000, when several firms went public over a period of a few months. This cohort of 2000 bioinformatics IPOs included Lion Bioscience AG (LEON), Genomica (GNOM), InforMax (INMX), and Pharsight (PHST). Some of these stocks were oversubscribed at offering time and raised more money than they had initially intended. As we saw at the end of chapter 4, however, after the IPO excitement passed, these IPOs plummeted. Now, the bioinformatics firms are small-cap companies vying for favor on Wall Street and revenues in the real world. Genomica has already been acquired and its assets sold.

Lion (LEON) has arguably led the pack in the number and value of deals as well as market capitalization. Lion, which is based in Germany and has a U.S. subsidiary, has signed agreements to provide a variety of data integration services to large drug makers including Novartis, GlaxoSmithKline, Merck, and Bayer. After Lion, the companies in this niche get very small, very fast, as measured by market cap. Notable among these small-cap players is Tripos Inc. (TRPS), which has managed to achieve profitability, albeit on a small revenue base, by selling a mixture of bioinformatics and chemistry services.

Bioinformatics firms do occasionally strike it rich for shareholders. Bioinformatics investors and executives look back with envy at Merck's purchase of Rosetta Inpharmatics in 2001. Rosetta had been one of the bioinformatics IPOs of 2000. Merck bought it the following year in a stock swap valued at $620 million—a price that represented an 82 percent premium over Rosetta's preannounce-ment close.

Aside from waiting around for a favorable acquisition, however, it's tough to see how investors can expect to be rewarded for betting on bioinformatics companies. It's a bit of a paradox. The manage-ment of data is clearly crucial to the success of every biotech firm. Yet, so far, bioinformatics vendors as a group haven't shown they can service this need in a way that builds profitable companies. It may be that there are just too many types of data, and too many ways to manage them for any one software product to become an industry standard. Even if a standard emerges, only investors who guessed or gambled on the right bioinformatics vendor would reap the rewards.

Tools Sector Summary

For most investors the tools sector represents a chaotic arena in which risk outweighs opportunity. There are simply too many small companies, focused on specialized pieces of the drug development puzzle, and, unless you have some special expertise in drug or com-puting technology, you are unlikely to be able to pick the winning companies and avoid the losers.

BioCentury, the authoritative industry newsletter, has addressed the general dilemma of the tools sector. "It doesn't take harsh assump-tions to conclude that for many biotech tools and services, the uni-verse of customers is actually quite small," the editors wrote about the tools space. *BioCentury* estimates there are only one hundred drug companies and five hundred biotech companies that can really afford any sort of expensive specialty tool or service. This relatively small buyers' market can almost always pick and choose between multiple vendors. "It doesn't take much creative accounting to whit-tle the real universe of likely buyers to 10 or 20 companies for some tools or services," *BioCentury* concluded. That estimate jibes with Incyte's oft-repeated pronouncement that nineteen of the world's twenty largest pharmaceutical companies had purchased subscriptions to its gene database. Remember, Incyte has revenues far in excess of most other companies in bioinformatics, and yet it is changing its business plan to move toward drug development.

The biotech industry will constantly invent new tool companies because there are so many problems to be solved, and so many ambitious academic and company scientists looking for the next breakthrough. A December 2001 article on bioinformatics in *Signals Magazine* (an excellent, free biotech newsletter available at www.signalsmag.com) counted more than one hundred privately held bioinformatics companies in addition to the public ones. The larger private players have been waiting for their chance to float IPOs, but there is no way the stock market can or should sustain most of them. Take the example of DoubleTwist, a California company that offered a variety of software and analytical services via a web-based subscription. It was poised to go public in 2000, but the window closed before it could float the offering; by spring 2002, the company had run out of cash and closed its doors.

The story is much the same in biochips. One venture capitalist with a stake in Fluidigm, a still-private microfluidics company, told me there were as many as fifty lab-on-a-chip companies in some stage of development—many presumably waiting to go public. In the microarray space, the existence of a large network of home-brew installations creates competition, and a training ground for potential start-ups that could further fragment the market available to the public vendors.

The bottom line is that the tools space is critical to the success of biotech, but few investors will have the patience or knowledge to be able to pick its winners and losers. If you are of a mind to scout for investments in this group, look only at the companies with revenues and strong revenue growth, and some prospect of profits in one to two years. Otherwise you're buying a promise, which is a polite word for hype.

Investor Tools: Tiers of Joy

One of the most difficult things about biotech investing is keeping track of all the little companies, not just in the tools sector but in every biotech niche. Well, I've got news for you. This proliferation of tiny companies doesn't just baffle you and me. It frustrates the pension and mutual funds money managers and other institutional investors who like to buy and sell millions of shares at a time. These institutional investors are professionals. Many have M.D.s or Ph.D.s in biology in addition to their financial skills. They understand the science behind biotech developments better than ordinary investors. Over time these professional investors have devised a strategy for dealing with the proliferation of small biotech companies. They ignore them. Oh, not completely. Professional money managers read scientific journals to stay current and many advances emanate from small companies. As a rule, however, large institutional buyers don't invest in small biotech companies. You need to understand Wall Street's preference for big biotech stocks—and how this preference will affect your investments if you trade in small and mid-cap companies. *One simple rule is that small-cap stocks generally lag behind big- and mid-cap stocks in performance.*

Portfolio managers invest hundreds of millions of dollars a year. Their fiduciary responsibility, not to mention their professional pride, requires them to study each stock they buy. Once they take a position in a stock, they have to track the issue throughout the year in order to add, trim, or liquidate the holding as circumstances warrant. But even professional money managers can research only a few dozen stocks at a time. If they tried to follow more companies, they would risk dividing their attention and missing a development they could have anticipated if they had kept a tighter focus. *Because institutional money managers control huge sums of money, they tend to take large positions and trade in large blocks, which effectively limits their activities to big-cap companies that trade a large volume of shares on a daily basis.* They have little choice. If they invested large

In Biotech Small Is (Not) Beautiful

Stocks with low market capitalizations tend to appreciate far less over time than mid- and upper-tier stocks. This doesn't mean you should never buy a small-cap issue. But realize that if it doesn't grow in market cap and break into the mid or top tier, it is likely to trade in tandem with the rest of the small issues.

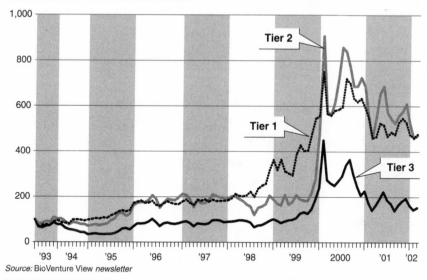

Source: BioVenture View *newsletter*

sums in small-cap companies, their buy-and-sell decisions would distort the market value of their target. If they made many small investments in tiny companies, they would have to spread their attention too thin—and perhaps miss a call on a big-cap holding because they were researching a start-up.

Just how big does a biotech company have to be to warrant attention on Wall Street? Of course the answer will vary from fund to fund. The manager of a $200 million fund will be able to look at smaller companies than the person managing $2 billion. By and large, a market capitalization of $500 million to $1 billion is becoming a minimum threshold for institutional interest. *BioCentury,* the industry newsletter, breaks publicly traded biotech companies in the United States into five tiers by virtue of market capitalization.

MARKET CAPITALIZATION	NUMBER OF COMPANIES
> $2 billion	35
$1 billion to $2 billion	26
$501 million to $1 billion	48
$201 million to $500 million	105
< $200 million	240

Many industry watchers would simplify that breakdown into three tiers. Anything over $1 billion would qualify as a big-cap stock. Anything under $200 million would be small cap. Everything in between would be mid cap, although there's obviously quite a difference between a company with market cap of $250 million and one of $750 million.

The important point for investors is that half of all public biotech companies fall into the small-cap ranking. You're bound to encounter these companies if you don't own them already. *The sad fact of life is that small-cap companies have a tough time getting attention on Wall Street.* Analysts tend not to cover their stocks. Institutional investors don't regularly trade in them. As a result, it's often tough for small-cap companies to raise follow-on financings if they need money to continue their work—and growing biotech companies always need money. This is particularly exasperating for small-cap companies with promising early-stage drugs they would like to put through clinical trials. If they can't raise the cash they need through a stock or debt offering on Wall Street, they're forced to seek a "partnership" with a larger biotech or drug company—which invariably tries to hog future profits. In these instances the shareholders in the small-cap companies must pay close attention to the terms of the partnership in order to determine how much profit the small company will get to keep, a topic we'll cover in detail in the Investor Tools section of chapter 7.

I'm not suggesting small investors should shun small-cap companies. In fact, individual investors who do their homework may actually pick out small, winning companies that Wall Street hasn't noticed. Take Cholestech Corp. (CTEC). The California biotech company was under $100 million in market cap in mid-2001, well below

Wall Street's radar. But it had recently won FDA approval to sell a new cholesterol-screening system that looked like a profitable product. The device relied on consumable test kits. Cholestech was the only supplier. The advantage of the system was that it provided the results of a full blood screening in just a few minutes as opposed to waiting days for the results. Cholestech had a natural market in health fairs, hospitals, and other outlets. The stock began to take off without institutional support, and Cholestech moved up several notches in market capitalization over a few months' time. Small companies can pay off—when investors can see some development that is likely to change their fortunes in the short run. In this case, it was immediate products and revenues.

But investors do face additional risk when they buy small-cap companies. Even if they're right and they've picked a winner, there's no guarantee that other investors will notice. Investor chat rooms are full of people who are convinced they've discovered the next Amgen. When you investigate a stock, its market cap should be one of the facts you note. It's easy to spot on Yahoo Finance. Type in the ticker symbol and choose the profile option. Scroll to the bottom of the company's profile page and you'll see the market cap number under the heading "Share-Related Items." On the left side of the profile page, under the "Ownership" heading, you can also find out what percentage of the company is owned by institutions. Big investors are not infallible, but in general the higher the percentage of institutional ownership, the more comfortable you should feel about owning a small-cap company. Under "Financial Links" on the same page you can also see which institutions and mutual funds own the stock. If you buy the stock, check this item regularly. If large stakeholders bail out of an issue, make it your business to find out why.

Big-cap biotech companies obviously command the greatest attention on Wall Street, and the mid-cap companies are constantly struggling to bulk up so that they can reach big-cap status. Size is becoming more important in determining a company's fortunes simply because biotech companies need capital to grow. Scott Morrison, biotech consultant for Ernst & Young, says small companies are finding it tougher to raise money. In 2001, for instance, the biotech industry as a whole raised about $12 billion, far below 2000's record take of nearly $33 billion. "And 90 percent of that money (was) raised by a handful of the biggest companies," Morrison said. "Down markets are very tough for the companies that have not yet achieved critical mass."

As for what constitutes critical mass, the bar is constantly being raised. A series of mergers in December 2001 provided a hint of where biotech is headed. First MedImmune (MEDI) offered $1.3 billion to acquire Aviron, a California company awaiting approval for an inhaled flu vaccine. A few days later, Millennium Pharmaceuticals (MLNM) anted up $2 billion to acquire Cor Therapeutics, another California company that markets the heart medicine Integrilin. Those deals were soon dwarfed by Amgen's $16 billion bid for Immunex, the Seattle firm that sells the arthritis medication Enbrel. All of these deals involved combinations of two large-cap biotech companies with products on the market or awaiting imminent approval. Most were profitable companies. Yet they thought they needed to get bigger to stay competitive.

Wall Street is fickle. There are times when investors throw money at biotech, but those are the rare spells. The default mode is caution, and when Wall Street is in a cautious mood, it prefers that biotech companies have strong products, profits, and pipelines. Amgen was already the world's largest biotech company when it bid for Immunex, but it wanted to bolster its position by adding Immunex's current and future products to its pipeline. The Med-Immune and Millennium deals were variations on the same theme. As the big-cap companies get bigger, the small-cap firms get left farther behind and the mid-cap companies face increasing struggles to climb the ladder. This dynamic is something that will continue to affect biotech companies and investors.

It all gets back to raising money. Biotech companies need a constant supply of capital to finance clinical trials, build manufacturing facilities, develop a sales force, and perform all the other tasks required to grow. Ironically, it's relatively easy for the biggest companies to raise money. That's no surprise. Banks love to loan money to anyone who doesn't need it. But the small- and mid-sized companies that have the greatest cash needs also have the most trouble raising follow-on capital.

In summary, here are some tips for how market-cap tiers affect your investing:

- Always know whether a company of interest is a big-cap, mid-cap, or small-cap player because you'll evaluate them through slightly different lenses.
- With small-cap stocks the key variables are cash position and burn rate; companies with two, three, or four years' worth of operating cash are healthy; companies with less than a year's operating cash must raise money to survive; know what money-raising options they have before you invest.
- Gauge mid-cap and large-cap stocks against the metrics provided earlier; if they are losing money, look at their pipeline, the status of clinical trials, their revenues and revenue growth rate, and cash position; if they are profitable, then earnings will be the key to stock movement.

6

Green Genes: Agricultural Biotechnology

Until now we've focused mainly on medical biotechnology. In this chapter we'll switch gears to look at how biotech tools and techniques have been—or could be—applied toward the improvement of agricultural crops and livestock animals. It cannot have escaped your notice that agricultural biotechnology is controversial. Europe has been the center of opposition to what consumers there call GMO foods—short for genetically modified organisms. Intense public opposition to GMOs has caused European governments to restrict the planting of biotech crops and demand the labeling of imported foods that contain GMOs. Europe's stance has provoked considerable friction with the United States, which supports agricultural biotechnology. In the United States there is far less public awareness and consumer opposition to genetically altered foods. However, U.S. critics have slowed the spread of the technology by convincing large food processors to shy away from using biotech foods, and they've also won popular support for labeling biotech foods (industry advocates oppose labeling as a tactic designed to keep products off store shelves). The rest of the world is still divided. Canada and Argentina have accepted some genetically modified seeds. China, India, and Brazil are in the throes of creating national policies. Japan has been generally hostile to biotech foods, but, as is the case in Europe, opposition there is tinged with protectionist sentiment.

The size of the market for genetically engineered foods, and the fortunes of the companies that make them, will depend on winning broad acceptance of these products both in the United States and abroad. Since the finances and the politics of the issue seem inextricably intertwined, let me try to give you an overview of the controversy. I have probably already offended some biotech food opponents by suggesting that Japanese and European opposition to the technology may be influenced by nationalism and protectionism. But what else can one think when one of the chief opponents to GMOs in France is sheep farmer José Bové, who became a folk hero in 1999 after he vandalized a new McDonald's outlet to dramatize opposition to what the French call *"la malbouffe americaine"* (lousy American food).

At the same time, as a society—and as smart investors—we shouldn't dismiss the environmental concerns of biotech food critics out of hand. Agriculture is being industrialized and centralized in favor of short-term yield improvements, and there is far too little research being done on how agro-industrialization is affecting the topsoil upon which food production ultimately depends. To some extent the debate over bioengineered foods is a continuation of earlier controversies over chemical fertilizers, pesticides, and herbicides, with the same constituencies on either side of the argument.

When it comes to the safety of eating biotech foods, many scientific studies have debunked the notion that genetically engineered crops represent a danger. In a July 2000 report entitled "Transgenic Crops and World Agriculture," the national scientific academies of the United States, the United Kingdom, Brazil, India, China, and Mexico, along with the Third World Academy of Sciences, stated: "To date, over 30 million hectares of transgenic crops have been grown and no human health problems associated specifically with the ingestion of transgenic crops or their products have been identified." Critics remain unsatisfied. They note that without labeling, consumers have no way to know whether an allergic reaction or some other ill effect might have been triggered from a biotech food.

This rancorous debate has already limited investment in the field. In a sense agricultural biotechnology isn't a niche yet. One company, Monsanto (MON), dominates the industry in terms of current sales of biotech food products, and is itself largely dependent on the success of biotech products, making it a pure investment play. The other large companies that are developing biotech crops are chemical or pharmaceutical giants for whom genetically engineered foods represent only a fraction of their overall revenues. There are a few small-cap start-ups in the field, but as it stands today, agricultural biotechnology is really just a set of techniques with the *potential* to create an industry.

Beyond this small realm of publicly traded firms there exists a large network of private companies and academic laboratories where scientists are trying to genetically engineer plants, fish, and farm animals to improve their growth characteristics or nutritional value. In the normal course of events we would expect to see these private companies go public, and watch academics seek venture financing to form companies. Public opinion will obviously affect this process, but we should expect to see many of these private efforts go public because there are enough scientists and financiers willing to take the extra risks involved in bucking the political tides.

There is money-making potential in this nascent industry. In 2000, genetically engineered crops generated about $3 billion in sales, according to financial analysts at Deutsche Bank. Roughly three-quarters of this volume was derived from sales of bioengineered soybeans and cotton. There are still no important commercial products in wheat, rice, fruits, and vegetables, much less cultivated fish or farm animals. The vast majority of these revenues were derived from sales in the United States, which is, so far, the only nation to embrace bioengineered agriculture in a big way.

So here's my plan to help you get a grip on the genetic revolution—and counterrevolution—in agriculture. First, I'll help you understand how and why biotech scientists are trying to modify plants and animals. In this primer I'll touch on the main elements of the controversy and the governmental regulations that control the introduction of biotech food products. Then I'll look in some depth at Monsanto, the pioneer (or villain) in agricultural biotechnology, and the other big agrochemical companies that have made varying degrees of commitment to genetic engineering. Finally, we'll look over the horizon, at the emerging companies and technologies for reengineering crops, fish, and farm animals.

A Biotech Foods Primer

The fundamental technique in biotechnology is the ability to splice genes from one species into the genome of another species. This was the tool Genentech used more than twenty-five years ago when it took the gene for human insulin and grafted it into bacteria to mass-produce medicine for diabetics. Biotech companies, notably Monsanto, have used the same gene-splicing techniques in a bid to improve agricultural products by introducing specific traits into plants and animals. Later, I'll take a stab at explaining why there seems to be almost universal support for gene-splicing in the pursuit of novel medicines, while controversy dogs its applications in agriculture. For now, however, let's see how plants are genetically engineered.

The process begins with the isolation of some gene that would introduce a desired trait into a plant. This gene might come from the same plant, a related plant, or another species entirely. (It is the last category that has aroused the most opposition, and led opponents to dub genetically engineered crops "Frankenfoods.") Some of Monsanto's successful genetically engineered products have resulted from splicing genes from an insect-killing bacterium (*Bacillus thuringiensis*) into corn, cotton, and other commercial crops. The added genes cause these BT plants to express proteins that kill insect pests. Thus, the altered plants produce their own insecticide. No matter where the desired gene comes from, once the addition has been identified, the trick is getting it into the plant's genome. This turns out to be no simple feat because the cell walls of grass plants, such as wheat, corn, rice, and barley, are tough and difficult to penetrate. Scientists rely on two main techniques to insert genes into plant cells. One technique involves the use of a "gene gun," which is conceptually akin to a shotgun. Instead of being loaded with buckshot, however, the gene gun fires tiny particles coated with copies of the desired gene. The particles blast through the cell wall, carrying some of the genes into the plant's DNA. The second technique is a variety of gene therapy. The desired gene is loaded onto a virus that infects plants. The virus penetrates the cell, bringing its cargo into contact with the plant's genome. Once the gene has been inserted using these or other methods, scientists coax the bioengineered plant cells to grow into seedlings. They then breed these seedlings with traditional plant varieties using conventional techniques. The idea is to blend the desired trait from the bioengineered plant with the other important characteristics (yield, drought resistance, nutritional characteristics, etc.) already present in traditional varieties. Once they've grown a stable bioengineered plant, scientists run field tests—in short, they plant the altered crop to make sure that in the process of adding the new trait they haven't broken something else in the plant's genome. They measure yield, check the plant's nutritional profile, and monitor for the presence of toxic or allergy-causing proteins they might have unwittingly created in the bioengineering process. Developing and field testing bioengineered foods can take about five to seven years, roughly half as long as it takes to develop a pharmaceutical product.

Much of the debate over genetic engineering with respect to foods has centered on whether this technique is simply an extension of thousands of years of breeding designed to improve output, as industry contends, or a revolutionary leap that raises new questions about human safety and environmental consequences, as opponents argue. But this debate masks an underlying disagreement that is far more important—how should genetically engineered plants be regulated before and after introduction? Where should the burden of proof lie in determining their fitness for human consumption, ordering any labeling requirements, and assessing the environmental risks? This is where the United States and Europe differ fundamentally. The United States has created regulations favorable to the introduction of genetically engineered crops because U.S. rules are governed by the presumption that genetically engineered foods are generally recognized as safe (GRAS). The U.S. Department of Agriculture (USDA), the Environmental Protection Agency (EPA), and the U.S. Food & Drug Administration (FDA) review new biotech foods before they can be introduced. But the GRAS principle favors their application and shifts the burden to regulators to show why the crop should not be introduced, and since genetically engineered foods are generally recognized as safe, the U.S. rule makers see no reason to enforce labeling after these products reach grocery shelves.

European GMO opponents want their governments to enact regulations based on a different and less favorable premise called the "precautionary principle." This may seem like a semantic difference, but it shifts the burden of proof in a substantial way. Opponents believe genetic engineering represents such a departure from past techniques that biotech companies should be required to prove that genetically altered crops are safe for humans and the environment. This would be a tougher standard and would make the introduction of a new biotech crop more like the process for winning approval for a new drug. Europeans also want strict labeling of foodstuffs that contain even traces of genetically altered ingredients. Since 1999 European governments have had a virtual moratorium on the approval of new genetically engineered crops while they argue over the regulations. Meanwhile, U.S. farmers have lost hundreds of millions of dollars in corn exports to Europe because there's currently no way an exporter can ensure that bioengineered corn doesn't get mixed up with traditional products. The United States and the various European governments have argued their differences through the World Trade Organization and other forums, but the parties remain on opposite sides of a philosophical divide. Should genetically engineered foods be generally recognized as safe or treated as novel products governed by the sort of precautions that greet the introduction of new medicines?

In the absence of agreement on this fundamental issue, the United States and Europe—and by extension biotech companies and their opponents—are engaged in a power play over genetically engineered foods. Victory for biotech means getting as many producer nations as possible to embrace genetically engineered crops, and increasing the acreage of biotech foods under cultivation to the point where these products dominate the market. The opposition strategy is to pressure brand-name food processors, companies like McDonald's, which buy potatoes by the ton, or Gerber, the baby food company, to proclaim that they will not use genetically altered crops as ingredients. It's a battle whose outcome is yet to be determined.

On the producer side, the number of nations that grow genetically engineered crops continues to grow, and some developing nations are embracing the technology. China is experimenting with genetically engineered foods though the acreage under cultivation remains tiny. As a practical matter, however, only three nations—the United States, Argentina, and Canada—plant genetically engineered crops in any volume, and the United States still accounts for better than 70 percent of global sales of genetically engineered products sold by biotech companies.

On the other side of the ledger, opponents have scored notable successes in their campaign to embarrass the industry and pressure food makers into keeping biotech foods off the shelves. One of their biggest coups was the StarLink corn episode. StarLink corn was genetically engineered to contain a protein that kills insects. In its premarket review, the Environmental Protection Agency was concerned that the insect-killing proteins in the corn might cause an allergic reaction in humans. As a result, when StarLink corn went on the market in 1998, it was designated for use *only* as an animal feedstuff. Farmers who grew StarLink were supposed to segregate this animal feed from any corn destined for human consumption. These precautionary steps apparently failed. Using genetic fingerprinting techniques, in the fall of 2000, biotech food opponents found traces of StarLink in taco shells, muffin mixes, and other human products, prompting a recall that embarrassed government regulators and the biotech industry. Although there do not seem to have been any serious illnesses caused by the StarLink contamination, the episode also proved financially disastrous for Aventis, the company that controlled StarLink. "While sales of StarLink maize (corn) are very small, only around $11 million in 1999," according to a report by Deutsche Bank financial analysts in 2001, "the compensation payments are likely to top $500 million and the reputational damage continues to be severe."

Investors should expect the biotech foods niche to remain something of a financial Vietnam, an arena marked by a continued battle for the hearts, minds, and checkbooks of farmers, consumers, food processors, government regulators, and financiers. Within the biotech industry there is a growing belief that, while their opponents may have won the first round in the PR battle, the next wave of crop improvements could tip the scales in favor of bioengineered foods.

Biotech proponents say the first generation of biotech foods delivered benefits to farmers but no advantage to consumers. BT corn, for instance, may have helped farmers limit crop loss to insect pests, but all the consumers could hope for was that bioengineered corn would be the same as the traditional variety. But over the last few years, biotech scientists have begun altering foods to improve their nutritional value. Perhaps the best-known example of these improved crops is the Golden Rice developed by Swiss academic scientists. In poor countries where rice is the diet staple, many people, especially children, suffer from vitamin A deficiency that can lead to blindness or even death. The Swiss scientists added genes to the rice to prompt the production of beta-carotene, a vitamin A precursor that could help alleviate the deficiency caused by diet. (The golden color of the rice comes from the addition of the beta-carotene.) The Golden Rice technology is being commercialized by the biotech firm Syngenta, which promised in its licensing agreement to make the seeds freely available to poor farmers in the Third World. Syngenta plans to recoup its investment in testing and refining the product by selling Golden Rice seeds in the developed nations, where beta-carotene supplements will be marketed to help stave off heart disease, cancer, and macular degeneration.

Golden Rice is only one of many nutritional fixes in the works at biotech labs. It also demonstrates the importance of patent law in biotechnology. In order to make Golden Rice freely available in the developing world, Swiss scientist Ingo Potrykus had to negotiate seventy patent licenses and legal agreements, according to a *New York Times* article. The patentability of biotech foods is an often overlooked but critical difference between genetic engineering technology and previous crop improvement techniques. Foods created by traditional breeding techniques enjoy some legal protection against unauthorized copying, but not the monopoly conferred by patents. Thus, when a biotech company creates a genetically engineered seed, it has the legal authority to set prices and restrict copycat products in ways previous food breeders never enjoyed. This patent power is the lure that continues to entice biotech companies into a politically perilous market. Conversely, critics see these patents as attempts to create monopolies on seeds, and make indigenous farmers dependent on technology imported mainly from the United States.

The Big-Cap Players in Biotech Foods

Any discussion of genetically engineered foods must begin with Monsanto, the company that pioneered the industry and continues to dominate the field. The company was founded more than one hundred years ago to manufacture food chemicals such as saccharin. Over time it has proven both inventive and opportunistic, branching out into industrial chemicals, human pharmaceuticals, and other research-driven markets. Some of its inventions have become household names. In the 1960s, for instance, Monsanto invented AstroTurf to create a playing surface after old-fashioned grass proved incompatible with Houston's air-conditioned Astrodome. In the 1970s, Monsanto entered the agrochemical market thanks to its invention of glyphosate, a hugely successful herbicide best known under the brand name Roundup.

By the early 1980s, Monsanto had embarked on a variety of projects to apply biotechnology to agriculture. In 1979, for instance, Monsanto began working with Genentech to create a genetically engineered version of bovine somatotropin. BST is a hormone that can boost milk production in dairy cows. Genentech helped Monsanto splice the BST gene into bacteria in order to mass-produce the hormone. This is the same technique biotech firms use to make protein medicines for humans. Monsanto obtained the rights to commercialize BST, and after a long and contentious campaign, in 1993 it finally won approval from U.S. regulators to sell BST to dairy farmers. Today, about a third of U.S. dairy cows take hormone supplements to boost milk production. Although the BST fight has faded from the headlines, the incident reads like the prequel to the current bioengineered foods debate. Before BST was approved in the United States, opponents from consumer, environmental, and organics food groups sought to block commercialization of the product, citing potential health risks to humans and cows. Long after approval, opponents continued to insist that milk derived from cows given BST should be labeled as a matter of consumer choice. U.S. regulators rejected mandatory labeling because it would suggest milk from cows given BST was less safe than milk from cows that had not taken the hormone. BST remains controversial outside the United States. The milk-boosting hormone has never been approved for use in Europe or Canada.

It was also during the 1980s, on a parallel track to the BST development, that Monsanto began the series of scientific, business, and regulatory initiatives that paved the way for the large-scale introduction of bioengineered crops. The company helped develop techniques for introducing genetic modifications into plant cells and then growing altered cells into seedlings. It acquired small biotech firms that specialized in agricultural applications, and also began to buy traditional seed vendors, thus obtaining both the technology to make genetic modifications and the distribution system to drive new crops into the market. Monsanto's actual product was the sack of seeds that carried the genetically engineered trait. Farmers who purchased these seeds agreed not to save seeds and replant them, but instead purchase new seed in the next season. These agreements were not unusual; American farmers were accustomed to signing such deals when buying seeds developed using traditional breeding techniques.

Finally, Monsanto worked with the Reagan and Bush administrations to craft regulations, issued in 1992 and 1993, that spelled out the regulatory framework governing the introduction of new biotech crops in the United States. Monsanto didn't win the race to bring the first genetically engineered crop directly to consumers. That prize went to Calgene, a now-defunct California biotech firm that, in 1994, began selling what it called the Flavr Savr tomato. The Flavr Savr was bioengineered to remain firm while it ripened on the vine, so that it wouldn't be damaged when picked. It was not a commercial success, however, in part because it was more expensive than competing tomatoes, and Calgene was eventually acquired by Monsanto. The true birth of the biotech foods industry therefore dates to 1995, when Monsanto won approval for several genetically engineered crops including what remains the dominant product in this infant industry, the Roundup Ready soybean.

The Roundup Ready soybean had a simple premise: Monsanto bioengineered the crop to resist the Roundup herbicide that killed other grasses. The product represented a win-win for Monsanto. It not only profited from the sales of Roundup Ready soybean seeds, it also sold more Roundup, as farmers switched from competing herbicides. Other agrochemical firms have since followed Monsanto's lead in modifying crops to withstand their own herbicides. Aventis's Liberty Link crops resist the company's glufosinate herbicide. U.S. soybean farmers rapidly adopted herbicide-tolerant seeds because they simplified weed control and reduced costs. Farmers could make one pass over a field and kill the weeds without harming the crop. According to the Deutsche Bank financial analysis, by the year 2000, a little more than half of all the soybean acreage under cultivation in the United States was planted in genetically engineered varieties. Herbicide-tolerant soybeans have also won over farmers in other nations that accept genetically engineered crops. According to the International Service for the Acquisition of Agri-Biotech Applications (ISAAA), headquartered at Cornell University, herbicide-tolerant soybeans are far and away the dominant genetically engineered crop on a global basis, representing 59 percent of all the area given over to biotech crops worldwide. Deutsche Bank estimates that herbicide-tolerant soybeans represented roughly half of the global market for biotech seeds, which stood at $3 billion in 1999. It is no exaggeration to say that herbicide-tolerant soybeans built the market for genetically engineered crops and remain its foundation.

Monsanto also helped pioneer another innovation, the engineering of pest resistance into plants, notably through the introduction of genes that would cause plants to express the pest-killing proteins produced by the *Bacillus thuringiensis* bacterium. These crops also proved popular with farmers because they allowed them to reduce the labor and expense of insecticide sprays. Deutsche Bank estimated that the global market for crops genetically engineered to cause insect resistance was worth $907 billion in 1999. At present, there are approximately forty bioengineered crops approved for sale in the United States, according to a tally by the Union of Concerned Scientists (UCS), one of the activist groups that is leery of biotech modifications. Corn was the most popular target for modification. The UCS tallied fifteen genetically modified varieties. Tomatoes, cotton, and soybeans together accounted for another twelve modifications. By company, Monsanto led the pack with eighteen modified crops approved. Aventis had eight approvals, Syngenta five, and Dow and DuPont two each.

As measured by sales, however, Monsanto utterly dominates the current market for genetically engineered crops, thanks again to its single masterstroke with the Roundup Ready soybean. Deutsche Bank estimated that Monsanto held 85 percent of the market for biotech seeds in 1999, notably the herbicide-resistant and pest-resistant varieties that constitute the bulk of current sales (Aventis and Syngenta had 10 and 5 percent market share, respectively). The bank's analysts believe Monsanto will increase its market share for these crops to 93 percent in 2004, when global sales are projected to reach $4.85 billion. Its competitors will divide the remainder. Despite all the controversy revolving around genetically engineered crops, Monsanto shares have outperformed the general biotech

Monsanto: Ag Biotech's Pure Play

Monsanto is shown here since its spinoff from Pharmacia. Despite being at the center of the controversy over genetically engineered foods, the new Monsanto has performed well against the American Stock Exchange Biotech Index, a basket of biomedical firms.

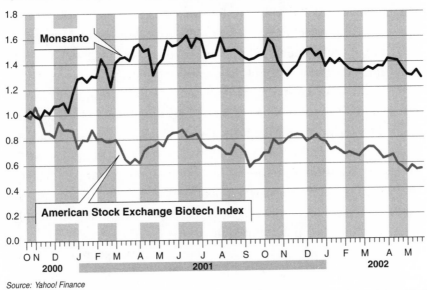

Source: Yahoo! Finance

sector, as measured by the American Stock Exchange Biotech Index. Monsanto's profits have obviously been more persuasive to investors than the qualms of its political opponents.

However completely it rules the current landscape, Monsanto's recent history has hardly been an unbroken string of successes. On the product front, Monsanto quietly pulled its NewLeaf potato off the market six years after it launched the product in 1995. NewLeaf had been bioengineered to produce a protein that repelled the Colorado potato beetle. But the genetically altered variety never got more than 5 percent of the potato seed market. In part, observers linked the disappointing performance to a persistent price slump in the potato market. Farmers simply weren't willing to pay premiums for the Monsanto seed. But indirect pressure from activists also played a role. Large French-fry buyers, including McDonald's, as well as potato chip makers like Pringles, a Proctor & Gamble brand, signaled farmers they would rather not be exposed to the controversy that surrounded genetically engineered varieties. On the corporate front, Monsanto went through a corporate transformation, brought on in part by the intense and often negative publicity surrounding bioengineered food. In April 2000, Monsanto merged with Pharmacia, a transnational drug giant. Pharmacia turned right around and spun out the agrochemical and biotech businesses as Monsanto, which now trades independently under the ticker symbol MON. (In July 2002 Pfizer made a bid to acquire Pharmacia.)

Given that its sales of genetically engineered seeds and technology account for roughly half of its revenues (estimated by Deutsche Bank in excess of $6 billion in 2002), Monsanto makes sense as a biotech foods play. The company's emerging products include a series of new Roundup Ready seeds for rice, rape, sugar beet, alfalfa, and wheat. Whether these will repeat the success of Roundup Ready soybeans or suffer the setbacks of NewLeaf potato is simply unknowable at this point. But Monsanto is clearly poised to drive its innovations into important new seed markets. Monsanto is also trying to popularize stacked traits in newer seeds, combining Roundup tolerance with resistance to insecticides or fungicides.

In addition to being the dominant biotech foods firm, Monsanto also provides a model for how such companies should do business, by combining pesticide and/or herbicide franchises with seed distribution channels and genetic expertise. For example, Syngenta AG was formed in November 2000 when Novartis merged its seeds and crops division with the agrochemical business that had been part of Zeneca. Syngenta (SYT) combines chemical crop amendments with seed production and genetic engineering know-how, including the Golden Rice technology, along the lines of Monsanto's business structure. Syngenta has several bioengineered varieties of corn on the market, but for now they represent only a little more than $100 million of its sales out of total revenues in excess of $6 billion, according to Deutsche Bank. Syngenta is positioning itself to be a leader in bioengineered foods in the future, but for the present its fortunes are hitched to sales of seeds and traditional chemical amendments, which are in turn dependent on the agricultural trends—factors that have little to do with biotechnology.

Bayer (BAYG.F), Dow Chemical Co. (Dow), DuPont (DD), and BASF AG (BF) all have research programs under way that involve applying biotechnology to agriculture. But these efforts take part inside large companies whose current fortunes depend much more on chemical markets rather than biotechnology. Bayer also has a large pharmaceuticals business. Nevertheless, Bayer, DuPont, and Dow all have seed divisions, agrochemical franchises, and biotech crop products on the runway, following the model of Monsanto and Syngenta in developing aggressive biotech strategies.

- Bayer is studying crop and insect metabolism to devise more efficient herbicides, pesticides, and fertilizers. Its agricultural products generated revenues of $3.27 billion in 2001, about 12 percent of the company's total revenues of $26.8 billion. In June 2002, Bayer acquired what had been Aventis Crop Sciences (formerly a division of the multinational drug firm Aventis). The deal brought Bayer seed and biotech expertise, which it merged with its existing agrochemical know-how to create Bayer CropScience. The new division will start with sales of roughly $6.4 billion, making it a powerful new competitor in biotech agriculture.

- DuPont acquired Pioneer Hi-Bred International, a giant seed vendor, in 1999, an acquisition that forms the heart of its agricultural biotechnology effort. DuPont's agriculture and nutrition divisions contributed revenues of $4.3 billion in 2001, or 15 percent of the company's gross billings of $24.7 billion in that year. (Pioneer seeds accounted for about 44 percent of DuPont's ag/nutrition revenues.)

- Dow's agricultural division delivered 2001 revenues of $2.6 billion, about 9 percent of the company's total revenues of $27.8 billion. Herbicides and pesticides accounted for most of the agricultural revenues.

- BASF, the world's largest chemical company, has an early research program into biotech agriculture. Its current line of agricultural and nutritional products, mainly fertilizers, herbicides, and pesticides, accounted for $5.24 billion in revenues in 2001, about 18 percent of total revenues of $29.2 billion.

Developments on the Horizon

The controversy surrounding agricultural biotechnology has greatly restricted the normal flow of academic research into venture-backed private companies, and from there to the public realm via IPO. Thus there are few options in agricultural biotechnology available to investors.

- Paradigm Genetics (PDGM) is one of the few young public companies with a focus on agricultural biotechnology. Founded in 1997 by several former executives from the Novartis Crop Protection division, Paradigm is applying functional gene analysis and bioinformatics tools toward agriculture. It is trying to discern the roles that specific genes play in plant growth and/or pest control, and has research collaborations with Monsanto, Bayer, and other firms. Paradigm is also applying its genetic toolkit to human health and industrial applications, so as not to get stuck with all its eggs in the fragile biotech foods basket. In 2001, the company reported a $16 million loss on sales of $24.5 million.

- The gene-research firm Exelixis (EXEL) has a division devoted to plant biotechnology and a series of research partnerships with Bayer and Dow AgroSciences aimed at developing new pesticides, fungicides, and herbicides.

- Sangamo Biosciences (SGMO) has also got its fingers in agricultural biotechnology—literally. Sangamo is working with zinc finger proteins as a way to switch gene functions on and off. It is doing some research into how it might exploit this gene-switching function in plants. Agriculture is just one of many ways the company is trying to make use of its zinc finger technology.

There are doubtless other genomics companies studying agricultural applications, but until and unless the political climate improves, they are likely to keep such programs quiet. For now there seems to be little upside in being billed as a biotech foods firm.

Even so, research continues on two fronts—genetic modifications to food animals and a new round of crop alterations aimed at improving the nutrition or limiting the fat content of foods. The animal research is still for the most part in the early stages, and is being carried on at academic laboratories and private biotech start-ups. Such research is centered at universities with strong veterinary traditions, including the University of California, Davis; the University of Wisconsin; the University of Georgia; and Virginia Polytechnic Institute and State University. These scientists are looking for ways to alter the genomes of domesticated animals to either improve their health (to create animals that get sick less or mature on less feed) or change their meat production characteristics (producing hogs or cattle with less fat). Some researchers are looking at ways to remove allergy-causing proteins from cow and goat milk. (A web search for "transgenic animals in agriculture" should lead you to a summary of a research conference that brings scientists in the field together every two years; the conference document lists speakers and topics and can be used as a lead to further research).

A handful of private firms are involved with various phases of animal genetics, often geared toward picking the best animals for breeding and in some cases accomplishing that breeding with technologies that move beyond the widely practiced art of artificial insemination of farm animals. Advanced Cell Technology, the Massachusetts company that claims to have cloned the first human embryo, has sold cloned cattle to farmers. Pyxis Genomics Inc., formerly known as AniGenics, is a Chicago company that is creating disease-resistant poultry through bioengineering. Today, poultry are bred in huge operations. To guard against the outbreak of avian diseases that could wipe out flocks, farmers routinely feed the birds antibiotics. The FDA wants this antibiotic use curtailed out of concern that it is increasing antibiotic resistance in humans, prompting the need for an alternative way of preventing infections that would otherwise decimate poultry flocks.

Most of these efforts are so early, and the researchers involved are so leery of publicity, that they seem intent on keeping their work under wraps. But one project has entered the public spotlight. A/F Protein in Waltham, Massachusetts, is a private firm that has developed a bioengineered salmon. By splicing certain genes from Arctic cod into salmon, A/F Protein found it could cause the salmon to pump out more growth hormone and thus reach maturity as much as a year faster than conventional salmon. The company wants FDA approval to market its bioengineered salmon to aquaculture farmers, who might be interested in a fish that would mature in less time and therefore cost less to rear. Biotech food opponents have opposed commercialization of the altered fish in part because they are concerned the bioengineered salmon might escape from the rearing pens and mingle with wild salmon, with unforeseen environmental consequences for the species. The A/F Protein application will set the tone for future regulatory treatment of other genetically engineered food animals, and therefore must be watched by investors interested in this field. A decision could come in 2003.

Although the experiments with animal modifications are interesting and could eventually spawn new public companies, it is the second-generation crop alterations that are most important from an investment point of view. Academic researchers and corporate scientists at Monsanto, Syngenta, DuPont, and other firms are working on plant modifications aimed at delivering some perceived consumer benefits. According to current thinking in the biotech industry, herbicide-tolerant soybeans and other genetically modified crops now on the market changed "input traits"—that is, characteristics of interest to farmers. The biotech industry hopes to win broader public acceptance of bioengineered foods by changing what it calls "output traits"—that is, characteristics important to consumers. For example, biotech firms are developing soybeans with less saturated fat and more monounsaturated fat, something that might appeal to health-conscious consumers. Golden Rice is another example of a product being developed for an output trait, in this case, as a beta-carotene supplement. Biotech scientists are trying to increase the sugar content in corn and strawberries to enhance their flavor. Efforts are also under way to remove the caffeine from coffee and add iron to rice through genetic engineering.

And so the list goes on, as biotech scientists experiment with new ways to enhance the nutrition or appearance of crops. Only time will tell whether these new bioengineered products gain consumer acceptance and remove any stigma associated with biotech agriculture, or increase the political pressure to label or segregate genetically engineered foods. The United States and Europe remain far apart regarding the regulation and approval of biotech foods. Meanwhile, biotech critics and advocates continue to spar over the role that biotechnology could play in the Third World, with advocates saying genetic engineering could lead to pest-resistant sweet potato, cassava, and other staple crops, while critics say global agribusiness firms are simply looking for new markets. The continuing political controversy is almost certain to create market uncertainties and add to the risks associated with investments in biotech agriculture.

Investor Tools: Understanding Patents

In a February 2001 document entitled "Economic Issues in Agricultural Biotechnology," U.S. Department of Agriculture economists cited patents as one of the most important factors driving private-sector investment in crop and animal research. The USDA noted that plant breeders have long enjoyed some legal protection for hybrids, thanks to laws passed by Congress in 1930 and extended in 1970 when the Plant Variety Protection Act became law. But the legal protections in those acts are inferior to the strong protections against copying or unauthorized use that are conferred with the issuance of a patent. The USDA economists were stating the obvious when they said that legal protections, "particularly the utility patent extensions" to plants and animals in 1985 and 1987, "have promoted private sector plant breeding activities."

Patents are the foundation not just of agricultural biotechnology but of every aspect of the field, from the discovery of new medicines to the development of novel tools and diagnostic tests. They are the legal basis for preventing copycats from competing with inventors. Given the importance of patents to biotech companies, I want to show you how to evaluate patents that might affect your investments. I also want to explain another law, the Orphan Drug Act, which has been very important for the development of biotech medicines. Finally, I want to touch on two emerging policy issues that revolve around patents: the need for legislation to govern the creation of generic biologic medicines and the smoldering antagonisms over the role that patents play in controlling access to drugs and diagnostic tests—and arguably to inflating the prices paid by consumers. Let's begin with the basics.

Patents grant inventors exclusive control over a technology for twenty years. During the life of the patent, inventors can set prices knowing that no one else can make the product or use the technology until the patent expires. Patent holders can license their technology under any terms, giving exclusive or nonexclusive rights in return for negotiated royalty payments. In the medical setting, a patent does not confer the right to market a product. Only the FDA can approve a new medicine. But a patent provides the inventor of a new medical product with a strong assurance that, provided they win FDA approval, they will have the legal right to set price and licensing terms for the medicine so long as the patent is in effect.

The widespread patenting of biological inventions is relatively new. It traces back to the 1980 decision in which the U.S. Supreme Court granted inventor Ananda Chakrabarty a patent on a genetically engineered bacterium. Prevailing legal wisdom up until then had been that living things could only be patented in the rarest of cases, and this made investors leery of backing biotech research since there was no guarantee that biological inventions would enjoy legal protections. The Chakrabarty decision galvanized the industry. Within months of the decision Genentech had floated the first biotech IPO and opened a floodgate of biotech investment. To this day, most biotech companies are formed around the intellectual property rights to some patented invention. The existence of a patent can't guarantee that an invention will be a commercial success. But if success comes, the patent holders control the reward.

In the biotech setting the most important types of patents are:

- Composition-of-matter patents. They protect a specific molecular formulation, that is, a drug or biologic medicine. Long before biotech was born, drug companies won composition-of-matter patents to protect their chemical drugs. Nowadays, biotech firms can get composition-of-matter patents on biological agents. "Composition-of-matter patents are the strongest patents in the drug setting because they cover the drug itself," says patent attorney John Storella. "No one else can make the product during the life of the patent."

- Process patents cover the steps used to create a drug or biologic, or the way that a chemical agent is used to treat a disease. Sometimes companies get process patents as well as composition-of-matter patents to give them a second way to protect an invention. But it isn't always possible to obtain a composition-of-matter patent for a biological agent. For instance, a naturally occurring protein might not be patentable because its molecular composition was previously known to scientists. But the process of making the protein in quantity might be considered novel and therefore patentable. And the ability to use the molecule for a specific purpose, for instance, dissolving a blood clot, might also constitute a novel invention. The important point for investors is that process patents are generally not as powerful as composition-of-matter patents, because it is often possible to devise an alternative to a process patent. It is also more difficult to prove infringement.

- Manufactured items and machines are also patentable. In the biotech setting a manufactured item might be a solid-state device like a DNA array, and a machine might be an instrument for analyzing DNA.

If a patent is going to form the basis for your investment in a biotech company, take the time to read it. Whenever the U.S. Patent and Trademark Office issues a patent, it assigns the patent a number. That number makes it easy to search for further information. If you visit www.uspto.gov/main/patents.htm, click on "Search Patents," and then plug in the number, you can read the full text of any patent. For instance, Genentech holds patent 4,777,043, which describes "novel, stable pharmaceutically acceptable compositions containing human tissue plasminogen activator," in short, a composition-of-matter patent covering a clot-buster medicine. That patent would be strong protection in itself, but Genentech also holds patent 4,853,330, which states that "human tissue plasminogen activator (t-PA) is produced in useful quantities using recombinant DNA techniques. The invention disclosed thus enables the production of t-PA." In other words, the second patent protects the process for manufacturing the medicine. Genentech holds other patents around t-PA, including one on the specific use of the medicine to dissolve a blood clot. *Redundant coverage of this sort should comfort investors, because it protects the product in different ways should any single patent be invalidated.*

When you're considering an investment in a young company that has its hopes pinned on a few patents, be sure to read the claims section of the patents for yourself. The claims are the heart of the patent. Do they seem to cover every instance in which the technology might be used, or are they limited by the language of the claims? When patent disputes end up in court, the battle often revolves around the patent claims. Fortunately, claims are rather simple to understand. For instance, Genteric Inc., a privately held company in Alameda, California, announced in 2001 that it had the commercial rights to patents issued on the process of putting insulin genes into the form of a pill, which could be swallowed to control diabetes. This development stunned gene therapy experts, who thought the body's digestive juices would dissolve any DNA that was taken orally. But the inventors, who also founded Genteric, proved that it was possible to try gene therapy through a pill, instead of the more exotic methods that had been pursued until then. Reading the claims to patents 6,225,290 and 6,255,289 suggests that Genteric has broad coverage over this technology not just for glucose control, its first objective, but in any instance "wherein the mammal is a human and the protein is a human protein."

As an investor you can't predict whether a patent will be contested, but a little research may help you anticipate potential disputes. Ask the investor relations staff at the company you're interested in whether they're aware of any conflicting intellectual property. (It wouldn't hurt to make such a request by fax and to ask for a reply in kind.) Take your research one step further by figuring out the key words in the patent of interest, and using these words to search the patent database for patents or applications with the same phrases. (The Patent Office also lists applications.) If you find another patent that includes the same key words, contact the inventor or the assignee (the entity that has legal control over the patent) and ask if he or she is aware of the patent in question and whether he or she sees any conflict. The potential for conflict shouldn't frighten you. The broader the patent, the more powerful and valuable it is and therefore the more likely someone will contest it. Fighting a patent case can easily be a $2 million exercise. So if you're making an investment on the basis of a patent, make sure your company has the war chest to defend it. A 1998 article in the American Intellectual Property Law Association's quarterly journal found that biotech patents were upheld in 56 percent of the cases in which they were contested in court. That's only slightly better than 50–50, and it puts a strong incentive on companies to settle disputes rather than risk court battles.

In addition to visiting the Patent Office website, some other places to monitor patent activity include the following:

- Biotech Patent News provides online and printed summaries of patent filings and news, on both a free and subscription basis (http://www.biotechpatent.com).
- European Patent Office offers search and tracking services similar to the U.S. Patent Office (http://www.european-patent-office.org/).
- The World Intellectual Property Organization will tap you into patent trends affecting international commerce (http://www.wipo.org).

Leaving patents for a moment, the biotech industry also benefits from the Orphan Drug Act, passed in 1983 to encourage the development of medicines to treat diseases that afflict fewer than two hundred thousand people. Under the act, a company applies to the FDA for orphan drug designation. If the FDA decides that the disease qualifies for orphan status, the first medicine to treat that disease has an exclusive market for seven years. The FDA is forbidden from approving another medicine for the same disease until the first approved remedy has enjoyed seven years free from competition. This can be even more powerful than patent protection, since other companies can produce rival medicines that don't infringe on patents. But there is no way around the seven-year grace period conferred by orphan drug status. Biotech firms such as Genentech, Amgen, and Genzyme have taken advantage of the Orphan Drug Act, and it continues to provide incentives to small companies. Getting a designation of orphan drug status does not guarantee that an experimental compound will be approved. But if it does pass muster with the FDA, it gives the sponsoring company an improved profit opportunity by preempting competition.

Looking at the biotech industry as a whole, there are several issues that are going to put an uncomfortable spotlight on patents. The first is the fact that there is presently no framework governing what happens when biological products—protein and antibodies—go off patent. Biotech medicines are new and are only just coming to the end of their patent life. When small-molecule drugs come off patent, generic manufacturers are able to come in and make the pills. At present, there is no legal structure to govern the manufacture of generic biologics. This is an issue Congress has been debating for several years. Legislation was not imminent at this writing, but eventually lawmakers will have to act. Given that generic biologics will affect current biotech patent holders, investors should monitor this issue through the general and financial press.

Another intermittent controversy involves the role patents play in pricing medicines or diagnostic tests beyond the reach of many people, both in the United States and particularly in the Third World. Activists in Europe and the United States have attacked drug companies for using patents to maintain high prices for AIDS medicine. Drug makers in India have offered to make unlicensed knockoffs of key AIDS drugs for a fraction of what the patent holders normally charge. The dispute has put the drug industry on the defensive. Although there is still broad public support in the United States for the notion that patents are a justified reward for undertaking costly research, public opinion can change and there is mounting frustration, even in affluent countries like the United States, over the soaring costs of prescription medications. In the United States, drug and biotech industry lobbyists are always fearful that Congress will institute some form of price controls on medicines as part of a future Medicare reform, though that prospect does not seem imminent. Even so, rising drug costs should concern investors because they have the potential for sparking a public backlash that could result in price controls. Any serious threat of price controls would spook the capital markets and probably send biotech and drug stocks tumbling.

Advances made through biotechnology are likely to fuel pricing complaints. Biotech medicines and tests are new and innovative, but they are also more expensive than preceding technologies. If patents are the goose that laid the golden egg, biotech investors will have to hope the industry as a whole exercises enough restraint not to kill it.

7

The New Factories:
Industrial Biotechnology

As I hope has by now become clear, the underpinnings of bio-technology are the ever-expanding ways in which scientists can modify and manipulate living organisms so as to cause these organisms to produce (or in scientific lingo, to express) proteins. Medicines have so far been the most lucrative product to emerge from this capability. In the previous chapter we saw how the gene-alteration techniques of biotechnology could be adapted to create plants and animals tailor-made for some perceived agricultural or consumer benefit. Now, we will look at the ways in which biotech-nology has been—and may in the future increasingly be—used to produce a wide variety of industrial chemicals or novel materials.

This field is often termed industrial biotechnology, to distinguish it from the medical or food-producing applications of gene-splicing. Industrial biotechnology is not an entirely new field, and that means investors interested in this area have at least a couple of mature companies they can evaluate as potential holdings. At the same time recent advances—including genomics and a technique called "gene-shuffling," which I'll explain later—have created some young com-panies for investors with a greater appetite for risk. We'll also review some of these young firms in the industrial biotech space. Finally, I'll expose you to some companies that are exploring new ways to make biotech medicines and other products by splicing protein-producing genes into living plants and animals instead of bacterial or mammalian cells. In essence, these companies are trying to create the next generation of biotech manufacturing "factories." Today's biotech products are made in giant vats in a fermentation process akin to brewing beer. Such fermentation factories can cost tens of millions of dollars to build. We'll look at the biotech firms that are trying to use goats to produce protein medicines in their milk and chickens to express therapeutic proteins in their eggs. Other companies hope to genetically engineer plants to produce therapeutic products—and in so doing create a new industrial process for making a wide variety of biotech products.

Some of the companies we'll review in this chapter are attempting to create novel materials that could never have been made by any previous industrial process. One young Canadian firm, for instance, is in the process of trying to mass-produce spider silk, a fiber that is incredibly strong and yet enormously supple. The company talks about one day using this spider silk to weave jackets and other garments strong enough to repel bullets. (Imagine the product liability disclaimers on bulletproof shirts!) Other firms hope to use the techniques of industrial biotechnology to create enzymes that can cost-effectively break down the stalks and stems of plants into ethanol, a clean-burning fuel that could be used to supplement or even replace petroleum. In a similar vein, industrial biotechnology is being applied toward the production of biopolymers—an emerging class of materials that could be refined out of plant waste and spun into fabrics to create ordinary clothing (of the non-bullet-stopping variety). So there's plenty of excitement and potential in the field.

But the trick to successful biotech investing is to balance the excitement with prudence. So while there are some truly fascinating developments that could be enabled by the techniques and companies in industrial biotechnology, I want you to head into this chapter with two principal cautions in mind. The first and more important is to focus on the product (i.e., the market) and not the technique. As we'll see later in this chapter, the classic products of industrial biotechnology are commodity chemicals. These chemicals are purchased by companies that use the products of biotechnology to help make soap, paper, or clothing. Corporate buyers are not going to pay a gee-whiz premium just because the chemical ingredient was produced by biotechnology. To the contrary, the industrial biotech firms are going to have to prove to these hardheaded corporate buyers that biotech chemicals are cheaper and/or better than chemical inputs derived from other technologies. That makes industrial biotechnology a niche in which the low-cost manufacturers win, a very different dynamic than exists in medical biotechnology.

Second, such low-cost manufacturing industries tend to concentrate in a handful of players. It is difficult to imagine that biotech start-ups, no matter how novel their techniques, will be able to develop into fully integrated producers of chemicals or other end-use products. Instead, they are more likely to be involved in research partnerships with some of the giant firms that are customers for their specialty products. In such relationships giants often absorb start-ups. Some of the young industrial biotech firms may therefore end up as divisions of larger companies, or the techniques of industrial biotechnology will simply be adopted by the large chemical companies, as has already occurred in the drug-discovery business. Thus, industrial biotechnology probably won't yield many pure-play biotech firms, and investors who decide to specialize in this area may end up investing in traditional chemical companies that adopt biotechnology techniques.

The Bio-Industrial Giants

At the present time the principal products of industrial biotechnology are enzymes, a class of proteins that triggers or enhances biochemical reactions. In other words, enzymes are catalysts. They help other processes occur more efficiently, at lower temperatures, or with the application of less energy. One everyday example of biochemical catalysts are the enzymes that are added to many laundry detergents to help clean nasty stains caused by substances like grass or blood. In a scientific sense, when blood stains a sock, certain proteins in the blood become stuck to the fabric. Industrial biotech firms have discovered naturally occurring enzymes that help lift these stain-producing proteins from the fabric. Biotech firms often enhance the natural enzyme by adding or subtracting groups of molecules that enable it to function better in cold water, or prevent it from leaching the colors out of fabrics. Although these enzyme-enhanced detergents have been on the market for years, soap makers have largely kept all this science hidden from consumers. So far consumers haven't been plied by television advertising campaigns promoting "biotech soaps." Biotech enzymes remain hidden, input commodities that follow the low-cost manufacturing rule. Two public firms dominate the production of biotech enzymes: Genencor (GCOR) and Novozymes A/S (ticker NZYMb.CO on the Copenhagen Stock Exchange).

Genencor was spun out of Genentech in 1982 as a joint venture with Corning, the glass-manufacturing giant. From the beginning, Genencor was organized around the notion of using biotech processes to create enzymes for industrial use. The company started developing its first product for Proctor & Gamble in the mid-1980s. The consumer products giant wanted to develop enzymes for its detergent and dish-cleaning products. Though this sounds like a trivial assignment, it actually involved a fair bit of scientific sleuth work. Genencor's molecular biologists first had to develop techniques to find potentially useful enzymes by seeking out bacteria that thrived in natural environments akin to the industrial or consumer environments where the enzyme would be used. If the enzyme was destined for a detergent, they focused their research on bacteria that thrived in an alkaline environment, isolated enzymes of interest, and tested them in the proper conditions. They actually set up tiny "washing machines" by connecting lab trays to agitators. They took into account factors like the temperature of the water in determining which enzymes were most appropriate for the task. An all-temperature detergent required different enzymes than a hot-water soap. Moreover, Genencor had to find enzymes that could be produced cheaply enough to compete with traditional chemical products.

Identifying the ideal enzyme was only the first step in the process, however. The enzyme then had to be mass-produced using the techniques of recombinant biotechnology. Genencor scientists had to isolate the gene responsible for encoding the enzyme and splice this gene into some growth agent such as a bacterium or a fungus that would reproduce rapidly and express large quantities of the enzyme. The production of industrial enzymes requires huge fermentation factories. Whereas the manufacturer of a biotech medicine might have to make only a few kilos of product per year, Genencor had to make tons of its enzymes to stuff into P&G soap boxes. Over the last fifteen to twenty years, Genencor has developed an extraordinary track record in identifying and manufacturing enzymes.

For most of its corporate life, however, Genencor remained invisible to the investment community, not simply because its products were more humble than the much-hyped biotech medicines, but because it was privately held. That changed in 2000 when the company floated an initial public offering like few others in biotech history. By the time it went public, Genencor had matured into a company with seven major factories in the United States, Europe, Asia, and South America. It had more than fourteen hundred issued patents; several hundred products on the market; a large base of blue chip customers, including the likes of Proctor & Gamble, DuPont, and Eastman Chemicals; and—best of all—strong revenues and earnings. Its size, maturity, and profitability instantly made Genencor one of biotech's big-cap issues on Wall Street. In 2001, Genencor reported earnings of 17 cents per share on revenues of $326 million. But the year-over-year comparisons were discouraging. Revenues in 2001 advanced just 3 percent over the previous year's figures, while net income was less than half of the 42 cents per share that Genencor earned in 2000. In the first half of 2002, Genecor's revenues rose 8 percent to $171.4 million, but net income plunged to just $86,000, or less than a penny a share.

Genencor's basic challenge is that it is a commodity manufacturer whose enzyme products are coming under price pressure from less sophisticated but cheaper alternatives produced by companies in China, India, and other emerging nations. Given that this competitive pressure is more likely to increase than decrease, Genencor is trying to move away from its industrial roots and toward diagnostic and therapeutic biotechnology. I'll have more to say about Genencor's transformation—and what it suggests about industrial biotechnology as an investment niche—later in this chapter. First, however, let's look at Novozymes.

Novozymes is a Danish company that traces its roots back to the 1920s. Like Genencor, it is a relative newcomer to public markets. Novozymes became an independently traded concern in November 2000, at roughly the same time as the Genencor IPO. Novozymes was spun out of two other Danish pharmaceutical companies—Novo Industri A/S and Nordisk Gentofte A/S—which had merged in 1989 to form Novo Nordisk A/S. Thus, it has access to technologies and facilities developed over many decades. At present, Novozymes accounts for roughly 40 percent of the world market for enzymes, roughly double Genencor's market share, according to a 2001 report from ABN-AMRO, the Dutch investment banking firm. Novozymes remains centered in Denmark, but it has factories around the world and a research division in Davis, California. The company has over four thousand issued patents and an even larger customer base than Genencor.

Together Novozymes and Genencor account for about 60 percent of the world market for industrial enzymes. But both of these dominant players are being challenged by a growing number of Indian and Chinese firms that also produce these commodity chemicals. Today, Novozymes and Genencor have closer relationships to the large purchasers of enzymes, and this gives them the inside track in developing new products and winning new contracts. Still, the existence and growing competence of these Asian rivals provides alternative suppliers for some enzymes that can only tend to depress prices. The ABN-AMRO report suggests that while Chinese manufacturers can't quite hit the high production standards demanded by end users like Procter & Gamble, "looking at the enormous progress made in Chinese society, including on the technological front over the last 10 years, it is hard to believe that the Chinese will not be able to overcome the challenges they face today." In fact, Novozymes and Genencor both have production factories in China, where they are, in essence, training a cadre of Chinese engineers in quality control.

In addition to increased competition from enzyme producers in emerging nations, Genencor and Novozymes will very likely face new challenges from some of the agrochemical giants we met in the last chapter. The ABN-AMRO report notes that Dow Chemical Company and Syngenta have both formed alliances with some of the industrial biotech start-ups to move into enzyme markets. Dow and Syngenta both have the size and manufacturing expertise to pose serious potential threats to the industrial biotech giants. "The expected entrance of Dow and Syngenta should send shivers down the spine of Novozymes—and Genencor for that matter," according to ABN-AMRO. Monsanto, DuPont, and BASF may also go after parts of the enzyme markets. *Industrial biotechnology is shaping up as a mature, low-margin, slow-growth industry over which industrial giants are poised to battle for market share.*

All of these competitive pressures have caused some concern about the investment prospects of the two industrial biotech giants. Judging by the stock charts, this nervousness has affected Genencor more than Novozymes. By spring 2002, Genencor's stock was worth roughly half of its 2000 IPO price. Although Novozymes's shares have slumped somewhat, the stock was still trading close to its IPO at the same time.

The current market for enzymes is mature and stable, and revenue growth is therefore tied to the needs of enzyme-consuming firms who use these chemicals to produce three main types of consumer goods: human food (mainly beer and bread); animal feeds; or soaps, starches, and textiles (the faded look of stone-washed blue jeans is produced by an enzyme). The fortunes of Novozymes, Genencor, and other enzyme manufacturers reflect the sales of these underlying consumer products and—except for stealing or losing market share—the revenues of these companies rise and fall on overall economic trends. People who invest in paper and other commodity industries are comfortable with the cycles of consumer demand. But biotech investors are accustomed to entirely different

Two Giants of Industrial Biotech

Genencor's shares have slumped as the company has signaled its intention to add a drug development capacity, while Novozymes has held steady in a turbulent market by staying with its industrial course.

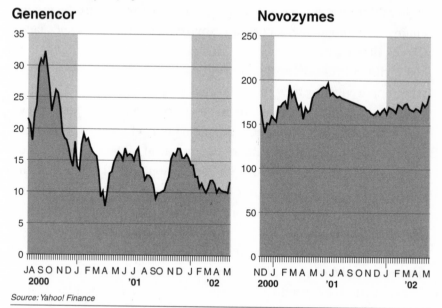

Genencor

Novozymes

Source: Yahoo! Finance

investment dynamics. The typical biotech firm creates a market for a novel therapeutic agent, sets high prices and margins during the period of patent exclusivity, and grows rapidly in revenues (when all goes well!). The industrial biotech landscape is quite obviously different.

Of course, Novozymes and Genencor are researching new breakthrough products. In 2001, for instance, both firms won competing research grants from the U.S. government to develop new enzymes that might make it economical to extract ethanol from the cellulose waste in plants. (Today, ethanol is made by converting the sugars in corn and other grain kernels.) If Novozymes or Genencor finds ways, at reasonable cost, to ferment plant waste, this would be a development with huge economic potential. It would open new markets to farmers and would potentially reduce U.S. oil imports. But don't rush to sell your oil stocks yet. There are a great many technical impediments to ethanol conversion from plant waste, and even if biotech scientists solve those problems by discovering or creating the cheap enzymes, it would still require huge investments in fermentation plants to create a large market for these enzymes. Remember that industrial biotech companies must produce huge volumes of low-cost, low-margin products, the exact opposite premise that underlies investments in medical and other biotech fields.

Given all of these considerations, Genencor is shifting its focus toward health care and personal care applications of biotechnology, while trying to retain its industrial base. The company has created a technique for identifying the specific portions of proteins that generate immune system reactions. Genencor is also in the process of creating a transgenic mouse that would have a human immune system. The objective is to create an animal model that could be used to test or develop human drugs. Genencor has other intellectual assets that it can leverage toward drug development. The company has extensive knowledge of a class of proteins called proteases. There are several hundred known proteases in the human body. As a class, proteases control other proteins. They cut, splice, or modify proteins. Genencor has, to date, manufactured proteases to cut protein stains loose from fabrics. It is now betting that its protease expertise can be redirected toward the development of protease-based drugs, like clot-busting medicines or AIDS drugs.

Genencor's initiatives in human health are in their early stages. The trick for the company will be to manage and grow the industrial parts of its business—which remain the basis for its revenues and any hope of profits—while it tries to enter the drug discovery arena. While the company has a great scientific and manufacturing track record, it is still a relative newcomer in medical biotech. It is not clear how Wall Street will interpret the company's split business focus, especially given that drug discovery is such a different business model.

Novozymes seems to be a different case entirely. Having made its bed in industrial biotech, it seems prepared to lie in it. "Put bluntly, Novozymes currently has a clear long-term focus on industrial enzymes, while Genencor in the longer term is placing its health care interests as top priority," according to the ABN-AMRO report. For investors interested in industrial biotechnology the behavior of these industry giants should provide food for thought—not only about potential investments in these two companies, but in evaluating the start-ups we'll address in the next section as well. *If industrial biotechnology offered such incredible growth opportunities, why is one of the incumbent leaders looking for greener pastures?*

To stay abreast of developments in this field, make it a habit to scan the trade publication *Chemical and Engineering News* (available at good business libraries), in addition to tracking the company websites.

The Industrial Biotech Start-ups

The newcomers in industrial biotechnology include three companies that played powerful roles in igniting the biotech IPO boom of 2000. Symyx Technologies (SMMX) and Maxygen Inc. (MAXY) actually went public in November and December of 1999, respectively. Symyx and Maxygen, therefore, helped to create the excitement and open the window that led to the record number of public offerings that occurred in 2000. Diversa Corp. (DVSA) floated its IPO in February 2000, which was still early in the rush. Wall Street was obviously impressed with the "story" these companies were telling about the use of biotechnology to create new materials and medicines. Even though these companies were new to the public markets, investors initially rewarded them with mid-range market capitalizations. Despite the many caveats in the foregoing section, these companies joined the universe of publicly traded biotech stocks amid great expectations. Their focus and genesis is on the industrial side of biotechnology, but they have also sought to apply their techniques to the discovery or improvement of medicines, along the same lines as Genencor.

The Symyx founding team included Dr. Alejandro C. Zaffaroni, one of biotech's best-known serial entrepreneurs, whose past credits include ALZA Corp., now part of Johnson & Johnson, and Affymetrix, the DNA chip maker that we met in chapter 5. The company uses—and also sells—a set of proprietary tools and techniques for finding or creating catalysts and other products with optimal characteristics. Symyx has research collaborations or sales relationships with Dow Chemical Co., Bayer, Merck, ExxonMobile Chemical, Agfa-Gevaert, BASF, and other well-known companies. Thus Symyx has a good executive pedigree and an impressive list of partners, two of the indicators investors use to assess early-stage biotech companies. Symyx also has the most impressive indicator of all: profits. In 2001 the company reported a net income of $6.3 million on revenues of $60 million—a most impressive showing for a young biotech company.

Maxygen's core technology is a process called molecular breeding or molecular evolution. In a simple sense, what the company does is take a set of genetic traits and shuffle them about to see what happens when the process results in slight variations of the genetic code. In other words, what Maxygen does is to mimic, on a greatly accelerated basis, the sort of mutations that occur in nature. Maxygen is working with Novozymes to improve enzymes by the use of gene-shuffling, and with Chevron to improve the synthesis of methanol. The company is also pursuing research in the agricultural biotech arena, working with DuPont and Syngenta on new bioengineered crops. Maxygen is also trying to apply its gene-shuffling expertise toward the improvement of pharmaceuticals. On the drug front, it has partnered with the biotech firm InterMune (ITMN) to work on improvements in the immune system compound Interferon Gamma. Maxygen is working with the Defense Advanced Research Projects Agency, the U.S. Agency for International Development, and other research institutes, on improved vaccines or treatments for malaria, dengue fever, and possible bioterror threats. The company reported revenues of $31 million in 2001 but posted a net loss of $45 million.

Diversa Corp. brings a slightly different focus to industrial biotechnology. Its specialty is hunting for novel organisms in extreme environments—hot thermal vents, rain forests, even garbage dumps. The idea is that microbes that can live in such environments probably express proteins and enzymes that can tolerate harsh conditions, and thus form the basis for improved industrial catalysts or pharmacological agents. In this regard, it is following in the footsteps of Genencor and Novozymes, which have also sought out enzymes from natural environments as the starting point for industrial products. Diversa's greatest innovation may be on the business front. Shortly after its public offering, Diversa established a fifty/fifty joint venture with Dow Chemical Company that the partners subsequently named Innovase LLC. The joint venture is aimed at producing enzymes for detergents, starch processing, textile manufacturing, and paper and pulp processing. Diversa will contribute the enzyme research; Dow will contribute the manufacturing expertise. Such a combination must be viewed as a serious potential competitor to Genencor and Novozymes because it combines a biotech innovator with an industrial giant capable of mass-producing novel products.

Diversa also hopes to enter various agrochemical and agricultural biotechnology markets. It has a stake in Zymetrics, a subsidiary formed by the ag-biotech giant Syngenta. Diversa is developing enzymes that Zymetrics will use to manufacture new animal feeds. In the human health arena it has relationships with GlaxoSmithKline and Celera Genomics. Diversa reported revenues of $36 million in 2001, and a new loss of $15.7 million.

One other company bears mentioning before moving on to the next section of this chapter, and a new set of technologies. Applied Molecular Evolution (AMEV) is another young biotech firm that uses the techniques of gene-shuffling, but the company is focused on using the technique to improve existing human medicines or create novel therapeutics. Some of the industrial biotech players are moving toward human therapeutics and so Applied Molecular may be a competitor.

Some of the industrial biotech companies have patents to cover aspects of the gene-shuffling technology, but unless or until one player succeeds in enforcing a broad claim over the field, then patent income, by itself, is unlikely to become a source of profitability. The various firms with molecular evolution skills will have to compete by using their gene-shuffling expertise to create profitable products.

In evaluating the companies in this niche, and potential newcomers, look at the following:

- Revenues and profits.
- Partnerships are important to validate a young company's approach, but try to figure out whether these deals are research-for-hire contracts or revenue-sharing relationships, and how much they are worth.
- Large-scale production is the key to success in industrial biotechnology; witness how Diversa and Symyx have tried to leverage their expertise by linking up with powerful manufacturing partners.
- Cash position is always a crucial indicator for any company that is not profitable.

Materials and Medicines from Transgenic Animals and Plants

The advance that launched the biotech industry more than a quarter century ago was the discovery that a gene from one species could be spliced into the genome of another species, and yet, in its new host organism, the transplanted gene could be made to express the same protein that it created in its normal environment. Early biotech scientists used bacteria as the hosts to produce the first medicinal proteins. Later, they discovered that some proteins had to be expressed in fast-growing cells drawn from mammals. Genencor has found that some enzymes can be raised only in fungal hosts. In recent years, biotech scientists have begun trying to produce biological materials and medicines in genetically altered animals and plants. They are called transgenic animals and plants because they have had a human gene spliced into them. Because this is ground-breaking technology, the FDA is sure to subject any medicine produced by a transgenic plant or animal to intense scrutiny.

The bioengineered plants and animals we'll discuss in this section are far too valuable to eat. If all works as planned, they will become living factories. The effort to develop animals and plants as production hosts stems in part from the escalating cost of creating biotech production facilities. As you may recall, biotech medicines are fermented in giant stainless steel vats, like a super-antiseptic brewing factory. It can cost tens of millions of dollars to build a biotech production plant. Getting the plant certified for the exacting standards demanded by the FDA is a process that can take many months. Production facilities must be staffed during this certification process. All of these are costs biotech companies must carry even before their medicine has been approved for sale. It is hoped that animal and plant production hosts will create large amounts of therapeutic medicines, at far lower costs for equipment and skilled labor.

But medicines are not the only targets for new plant and animal production. Biotech firms are also trying to use their gene-splicing techniques to create animals and plants capable of mass-producing new materials. One Canadian company in this alternate production niche—Nexia Biotechnologies (NXB.TO on the Toronto Stock Exchange)—has bioengineered goats to produce spider silk in their milk. Spider silk is a strong, lightweight fiber that, hitherto, couldn't be produced on a commercial scale. Unlike silkworms, which have been cultivated for centuries, spiders simply don't function in colonies. They eat one another. So Nexia, which went public in 2000, has tried the biotech approach. The company identified the spider genes that produce silk. It ruled out trying to use bacteria or other traditional biotech production vectors because they could not make the long silk fibers that were desired. So Nexia has focused on bio-engineering goats to express the spider silk in their mammary gland when they produce milk. The spider silk would be refined out of the milk and spun into fibers. A great deal of cutting-edge bioscience has gone into the creation of Nexia's silk-producing goat. The company has used cloning techniques, similar to those that created Dolly the sheep, to create additional goats with the capability of producing spider silk. Nexia is also experimenting with the use of plants to grow spider silk. The idea would be to splice the silk-producing genes into some plant host and see if the plant will express a useful fiber.

All of this is still experimental and there are as yet no guarantees that Nexia will be able to harvest spider silk economically using these animal or plant vectors. Again, cost-effective production is the key word. *The objective is not to impress the world but to produce products.* That means the process must yield spider silk in sufficient quantity to create some product for which the company can charge enough to stay in business. I hate to dwell on what should be an obvious point, but people tend to get so excited by novel technologies that they forget the practicalities. Nexia is currently focused on medical applications for its spider silk (which it calls BioSteel), products that would presumably command a premium price. These uses would include sutures that would be strong and thin, as well as artificial ligaments. Nexia is also working with the U.S. and Canadian armed forces to create BioSteel vests that might one day compete with Kevlar. But I suspect it'll be a good long while before Nexia can produce sufficient spider silk at any reasonable cost to popularize a bulletproof windbreaker. The company reported a $6.7 million loss on 2001 income of $1.6 million.

Most experiments in the use of transgenic animals and plants focus on the production of novel medicines, as the products with the highest potential market value, but developments so far have not been encouraging. For instance, GTC Biotherapeutics (GTCB) has undertaken human clinical trials to test the use of animals to produce a variety of biotech medicines. GTC, which used to be called Genzyme Transgenics, is an offshoot of the biotech giant Genzyme General (GENZ). GTC changed its name in 2002. This small-cap company is trying to produce therapeutic proteins using rabbits, mice, goats, and cows that have been genetically altered to express medicines in their milk. GTC says it has successfully produced experimental quantities of several dozen therapeutic compounds, including monoclonal antibodies and proteins. Since these are medicines destined for human use, they will all have to undergo human clinical trials prior to seeking review by the FDA. In 2001, GTC was disappointed when the FDA asked for additional clinical trials on an animal-produced anticoagulant protein known as rhATIII. The compound had already been through Phase III tests for use in patients who did not respond to current anticoagulants, so the request was a setback for GTC, which thought its product was poised for approval. Rather than proceed with the FDA process, GTC shifted its geographic focus to Europe and targeted a different use—providing rhATIII to people born with an inherited deficiency of this natural anticoagulant. GTC believes it can get its animal-produced protein approved more quickly in Europe than in the United States. If successful there, it plans to return to the U.S. market.

PPL Therapeutics (PTH.L on the London stock exchange)—the company that helped clone Dolly the sheep—is also experimenting with the use of animals as protein medicine factories. But the stocks of PPL and GTC both slumped miserably from 2001 into early 2002, reflecting investor pessimism with the field. One of the underlying problems seems to be that transgenic animals don't necessarily produce reliable quantities of the desired protein. The challenges have been so fierce that in 2001, Pharming, NV, a Dutch firm that was a pioneer in the field, went bankrupt. Nevertheless, young biotech companies continue to experiment with new ways to turn animals into medical production plants. For instance, a private Canadian start-up, TGN Biotech in Quebec, is developing a process to create gene-spliced boars that would produce therapeutic proteins in their semen. AniGenics Inc., a private biotech firm in Athens, Georgia, is in the early stages of determining whether chickens can be genetically engineered to express medicinal proteins in their eggs.

Meanwhile, gene-splicing technologies are being tried on plants, to see whether these fast-growing life-forms can be harnessed for biomedical production. One of the most advanced experiments in this regard is being conducted by Large Scale Biology Corp. (LSBC), a small-cap biotech firm in California. The company uses a virus to insert a human gene into a plant. In essence, the virus "infects" the plant with the human gene, causing the plant to express the human protein. Large Scale Biology has completed a Phase I clinical trial to ascertain whether this process might be a cost-effective way to produce a protein medicine that a Stanford University professor has devised to treat a form of non-Hodgkin's lymphoma. To date, no one has come up with an economical way to manufacture the treatment. Large Scale Biology's clinical trial is something of a litmus test for the young field of plant-produced medicines, which needs a success to encourage further investment and experimentation. Large Scale Biology is a very small company. In 2001 it lost $20.7 million on revenues of $17.7 million.

The notion of genetically altering plants to produce medicines and materials is so new that much of the innovation is being carried on at privately funded start-ups. The effort to turn plants into protein factories brings us full circle to industrial biotechnology, because some of the experimental uses under development aim to use plants as enzyme factories. For instance, ProdiGene is a private firm in College Station, Texas, that is developing a wide array of possible uses for transgenic plants, including collaboration with Genencor to produce industrial enzymes. The Texas start-up is also working with Large Scale Biology to produce therapeutic antibodies. It has won support from the National Institutes of Health to research the potential for edible vaccines for certain viral diseases. Another private player in this space is Epicyte Pharmaceutical Inc. of San Diego, which has trademarked the term *Plantibodies* to describe its efforts to use transgenic plants as manufacturing plants. Among its many initiatives, Epicyte is collaborating with Dow Chemical Company and Dow AgroSciences on industrial biotech products, and it has a series of deals with medical biotech companies to explore the use of Plantibodies as human medicines. This field could change the way medicines are produced. But the work is at such an early stage that potential products could be five to ten years away. Investors should approach this area with caution and make sure that any company they follow has the cash to carry it through many years of probable losses.

Investor Tools: Analyzing Alliances

Earlier in this book I mentioned that one of the definitions of biotechnology had to do with the size of the company. Today drug and biotech firms use the same techniques to invent medicines, discovery tools, and new materials. The inescapable difference is that the biotech players are almost always newer and smaller, and they very often find it necessary or desirable to form alliances with larger companies. A large part of the reason for these alliances is the need to raise money. "About 10 percent of the money in biotech comes from venture capital," says Mark Edwards, managing director of Recombinant Capital, a biotech consulting firm in Walnut Creek, California, that specializes in tracking alliances. "Another 40 percent comes from public equities and convertible debt. Much of the remaining 50 percent comes from alliance partners," who underwrite clinical trials or otherwise bear many of the expenses involved in biotech product development. Obviously the formation of such alliances is a pivotal point in a biotech firm's history. The relationships not only provide cash, but they tend to legitimize young companies. "A big company does due diligence on twenty-five to forty deals before making an alliance," Edwards says. They have their scientists study the start-up's technology, assess the caliber of management, look at its balance sheet, and weigh each potential partner against its competitor. For these reasons, investors trying to decide whether to take a stake in a start-up find it comforting when a large drug company or biotech firm makes a bet on the same company.

Trouble is, says Edwards, some deals are far less than they're cracked up to be, and bad deals can ruin a young company, so investors need to analyze these alliances rather than assuming that because a big company has invested in a little outfit, you should, too. For instance, every biotech firm that gets an experimental medicine through a successful Phase II trial faces a costly dilemma. It must fund an expensive Phase III study and at the same time it must begin setting up a manufacturing process to make the product. This way, when it presents what it hopes will be successful Phase III data to the FDA, the company can also have regulators certify the process that will make bulk quantities of the medicine. The biotech company's whole future is riding on the nature of the alliance it strikes at this time, Edwards says. Does it give up the lion's share of the revenues to the alliance partner, who is, after all, bearing most of the expense? Or does the biotech firm manage to retain control and make its backer the junior partner in the alliance? "This is the make-it-or-break-it point for many young companies," Edwards says. "As an investor, you want to make sure they haven't had to give up control of the profits to make the product a reality."

In an article entitled "Ten Deals That Changed Biotechnology" (search the archives of the online publication *Signals Magazine* at www.signalsmag.com), Edwards cited one of the best deals ever struck, the 1984 arrangement by which Amgen secured the backing of Japan's Kirin Corp. to develop Epogen, the blood-boosting compound that made Amgen what it is today. The key factor, according to Edwards, was that Amgen retained the rights to control the U.S. market, and won Kirin's backing by giving the Japanese firm control of the marketing rights in Japan. Edwards quoted Amgen cofounder George Rathmann: "The key to the best deals has to do with how much downstream value you retain."

Trouble is, it's often difficult for investors to learn the nitty-gritty details of these crucial alliances. "They (biotech companies) are very sneaky as a group," Edwards says. This is especially true with early-stage research alliances, a common type of deal in which young companies team up with larger players. Often the small company contracts to discover drug targets or screen medicinal compounds that the large company will take into drug development. Such partnerships offer the young firm a way to generate income while validating its technology. In addition to considering the total announced value of the deal, and the prestige of the senior partner, investors should also note:

- The duration of the deal; how many years is it supposed to run?
- The purpose of the deal; who is supposed to do what?
- The up-front payment; the senior partner often pays a fee or makes an investment in the smaller company; bigger is usually better.
- The conditions for future payments; small companies must usually meet "milestones," that is, do whatever they've promised; try to discover what they have to do, when they have to do it, and what they'll be paid if they succeed.
- The potential for royalties; it's usually a good sign when a junior partner retains a piece of the action if its discoveries eventually

become products—provided it still gets milestone payments and isn't saddled with carrying on expensive research against the distant hope of a payoff.

- The cash position of the junior partner at the time of the deal; check the start-up's balance sheet, note its most recent cash balance, and calculate how many years of cash it has left (divide cash by annual loss); if a start-up has two, three, or five years of cash when it strikes a deal, it was probably in a strong bargaining position; conversely, a company running low on cash probably had to make concessions.

Alliances are generally announced by press release and the stocks of the small companies involved often pop on the news. But prudent investors don't act until they understand the details. Sometimes this means waiting until a company reports the alliance in an SEC filing. If the target is a company going public, the registration form, or S-1 filing, is the best place to look. Companies that are already public may detail a new alliance in a form 8-K (notice of a special event), a quarterly report (10-Q), or annual report (10-K). All of these forms are freely available at www.sec.gov.

But SEC documents may not spell out all the fine print governing alliances. Therefore, Edwards recommends that when investors become interested in a company because of a newly announced deal, they should go back and look at its deal track record. Visit the company's website and read the press releases of past announcements. Note how much they were supposed to be worth and over how many years. Then estimate how much revenue the company should be reporting annually. If a company has announced a series of deals worth a total of $120 million over a three-year period, you should expect to see roughly $40 million a year in revenues. Compare this estimate to the company's quarterly and annual statements. "Most companies have half a dozen or fewer revenue-generating partnerships," Edwards says. "It's not very hard to figure out whether the revenues are consistent with the deal promise."

Investors get two rewards for performing such analyses. First, they get a deflation factor for assessing any future deals announced by the same company. If the company in this example reported $20 million in revenue, you might want to discount the current announcement by 50 percent. Studying the deal track record also gives investors a broader insight into the character of the management. If the revenues are consistent with the deal announcements, it suggests you're dealing with a management whose pronouncements are reliable. Conversely, if you see huge disparities, you might suspect that the outfit is full of hype when it makes other announcements, such as reporting a "positive" clinical trial, without providing all the data.

When evaluating competitors in the same niche, it's wise to compare their partnerships. "Who has the most deals, who has the best deals, who has the partners with the best reputations," Edwards says. "These are great clues about where the smart money has placed its bets."

Of course, the smart money isn't infallible. In September 2001, Bristol-Myers Squibb paid $1 billion for a 20 percent stake in ImClone Systems in order to gain marketing rights to a much-touted anticancer treatment called Erbitux. The Bristol-Myers deal was a huge validation for investors who had seen ImClone's shares rise from the single digits in 1998 to the $50 range before the alliance was announced. But ImClone came under a cloud in 2002 after the FDA rebuffed its application to sell Erbitux, and investors—including Bristol-Myers—started asking when ImClone knew, or should have known, that it had problems with the FDA.

Few alliances blow up as spectacularly as the ImClone deal. Bad ones simply peter out when the biotech firm fails to meet its milestones, but many alliances succeed. In 1993, William Haseltine put Human Genome Sciences on the map—and established the value of genomic research—with a $125 million deal to develop a large number of gene targets for SmithKline Beecham. In 1998, Millennium Pharmaceuticals did even better when it signed a $465 million deal to provide 225 new drug targets to Bayer over five years. Hindsight always tells you which deals were good, but if a new alliance catches your eye, take the time to examine the fine print. This may involve going through the sort of analysis described here, or the companies may spell out the arrangement in sufficient detail to make you comfortable. As Edwards says: "If you have a good deal, you tend to let people know. Those who will not disclose didn't do real well."

8

Brave New Worlds: Stem Cells, Clones, and Other Frontiers

Biotechnology was born in controversy. When the fundamental technique of gene-splicing was invented in the 1970s, it seemed such an awesome power that leading scientists called a moratorium on what they called recombinant DNA experiments until the scientific community could design self-monitoring systems to ensure that researchers did not unwittingly create dangerous organisms. With the benefit of some thirty years of hindsight, we can see that this early caution helped create the atmosphere of public trust that has allowed the biotech industry to grow, innovate, and prosper. There have been exceptions to the rule, notably the fears that biotech critics express about so-called Frankenfoods and Frankenfish. But the vast majority of biotech firms remain focused on medical inventions, an activity that enjoys a halo of public approval that goes a long way toward explaining why so many investors tolerate the volatility and spotty performance of biotech stocks. They feel they're part of an industry that is doing good.

However, just as gene-splicing did in the past, powerful new biotechnologies are causing the world to draw in a sharp breath. In this chapter I want to look at stem cell therapy, cloning, gene therapy, biological warfare countermeasures, and other controversial technologies. These cutting-edge fields—and others that may arise in the future—conjure up political, religious, and moral misgivings that compound the normal investment uncertainty and risk. If you are a cautious investor, with a minimal appetite for volatility, these niches simply aren't for you—not yet, and not for many years to come. But biotechnology is moving so quickly that what seems like science fiction today could become mainstream tomorrow. In any event, some of these technologies, particularly stem cell research and gene therapy, have the potential to affect future medical research as profoundly as gene-splicing did thirty years ago. Their promising—and controversial—nature practically guarantee they'll make headlines. And depending on the tenor of the coverage, even cautious investors may be tempted to dabble in companies pursuing these approaches. Better to inoculate yourself with a bit of knowledge now rather than catch an expensive fever later!

The same advice is even more applicable to daring investors who sense the long-term potential in these fields. For those who are intrigued rather than repelled by novel technologies, the trick is to avoid getting so blinded by the promise that one fails to ask how many years it will take to figure out whether these are paths to riches or blind alleys. Let's look at some of the public and private companies exploring the edge of what is possible—and treading the same ethical and scientific swamps that made early biotech investing so risky.

Stem Cells: Hope or Hype?

The field of stem cell research has been intensively covered in the media, and yet it remains an area that is profoundly misunderstood. That is not surprising. The science underlying the field is incredibly complex, and controversy has made it difficult to consider the work dispassionately. As a new area populated by a handful of small companies, it is not well covered by financial analysts. To help you evaluate potential investments in this area, you must understand the two main divisions inside the stem cell niche:

- Embryonic stem cell research, which uses cells drawn from human embryos; this has been the center of controversy.

- Adult stem cell studies, based on material extracted from tissues after birth.

Let's start with definitions. Simply put, stem cells give rise to other cells. It takes more than two hundred different types of cells to make our bodies tick. Nerves, muscles, blood, bone, and skin are examples of large families of cells. Each of these families is further divided—or as scientists like to say, differentiated—into cell types with specialized functions. Among blood cells, for instance, there are the oxygen-carrying red cells and the disease-fighting white cells; under the white cell heading there are five specialized varieties, and so on. The body is a network of literally trillions of cells, organized into neighborhoods, such as the heart and the liver, which scientists call organs and tissues.

The most powerful stem cells—and the ones at the center of the controversy—are those that are formed shortly after a sperm cell fertilizes an egg. The fertilized egg divides, creating a small group of what are called embryonic stem cells. In a routine pregnancy, these embryonic stem cells would continue to divide and differentiate, creating larger numbers of new and more specialized cells, which further divide and differentiate to form even more specialized cells until, at the end of the normal gestation period, a baby composed of two hundred different tissue types would emerge.

The fundamental breakthrough came in 1998 when scientists extracted human embryonic stem cells from their natural settings and caused them to grow in a tissue culture. Because embryonic stem cells can give rise to any type of cell, scientists hope to discover how to prompt these undifferentiated cells to produce specialized cells to repair damaged organs or tissues. For instance, paralysis results when the spinal cord is severed. What if embryonic stem cells could be transformed into nerve cells to repair the break, like using solder to splice two wires? Opponents object to embryonic stem cell research because it involves the destruction of human embryos for use as spare parts.

The debate about embryonic stem cell studies has largely revolved around whether federal funds should be used to fund experiments that would destroy human embryos. It is not illegal to experiment with embryonic stem cells provided the work has private sector rather than federal backing. In fact, Geron Corp. (GERN) supported much of the fundamental science in the field and now controls important commercial rights on potential uses of the technology. But federal funding is important to legitimize the field and to focus academic research on overcoming the many challenges involved in turning undifferentiated cells into therapies. In August 2001 President George Bush, over the objections of pro-life groups that have been the most determined opponents of this technology, said the federal government would fund experiments involving several dozen embryonic stem cell lines already in existence. It was a compromise that allowed the research to go forward, without settling the underlying debate.

The controversy surrounding embryonic stem cells has overshadowed the related field of adult stem cell studies. Stem cell activity does not cease at birth. Scientists have discovered reservoirs of stem cells in a variety of tissues, including bone marrow, blood, eyes, the brain, skeletal muscles, dental tissue, the liver, the skin, and the lining of the intestinal tract. These adult stem cells give the body a limited ability to repair damage caused by the wear and tear of living. Adult stem cells are only able to differentiate into specific cell types. Stem cells found in bone tissue develop into bone cells; those found in nerve tissues develop into nerve cells; and so on. However, new discoveries hint that certain types of adult stem cells may be more capable of differentiating into different cell types than previously supposed. Scientists call this transformational ability "plasticity." A primer on stem cells put out by the National Institutes of Health (www.nih.gov/news/stemcell/scireport.htm) explains how adult stem cells, drawn from bone marrow, were coaxed into forming neurons and other brain cells. "The concept of adult stem cell plasticity is new and the phenomenon is not thoroughly understood," according to the NIH report. "[However,] evidence suggests that, given the right environment, some adult stem cells are capable of being 'genetically reprogrammed' to generate specialized cell types that are characteristic of different tissues." Opponents of embryonic stem cell research have seized upon these hints to argue that there is no need to destroy embryos to create new cell therapies—not if adult stem cells, harvested from bone marrow or other sources, might prove plastic enough to make a wide array of repair tissues. However, the weight of scientific opinion rejects that argument and insists that embryonic stem cell research should be carried on in parallel with the adult stem cell studies—and may the best stem cells win.

I'll leave the argument at this impasse and shift my focus to the companies that are pursuing various stem cell studies. In so doing, I don't wish to minimize the importance of the debate. In the investment context, however, the crucial point is that the controversy adds to the uncertainty about whether stem cell companies will be able to develop products that can be sold safely and at a profit. But I don't believe politics is the greatest risk affecting investments in this field. These are sciences in their infancy, particularly the embryonic studies, which only began in earnest in 1998. That's yesterday in biotech time. Consider how long it took to develop monoclonal antibodies. They were first discovered in the mid-1970s. It was the mid-1980s before biotech firms like Genentech began serious commercial development. And it was not until 1997 that the FDA approved the first monoclonal antibody, Rituxan. That's twenty years from the lab to the pharmacy!

Moreover, cells are unlike other medicines because cells grow. What if a patient took a dose of stem cells contaminated with unwanted or defective cells? The FDA will demand assurances that cell therapies have been exhaustively screened for defects. Regulators will also scrutinize stem cell medicines in light of what has been learned by exploring previous cell-based technologies, notably fetal tissue research. A decade before stem cells became the cause célèbre, many scientists were convinced that fetal tissues could be used to treat a variety of ailments. The fetal tissue debate was a dress rehearsal for the stem cell controversy. Opponents feared the research would create a market for aborted fetuses. Proponents held forth the promise of cures for conditions like Parkinson's disease. Congress banned the use of federal funds for fetal tissue research, handicapping the science, but some experiments proceeded with private funding. On May 7, 1992, the *New York Times* reported that two preliminary studies "on small groups of patients provide what experts say is intriguing evidence that fetal tissue transplants can alleviate symptoms of Parkinson's disease." The theory was that the fetal cells would supply the dopamine that Parkinson's sufferers lack. But on March 8, 2001, the *Times* followed up one of those experiments with this report: "A carefully controlled study that tried to treat Parkinson's disease by implanting cells from aborted fetuses into patients' brains not only failed to show an overall benefit but also revealed a disastrous side effect." The article went on to report how, in about 15 percent of patients, the fetal cells produced an excess of dopamine, causing debilitating spasms.

Politics aside, when cellular therapies come before the FDA for review, the hurdle for approval will be high.

The Regenerative Medicine Companies

The basic reason to consider any of the companies in this perilous space is that success would lead to a tremendous breakthrough in how we treat disease. Today, at the very best, doctors try to limit the damage caused by disease, or slow the spread of the ailment. Cell-based therapies hold out the hope of being able to reverse the effects of heart disease, stroke, and other infirmities. This would be an utterly profound change in medicine, and it is that hope that keeps some companies and investors interested despite the many obstacles. In a bid to escape the aura of controversy surrounding stem cells, the companies in this niche like to think of themselves as pioneering a new field called regenerative medicine. To the extent the new label sticks, it would help companies overcome the stigma that complicates their work. But in a practical sense it's important to know who's doing what, so I'll introduce the embryonic and adult stem cell companies in that order.

- Geron Corp. (GERN) is the pioneer in embryonic stem cell development. Before the federal government began funding such work, the California company supported the two scientific teams that isolated embryonic stem cells in 1998. These discoveries were patented by the University of Wisconsin and Johns Hopkins University. Geron—by virtue of its early support for the research—obtained commercial rights to develop embryonic stem cells as therapies for ailments such as heart disease, diabetes, and nerve disorders. In early 2002, the company agreed to limit its commercial claims and allow key stem cell patents to be licensed to other companies, thus defusing political concerns that one company might monopolize the field. The ultimate home run for Geron would be to develop embryonic stem cells into regenerative medicines. But clinical testing and FDA approval remain distant hurdles. Meanwhile, the company is attempting to develop near-term markets, such as the creation of liver cell cultures for use in screening experimental drugs. Liver toxicity sinks many compounds in clinical trials. An early and reliable test to screen out toxic drugs would presumably appeal to drug developers.

As a company, Geron is about more than stem cells. It holds strong patent positions in the use of telomerase, an enzyme that allows cells to keep growing indefinitely. Although this may seem like a fountain of youth, telomerase overactivity seems to work against us, by making cancer cells immortal. Geron is exploring the connection between telomerase and cancer, hoping to find small-molecule drugs that would inhibit telomerase in cancer cells. It is also trying to teach the immune system to kill tumor cells that overexpress the enzyme and multiply out of control. Finally, Geron controls a broad array of cloning patents including the technology used to produce Dolly the sheep. Geron hopes to exploit these patents in a variety of agricultural settings, from the cloning of food animals to the creation of herds designed to express therapeutic or industrial proteins (as we discussed in the previous chapter). With three such futuristic technologies as stem cells, cloning, and telomerase, Geron has alternately been a public sensation—and a pariah—and its stock has fluctuated accordingly. It remains a money-losing, small-cap company with huge challenges to match its big ambitions. (And as we'll see later in this chapter, Geron's cofounder has moved on to a private Massachussets firm where he seems intent on challenging his former company.)

- After Geron, the field of public embryonic stem cell plays thins very quickly. One alternative is a small-cap company called BresaGen, a publicly traded Australian biotech firm with offices in Athens, Georgia. BresaGen has access to four stem cell lines approved for use in federally funded experiments. The company also claims to have derived embryonic stem cells using a technology distinct from that used by the University of Wisconsin or Johns Hopkins. Thus it may create an independent patent position and be able to challenge Geron in that company's chosen therapeutic turf. But that remains speculative for now.

- Reliance Life Industries in India also controls several federally approved stem cell lines. It is a subsidiary of Reliance Industries, an Indian petrochemical conglomerate, but is a very small part of a huge company whose stock will likely rise or fall on other factors.

- CyThera Inc. is a small, privately held firm in San Diego that has nine approved stem cell lines. The company's website (www.cytheraco.com) says its internal development is focused on the creation of pancreatic islet cells for the treatment of diabetes, but little is known about its backers, plans, or prospects.

- The rest of the federally approved cell lines are dispersed among academic institutes in Sweden, the United States,

Geron's Turbulent Ticker

Closing price

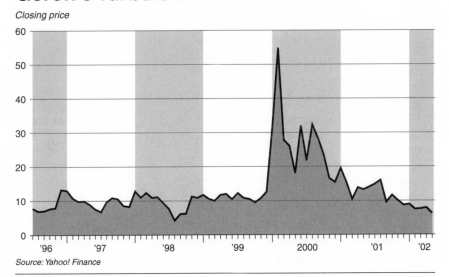

Source: Yahoo! Finance

Israel, and India. The National Institutes of Health keeps a registry of approved human embryonic stem cell lines at http://escr.nih.gov. It's a good central point to start investment research for new players in the field, since access to federal funding will make a big difference in the early stages of research.

In the field of adult stem cell therapies, we also find a handful of tiny public firms that, taken together, had a market capitalization of $120 million in May 2002! In the Wall Street scheme of things these aren't small-cap companies, they're micro caps. They are as follows:

- Curis Inc. (CRIS) is a Massachusetts company that is collaborating with a privately held Montreal firm, Aegera Therapeutics. They are experimenting with a type of adult stem cell found in the skin that seems capable of forming nerve and muscle cells, among other tissue types. This work is in its very earliest stages. Curis also has programs in tissue engineering and small-molecule drugs. The company has negligible revenues and is still in a money-losing, research mode.

- StemCells Inc. (STEM) is a California company experimenting with adult stem cell therapies for the central nervous system, the pancreas, and the liver.

- NeoTherapeutics Inc. (NEOT) of Irvine, California, is trying to develop growth factors that would stimulate the activity of the stem cells that naturally reside in the patient's body. Its first target has been the attempt to stimulate the stem cells of the brain to produce new neurons, with the eventual hope of treating disorders such as Parkinson's disease.

- Nexell Therapeutics Inc. (NEXL) is another Irvine firm that is developing cell-sorting and selection technologies. One of the problems that will face adult stem cell companies will be isolating stem cells—which are exceedingly rare—from their host tissue. Those companies that succeed in causing stem cells to differentiate into therapeutically useful cells will also have to gather the proper cells and exclude any contaminants. Nexell is working on these challenges.

- Aastrom Bioscience Inc. (ASTM) is a tiny company in Ann Arbor, Michigan, that is working on cell-sorting technologies and cell-based therapies. The cell-sort problem won't be unique to stem cell companies. There is an emerging market for cancer vaccines that will use altered cells in an attempt to augment the body's response to cancer. For any cell-based therapy, it will be essential to exclude any undesired or aberrant cells. Aastrom is currently active on the cancer vaccine and adult stem cell fronts, and its sorting technologies could prove useful in both fields.

In addition to these micro-cap players several private biotech firms are working on adult stem cell therapies, and presumably waiting for the proper market conditions to go public. The best way to stay abreast of developments will be through their Web pages.

- ViaCell Inc. is a Massachusetts company that began as a cord blood registry (saving the umbilical cords of newborns for potential transplants). From that base it branched into adult stem cell research. ViaCell is testing its potential stem cell therapy in early-stage clinical trials.

- VistaGen Inc. is a private firm in Burlingame, California, that is developing stem cell systems as drug screens—that is, using stem cells to create batches of bone marrow, nerve, heart, and other cell types to test the efficacy or toxicity of experimental drugs.

- NeuralStem Inc. of Gaithersburg, Maryland, is focused on the development of brain stem cells for the potential treatment of Parkinson's disease, Alzheimer's disease, stroke, multiple sclerosis, epilepsy, and other nervous system disorders.

- Osiris Therapeutics Inc. is a private firm in Baltimore that has human clinical trials under way to test the therapeutic potential of what seems to be a particularly "plastic" variety of mesenchymal stem cell derived from bone marrow. Preliminary work indicates mesenchymal cells have the ability to form bone, cartilage, cardiac cells, and various connective tissues. Osiris has developed ways to extract these mesenchymal cells from bone marrow. The company also believes these cells may not have the molecular markers that might otherwise provoke an immune system reaction if and when stem cell derivatives are transplanted into patients.

Cloning and Stem Cells

I saved this point, about the possible immune system complications of stem cell therapies, for last because it is a technical challenge that bedevils the entire field—and because it ties the stem cell debate to the explosive question of human cloning. We know about immune system reactions from our long experience with organ transplants. Patients who get heart, lung, or liver transplants must take drugs to suppress their normal immune system reactions. Otherwise, the immune system would consider the transplanted organ an infection and reject it. But immune system signals are embedded at the cellular level. Thus a cell transplant would presumably provoke an immune system response. Even as they struggle with the many other challenges facing the field—isolating stem cells in sufficient quantity, guiding them to specialize into a desired cell type, and then sorting the cells again—stem cell scientists are looking ahead to how they might be able to overcome the anticipated immune system rejection. One of the ways they anticipate being able to overcome the immune system hurdle is through cloning or, as it is scientifically called, nuclear transfer.

The process of nuclear transfer involves taking the nucleus out of one cell and replacing it with the nucleus extracted from another cell. If the host cell were an egg, this nuclear transfer could also trigger the development of an embryo that would derive all of its genetic instructions from the transplanted nucleus. In short, it would be a clone of whatever organism provided the nucleus. Nuclear transfer was the process used to create Dolly the sheep. But, in theory, nuclear transfer could also be used to splice the nucleus from a patient's skin cell into a batch of stem cells, or an egg destined to produce a colony of stem cells. In this case the nuclear transfer would be intended to create stem cells that were a genetic match for the patient's immune system.

Nuclear transfer (or cloning) to make babies is controversial and Congress has mounted at least two serious efforts to ban the practice. But lawmakers have been unable to pass a bill because the cloning debate has become entwined with the stem cell controversy. There is general agreement in Congress that reproductive cloning should be banned, at least for now, because of health risks to the offspring. But there is a huge divide when the debate turns to cloning experiments involving stem cells. Leading scientific bodies have asked lawmakers to create an exception to any cloning ban so they can use nuclear transfer in research. This might mean creating cellular medicines that overcome the immune system barrier or it might involve cloning stem cells for study purposes. The biotech industry has supported this call for a split ban: "no" on reproductive cloning, "yes" to therapeutic or research cloning. However, many cloning opponents fear that any exception to the ban will quickly move cloning from the laboratory into the delivery room. With neither side able to muster a majority, Congress has so far failed to act. The link between cloning and stem cell debates adds to the political uncertainties facing the nascent stem cell industry.

One small private company has become a continual source of innovation—and irritation—in the stem cell and cloning debates. Advanced Cell Technolgy of Worcester, Massachusetts, has performed a series of high-profile experiments, some of which it has publicized in the mainstream media, others of which it has revealed through traditional scientific journals. The company has consistently pushed the envelope of what is technically possible in regenerative medicine, while simultaneously challenging public opinion. ACT generated intense publicity in November 2001 when it revealed that it had cloned a human embryo. The company's stated objective was to demonstrate that cloning could lead to therapeutically useful stem cells that overcame the immune system hurdle. In that regard the experiment fell short, because the cloned embryos proved short-lived and did not generate sustainable stem cell colonies. But one should assume ACT is still trying.

In similar fashion ACT has pioneered a technique called parthenogenesis—the process of stimulating an egg to develop into an embryo without requiring fertilization by a sperm cell. In 2002 the company reported in the journal *Science* that its scientists had collaborated with several academic groups to create a line of embryonic stem cells by initiating parthenogenesis in a monkey egg. The company said it had kept the primate stem cells alive for months and had caused them to differentiate into a variety of cell types, including neurons and muscle. That success in primates is only one step shy of reporting a similar advance with human embryonic tissue—creating another potential detour to the existing patents upon which Geron, for one, currently depends. And, like Geron, ACT is active in the area of cloning technology for use in the production of livestock animals.

The convergence with Geron is probably not accidental. ACT chief executive Michael West cofounded Geron in the early 1990s and launched that company's research into telomerase and human embryonic stem cells. West joined ACT after being eased out of Geron in 1998—in part because he was perceived as being too provocative. At ACT, West has focused on the same technologies that had inspired him to found Geron.

Gene Therapy

The field of gene therapy is a perfect example of the cyclical nature of biotechnology. Many new niches are born to incredible hype, only to fall out of favor during the long years of failure and experimentation. But some technologies rebound. That could—emphasis on the conditional—be the case with gene therapy.

When the first human gene therapy experiments began in 1990, there was an almost euphoric belief that biotech scientists had found the magic bullet. Many diseases, including cancer, result from the absence or abnormality of the genes that a person inherits. A whole series of rare disorders occur when children inherit gene defects that prevent their cells from making enzymes to create fuel or eliminate waste. Hemophilia is the most commonly known genetic disorder. Hemophiliacs lack the gene needed to make one of the proteins that clot blood. In theory, if scientists could insert the missing or defective gene into the proper cells, the patient should be cured.

Even in gene therapy's euphoric days, however, it was clear that the field faced many technical challenges, beginning with getting the right genes into the proper cells. To solve this microscopic delivery problem, scientists borrowed an idea from nature. Certain viruses have a natural ability to penetrate human cells. Adenovirus, which causes the common cold, is one such example. Scientists theorized that if they could insert specific genes into a modified adenovirus, the microbe would deliver this gene therapy at the cellular level.

By now it should go almost without saying that every aspect of these theories proved difficult to put into practice. But it wasn't the technical challenges that have all but buried gene therapy—and make no mistake, this is one niche that has fallen off the radar screens of most biotech investors. Instead it was a scandal that tarred the field.

In 1999, an eighteen-year-old Arizona man named Jesse Gelsinger died as a result of being injected with an experimental gene therapy. Subsequent investigations suggested that his immune system had had a deadly reaction to the high dose of adenovirus used as the delivery vehicle. (Gelsinger had a rare genetic defect that prevents the body from cleansing the bloodstream of ammonia.) In a technical sense the death was a setback for the field, because adenovirus is used to deliver many gene therapies. But the tragedy was compounded by revelations that the principal scientist behind the experiment, an academic at the University of Pennsylvania, had founded the biotech company that was supporting the experiment. The affair suggested that the researcher had taken safety shortcuts to push an experiment in which he had much to gain—and in which one young man lost his life. The Gelsinger tragedy soured the outlook for gene therapy.

But in the spring of 2002, French researchers reported that they had apparently cured four children of a severe immune system disorder using gene therapy. The four children had the same condition as David, the so-called bubble boy, who had lived in a sterile environment until he died in 1984 at the age of twelve, a victim of his body's genetic inability to ward off disease. According to a report in the *New England Journal of Medicine,* the French researchers first extracted bone marrow from the affected children. Then, in the laboratory, they inserted the corrective gene back into the extracted cells. The French scientists grew large quantities of these gene-enhanced cells, and injected them back into the children, who went on to regain disease-fighting ability.

The French success gave the field a lift, but only briefly. Shortly after the "cures" were reported, one of the children in the French study developed a condition akin to leukemia. Suspecting that the gene therapy may have been the cause, U.S. and French officials halted several studies similar to that experiment and the goodwill was lost. Even so, several considerations compel me to bring gene therapy to your attention. First, a handful of biotech firms have patiently pursued clinical trials through this bleak spell, and one of those efforts could eventually break the gene therapy jinx. And if some company gets a gene therapy approved by the FDA, its achievement will probably lift the entire biotech sector. That's what happened in 1998 through 2000, after the FDA approved the first monoclonal antibodies. Biotech was in the dumps in the late 1990s. But the sector began to rise in 1999, as sophisticated investors realized that monoclonal antibodies represented a new product category for biotech firms. The frenzy caused by the Human Genome Project poured fat on the fire in 2000, but the flames of biotech's recovery were lit by the recognition that monoclonal antibodies were about to hit pay dirt. The same sector-wide excitement could occur if gene therapy rises from the dead.

One last caveat before I briefly highlight a few companies. Given the previous failures, the FDA will subject gene therapy pioneers to utmost scrutiny. Companies that report favorable Phase III results in gene therapy trials will face intense safety reviews by FDA advisory panels. And even if these advisors recommend approval, the FDA will think long and hard before it sanctions a therapy that puts viruses into patients. So be prepared for volatility as you look at players such as the following:

- Avigen Inc. (AVGN) is a California firm that has launched two Phase I clinical trials to test a gene therapy aimed at hemophilia. Though still in its early stages, Avigen's program has a couple of plusses. Hemophilia is a relatively simple disorder to treat. Moreover, the firm uses the AAV virus to deliver its gene therapy, rather than the adenovirus, which killed Jesse Gelsinger.

- Targeted Genetics Corp. (TGEN) is a Seattle biotech firm exploring two separate gene therapy technologies. Its first effort uses AAV to deliver a gene to alleviate the effects of cystic fibrosis, and the therapy is in a Phase II clinical trial. Its second gene therapy approach uses certain lipids (fats) as delivery vehicles to carry therapeutic genes to cancer cells. The company is testing this lipid-delivery system in Phase I and Phase II trials against several cancers.

- Introgen Therapeutics (INGN) is a Texas firm that uses both viral and nonviral systems to deliver gene therapies against an array of cancers. The company has completed approximately twenty Phase I and Phase II clinical trials. Its most advanced effort, a modified adenovirus gene therapy designed to attack head and neck cancers, is in Phase III clinical trials. Provided those trials are successful, Introgen will begin seeking FDA approval in 2004.

- GenVec Inc. (GNVC) is a Maryland biotech firm that has taken two gene therapy treatments through the Phase II stage. GenVec hopes to repair the damage caused by clogged arteries. Its approach uses a modified adenovirus to deliver a gene that stimulates the growth of new blood vessels to relieve blockages in the heart and the lower limbs. But in 2002 the company suffered a setback when Pfizer, which had been its development partner, ended financial support for the trials, saying the project didn't fit its current focus. The question going forward is whether GenVac can push its gene therapy into Phase III

Xenotransplantation

How could biotech possibly top stem cells, cloning, and gene therapy when it comes to controversy? Without necessarily intending to try, it's a good bet the industry will eventually do just that. Biotechnology is the transformation of living organisms toward some commercial end, and while many biotech innovations will command the support of investors, patients, and the general public, the very novelty of some techniques is likely to provoke soul-searching if not opposition. Xenotransplantation is one of the emerging technologies that falls into this category.

The term stands for foreign transplants, and the objective in a nutshell is to bioengineer animals so that they could serve as organ donors. Despite sounding like science fiction, xenotransplantation research has been going on for more than a decade. At least one publicly traded company, PPL Therapeutics in Scotland (PTH.L on the London Stock Exchange) is trying to bioengineer pigs—the preferred animal for xenotransplant—in order to overcome the immune system issues that would normally cause humans to reject any transplant, much less one from a nonhuman source. Other firms, Geron included, are interested in xenotransplantation.

Several trends are converging to make this process seem more technically feasible. Biotech scientists have a better grasp of immune system functions, more experience with making genetic modifications, and access to cloning technology to make replicas of animals that have been bioengineered to meet human needs. And the need remains urgent. In 2000, when the FDA updated its guidelines covering xenotransplantation research, the agency noted that "in the United States alone, thirteen patients die each day waiting to receive a life-saving transplant to replace a diseased vital organ." Dying patients can be counted upon to be persuasive advocates in support of the biotech industry's research.

Against this formidable technological push, xenotransplantation will likely face the sort of visceral opposition that has arisen against genetically engineered foods and stem cell research. Antivivisection groups, which object to the use of animals as research tools, will surely object to this new purpose and seek to sway public opinion. But there are many scientific reasons for caution, some of which the FDA spelled out in its draft "Guidelines on Infectious Disease Issues in Xenotransplantation" in 2000. "The use of live nonhuman cells, tissues and organs for xenotransplantation raises serious public health concerns about potential infections . . . with both known and emerging infectious agents." In the simplest terms possible, health officials fear that viruses, in particular, will jump from animals to humans, a concern that is compounded by the fact that xenotransplant recipients will probably have to take immunosuppressant drugs—handicapping their ability to fend off any such infection. The FDA noted that human transplants have been shown to pass infections such as HIV/AIDS, Creutzfeldt-Jakob disease (the human analog to mad cow disease), rabies, hepatitis B, and hepatitis C. The FDA said any future human trials of xenotransplants will have to be carried on in such a way as to limit the possibility of a virus jumping from the donor species to the human. Pigs will probably remain the xeno-donors of choice for several reasons, beginning with the fact that their organs are appropriately sized. Humans also have some experience using pig tissue in medical settings; pig insulin was routinely supplied to human diabetics before the biotech industry produced the genetically engineered variety, and surgeons have used pig valves in human heart operations. The FDA already allows transplant specialists to filter human blood through pig livers as a temporary measure when a patient awaiting a human liver transplant experiences the sudden failure of their own organ.

Early in 2002, two rival scientific teams pushed xenotransplantation ahead a few inches when they independently announced that they had genetically engineered pigs that lacked a particular gene. Biotech scientists call this gene-knockout technology. In this case the scientists knocked out a gene that gives pig cells a sugary coating that is known to trigger an immune system response in humans. The advance was apparently first achieved by scientists at the University of Missouri–Columbia, working in collaboration with Immerge BioTherapeutics, a private biotech firm in Charlestown, Massachusetts. Just as the journal *Science* was about to publish a scholarly paper detailing the Immerge achievement, however, PPL Therapeutics—the Scottish firm that cloned Dolly—announced that it, too, had knocked out the same gene. These rival announcements indicate that there is commercial interest in xenotransplantation. Immerge, although a private firm, has public parents. It was created in 2001 by Novartis, the Swiss drug giant with a transplant medicine franchise, and BioTransplant Inc. (BTRN), a small-cap biotech firm in Massachusetts. Novartis controls 67 percent of Immerge, while BioTransplant owns the remainder. The partnership set up Immerge as a start-up focused on xenotransplantation, with the backing of one of the world's pharmaceutical giants.

Countering Bioterror

In the aftermath of the September 11 attack, a series of mysterious and deadly letters containing anthrax spores forced Americans to confront their potential vulnerability to biological warfare agents— weapons of mass destruction that are, alas, relatively easy to produce. The anthrax scare focused investor interest on ways that biotechnology could be used to detect, treat, and/or vaccinate people against biological threats. A handful of companies with products for detection or remediation of bioterror threats experienced brief pops in their stock prices. On the detection front, Cepheid (CPHD), Nanogen (NGEN), and Bruker Daltonics (BDAL) all rose and fell in short order. The same was true for therapeutic plays like Abgenix (ABGX) and Avant Immunotherapeutics (AVAN). Although these companies had plenty of promise, they didn't have enough product to ship within a reasonable time frame. The one firm to emerge from the terror scare with appreciable and sustained gain was Acambis, a British biotech firm that trades on the Nasdaq (ACAM). And no wonder. Acambis won contracts, worth on the order of $861 million, to supply the U.S. Centers for Disease Control with 209 million doses of smallpox vaccine and to refresh this stockpile over twenty years. The company also has a series of vaccines in late-stage clinical trials, so its fortunes aren't tied to a single product—which we all surely hope is never needed.

Although interest in biotech countermeasures has waned, it will inevitably rebound if another incident dramatizes the threat. Aside from ghoulishly waiting around to trade on fear or disaster, however, the intelligent way to play this trend is to focus on the underlying niche—the companies that target viral, bacterial, and other infectious diseases (see Infectious Diseases in Appendix II for more company names). This is an approach suggested by Dr. Scott Gottlieb, editor of futurist George Gilder's *Biotech Report*. "Anti-infectives are the fourth largest pharmaceutical market and account for $20 billion in worldwide sales, of which $15.8 billion is anti-bacterial agents," Gottlieb wrote in December 2001.

Two powerful trends, above and beyond the bioterror blip, make infectious disease companies a sensible, long-term investment focus. The first trend is the emergence of bacterial and viral infections that have become resistant to current medicines. Disease-resistant microbes have arisen for a variety of reasons, including the presence of bacterial agents in animal feeds. Over time, gonorrhea, malaria, and even childhood ear infections have become difficult to treat using standard antibiotics. Just in time to meet the threat of disease-resistant bugs, however, biotech firms have developed the tools to analyze the genetic and molecular structure of diseases in order to design more effective treatments. This is called rational drug design, and it is the second trend that makes infectious diseases a sensible investment focus. Rational drug design isn't a new concept; companies were talking about this in the late 1980s. The difference is that now it isn't just talk. Rational drug design has led to approved products.

Gottlieb focused on Gilead Sciences (GILD), which used genetic data to map two different strains of flu virus in order to discover one medicine that would attack both. The genetic analysis pointed Gilead to a particular receptor that was common to both strains. Company researchers used the receptor gene to express the protein, and then crystallized that protein to discern the actual shape of the receptor. As we discussed earlier, shape is the key to designing a small-molecule drug to "dock" with a receptor. Using computational chemistry, Gilead designed and ultimately tested a drug called Tamiflu that was shown in clinical trials to blunt the infectious power of both strains of flu virus; the FDA approved the drug in 1999. Gilead markets the drug with Roche, the German pharmaceutical firm. By using the modern tools of biotechnology, Gilead "not only found a drug that traditional techniques overlooked, it did it in less than half the time and therefore a fraction of the cost," according to Gottlieb.

Gilead's experience with Tamiflu is an example of what is possible in the way of new treatments for infectious diseases. But finding other, as-yet-undiscovered stocks will require a lot of sifting and winnowing. Infectious diseases is a huge category that has attracted significant interest. BioCentury's database of companies broken out by niche identifies seventy-nine companies in the group.

- You can begin to narrow the field by visiting the Pharmaceutical Research and Manufacturers of America website (www.phrma.org) and clicking on the "Search for Cures" link, and then clicking again to the "New Medicines in Development" link. This will lead you to a series of special reports, including one for infectious diseases. The last report was a bit dated (2000) but it is still a valuable road map that will identify which companies are at what phase of clinical trial for a variety of products from antibiotics to vaccines.

- As I've suggested before, you'd be wisest to focus on companies with products in Phase II or Phase III clinical trials. At the top of the same PhRMA website where you found the Infectious Disease report, you'll see a link that reads: "Explore the New Medicines in Development Database." You can search the database for more recent information concerning any company, experimental medicine, or disease category that catches your interest.

- If you decide to investigate the infectious disease niche, you'll also want to become conversant with the Interscience Conference on Antimicrobial Agents and Chemotherapy, which goes by the acronym ICAAC (pronounced ik-ak). Each fall ICAAC holds a conference that is the clearinghouse for new clinical trials (see www.icaac.org for details). Stocks often move in advance of the event, when ICAAC posts conference abstracts that hint at whether a company with a closely watched trial is going to reveal positive or negative news—or perhaps be left out of the proceedings because it had no data deemed significant.

Companies that win approval for novel medicines to fight infectious diseases should command premium prices during the period when they are patent-protected against generic rivals (the company's annual 10-K report filed with the SEC should detail when key patents expire; if you can't find the information, query investor relations). For instance, a 2002 article on flu treatments in *American Family Physician* magazine reported a $60 price for Tamiflu, versus $2 to $10 for the two older flu medicines. (Tamiflu competes with a second, novel flu medicine called Relenza, priced at $48 in the same survey article, so in this case an investor would have to monitor news articles and company earnings reports to detect any market share shifts between the two new medicines.) Higher prescription prices should translate directly into better share prices for companies that succeed in winning approval for new medicines.

Finally, the companies in the infectious disease niche are targeting some of the Third World's worst killers, including malaria and tuberculosis. These haven't been considered lucrative markets in the past, but with philanthropic groups such as the Bill & Melinda Gates Foundation focusing money and attention on Third World medical needs, there are prospects for growth. Getting medicines to the neediest won't be easy. Ultimately, someone has to pay the pills. But world health officials, philanthropists, and biotech industry leaders have already started talking about ways to combine pricing discounts, philanthropic gifts, international aid, and direct purchases by Third World governments to bring new medicines and vaccines to the places where they are needed most. Such an outcome would be a fitting and positive way for the biotech industry to stand the bioterror threat on its head.

Investor Tools: Tracking Science and Disease

The careful investor faces the constant challenge of staying informed about the theories, personalities, scholarly journals, and annual meetings of the many scientific communities that help determine the fate of early-stage biotech companies. Many companies go public long before they have products to sell. Indeed, going public is one of the ways companies raise money to fund experiments and clinical trials. The share prices of early-stage companies are heavily dependent on their scientific and medical publications. Scientists, like other scholars, operate on the "publish or perish" principle. Getting work published in scientific journals establishes and embellishes a researcher's reputation with his or her peers. Scientific journal articles are "peer-reviewed"; that means any article describing an experiment is read and approved by a panel of experts before it is printed. This puts an imprimatur on the work, with the most prestigious journals having the greatest impact.

At the top of the pecking order are *Science* and *Nature,* the leading journals in the United States and Europe, respectively. When the first drafts of the human genome map were published, *Science* carried the report of the Celera scientists and *Nature* laid out the work of the public scientists. *Science* and *Nature* are general-interest journals that publish experiments on particle physics and global warming in addition to biomedicine, so these journals set a high standard for the importance of a finding. Hence, any study involving a biotech firm that is published in *Science* or *Nature* has a special cachet. (*Nature* also publishes more than a dozen specialized offshoots geared toward aspects of biotechnology from cancer to general medicine to structural biology; check www.nature.com for details.)

Three key medical journals often have a great influence on biotech stocks because they publish the results of clinical trials and can influence the way doctors prescribe medicines and treat disease. They are:

- *Journal of the American Medical Association*
- *New England Journal of Medicine*
- *The Lancet*

Beyond these top publications, hundreds of specialized journals provide peer-reviewed forums for scientists in the many niches of biotechnology. An experiment involving a leukemia treatment might appear in *Blood,* the journal of the American Society of Hematology. Experiments involving heart disease might be published in *Circulation,* published by the American Heart Association. One of your first tasks when you take an interest in a new company or a new disease will be to determine which scientific societies and journals are the arbiters of excellence in that particular field.

- Ask the company's investor relations staff which journals and scientific conferences you should follow; it's their *job* to help you.

- Once you have identified key journals, find a public or university library that will let you come in and read their subscription. These are expensive publications, and unless you're a professional investor with a research budget, you probably can't justify your own copy.

- The ISI database (www.isinet.com) ranks journals, research institutes, and individual scientific papers. Most of ISI's services cost money, but the website offers an enormous amount of free information that can help you understand the relative prestige of the scientists whose work is important to the companies you follow.

Early in a company's evolution, when it is doing preclinical or animal studies of a novel therapy, publication in a peer-reviewed journal is an important way for the firm to demonstrate that its work is valid. Later, when a company is conducting human clinical trials, the emphasis shifts slightly. The premier place to tout findings from a Phase I, Phase II, or especially a Phase III clinical trial is before the medical community that treats the given illness. Thus, if you look at the website of Avigen Inc. (AVGN), a gene therapy company with a lead product to treat hemophilia, you'll see a long list of publications in journals such as *Nature, Medicine,* and *Blood,* as well as a list of abstracts, which are distilled reports of experimental findings that were presented at medical or scientific gatherings. Avigen has presented several times before the American Society of Hematology, the organization of scientists and physicians who specialize in hemophilia and other blood-borne ailments. The audience at such presentations is made up of the clinical doctors who will end up prescribing—or refusing to prescribe—a new medicine.

Getting a favorable showing before the appropriate community of physicians and scientists is even more essential when a company is trying to launch a novel medicine against an entrenched alternative, or when a series of new medications are poised to hit the market more or less simultaneously. For instance, when Biogen and Genentech were developing rival treatments for psoriasis, the two biotech giants campaigned for the hearts and minds of the specialist community at meetings of the International Psoriasis Symposium. Conference presentations generally allow the specialists in the audience to ask questions of the scientists presenting data. Wall Street analysts and money managers often attend the conferences to gauge the reaction of the physician community to a new medicine. As an individual investor you may not have the travel budget to warrant attendance, and there are often steep admission charges. But if you have a large stake in a company that is presenting findings—especially Phase III studies—at a vital scientific conference, consider attending. Even if you can't follow all the scientific details, you should be able to detect whether the event was a love fest or a hostile interrogation.

Even if you can't attend conferences, you should still be aware of when they are being held and whether your company or its competitors are presenting data. Schedules and abstracts for important conferences are usually posted online. Familiarize yourself with the conferences important to the companies or niches you are investigating (if you have any doubts, ask each company's investor relations staff).

Above all, be mindful of the quirks of the conference process, and how biotech stocks tend to move around such events. For instance, the annual meeting of the American Society of Clinical Oncology (ASCO), generally held in the spring, is a vital event for companies in cancer medicine. Being invited to present data is an honor that can boost a small company's stock. ASCO publishes abstracts of presentations before the conference. Some financial reporters have criticized ASCO because its members can read the abstracts online before the general public. Invariably some of these abstracts leak to institutional investors who trade on the information. In 2002, for instance, Genentech shares dropped 12 percent in a single day, wiping out $2.8 billion in market capitalization, when some traders got hold of an ASCO abstract suggesting that a new cancer treatment might have safety issues.

Although ASCO's policy of preferential access puts retail investors at a disadvantage, the SEC does not regulate nonprofit scientific societies, so this remains an unsolved problem. Some scientific societies are trying to change their conference practices because they realize that the release of their abstracts can affect biotech stock prices. The American College of Cardiology, an important society in cardiovascular research, provides its abstracts in advance of its meetings to all comers, without preference. The moral is to be aware of the rules governing the conferences important to the companies you follow so that you know whether you're on par with institutional investors.

Finally, expect that the shares of your company or its competitors will be volatile around the conference cycle. This is especially true of small-cap, early-stage companies. They don't have many metrics for investors to judge them by, and they tend to bounce around a lot whenever there's news and rumor in the air.

In a way the scientific process in biotechnology is a confidence game, though not in any illegal sense. Biotech scientists are trying to convince an ever-widening circle of onlookers that their theories

Genentech's Spring Surprise

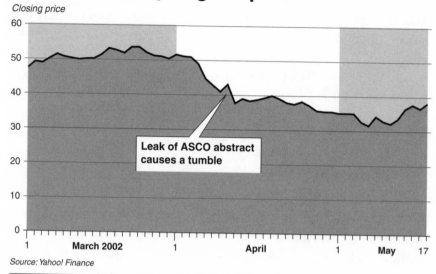

Closing price

Leak of ASCO abstract causes a tumble

Source: Yahoo! Finance

will lead to profitable products. Getting articles placed in peer-reviewed publications builds confidence. So does presenting data at scientific conferences. Adding prominent scientists—often called "thought leaders"—to a company's scientific advisory board is yet another way that a firm says: "See, these smart people think we're on the right track." In distinguishing between competing companies in a niche, or in deciding whether to place a bet on a novel company, use scientific endorsements as a clue. But always do your financial analysis as well. A company with great scientists but a lousy cash reserve is a weak bet. Remember, the smartest scientists in the world are not infallible, and sometimes following the thought leaders may simply mean you're in good company when a stock fails to perform.

9

The Biotech Clusters:
Follow the Leaders

So far we've looked at biotech companies as competitors in a series of industry niches because that's the most sensible way to categorize potential investments. To deepen your understanding of the industry, however, you should look at companies in a different light—as organizations that grow up in particular environments. If you were investing in steel or automotive firms, you'd look for companies located near coal and iron deposits to provide raw materials, and close to rail lines or highways to transport finished goods. Biotech is a knowledge industry, but it still has its environmental necessities. "The raw materials for biotechnology are really smart people," said Craig Venter, founder of Celera Genomics, the company that mapped the human genome. To the raw materials' list Venter should have added capital—and lots of it—because biotech firms typically operate at a loss for years and need regular cash infusions to continue their research.

Just as automakers gravitated to Detroit, and steel mills arose around Pittsburgh, biotech firms tend to gather in metropolitan areas where they can find trained workers, talented academic collaborators, and risk-tolerant investors. A handful of metropolitan areas in the United States have emerged as biotech clusters on the strength of their local research and investment resources, including San Francisco, Boston, San Diego, Seattle, and suburban Washington,

D.C. Outside the United States, regional clusters have grown up in the United Kingdom, Germany, France, Scandinavia, India, and a handful of other nations. Whether based in the United States or abroad, these clusters are generally dominated by a few successful companies that become role models and champions for subsequent start-ups. The department heads and middle managers of these successful companies often go on to found or run the next generation of start-ups. In northern California, where the biotech industry was born, Genentech and Chiron play this role; one *San Francisco Chronicle* article counted roughly thirty biotech companies that were either founded or run by former Genentech scientists or managers, and another fifteen firms in which Chiron alumni played a similar role. In the Boston area, successful companies such as Biogen, Vertex, and Millennium Pharmaceuticals play a similar role of seeding the executive and scientific talent pool.

For long-term investors the need to understand geography of biotech seems obvious. Investors who buy and hold want to know everything they can, including the strength their holding can derive from being part of a larger community of companies—or the challenges of investing in firms that are off the beaten track. Even active traders who flip their holdings regularly need to have a thirty-thousand-foot view of the biotech landscape. This is an industry built on reputations and pedigrees. Investors making a bet on a start-up are really buying the reputation of the company's scientific founders and the strength of the firm's patent portfolio. Even later-stage companies are valued heavily on the track records of their management teams and venture backers. To be a smart trader, you'll have to know where the company's core leaders came from and how their backgrounds stack up in the industry's pecking order. Take Scios, for instance, a California biotech firm that took nearly twenty years to develop its first drug. The catalyst for change at Scios was the hiring of a new CEO who had been a senior executive at Genentech; his experience helped guide the completion of a clinical trial and the building of a sales force to drive the company's first drug into the market. Investors who don't know where the players come from will operate at a severe disadvantage in a market where personality and reputation often have a direct bearing on stock price.

A firm grasp of biotech geography is essential to investors who plan to follow companies outside the United States. With roughly 360 public companies to pick from in the United States, it's questionable whether U.S. investors should even look abroad for biotech stocks. For one thing, currency fluctuations complicate foreign investments. The fact is, however, U.S. investors won't be able to ignore foreign biotech for long because many of the industry leaders will hail from beyond the United States. One of the top proteomics companies, Oxford GlycoSciences (OGSI), is based in the United Kingdom. Qiagen (QGENF), a leading vendor of supplies for purifying DNA and RNA, is based in the Netherlands. U.S. investors who don't plan to buy foreign stocks will still need to be aware of overseas competitors. Some U.S. investors may also dabble in overseas biotech stocks, at least in Europe, which has the strongest concentration of biotech activity outside the United States. I'll have some special tips for them at the end of this chapter.

But as I'll show, many other nations have had difficulty copying the legal and financial incentives that have driven biotech in the United States. It isn't that U.S. scientists or executives are cleverer. Rather, U.S. firms enjoy an environment that allows them to capitalize on their ideas more aggressively than biotech entrepreneurs elsewhere. It all gets back to understanding the factors that allowed biotech firms to arise and flourish in the first place, beginning with the industry's birthplace in the San Francisco Bay area.

Silicon Valley Redux

Genentech is arguably the world's first biotech firm. Its founding in 1976 set the pattern for the many companies that have followed. As you may recall, Genentech was founded to use gene-splicing techniques to produce protein medicines. Gene-splicing was acknowledged as a scientific marvel when it was discovered in the mid-1970s. But techniques don't automatically spawn industries. Credit for commercializing the science belongs to a young venture capitalist named Robert Swanson. It was Swanson who sought out Herbert Boyer, one of the scientists who discovered the technique, and convinced him to start a company—something that was unusual for academics to do in those days. There was certainly an element of luck involved in the founding of Genentech. There was intense competition among academics in the 1970s to manipulate DNA. If Boyer hadn't been part of the team that perfected gene-splicing, other scientists surely would have made the breakthrough in short order. Researchers at Cambridge University in the United Kingdom were leaders in DNA studies going back to the discovery of the structure of DNA in 1953. The Massachusetts Institute of Technology was another hotbed of DNA science. Gene-splicing could have been discovered in either locale as easily as in northern California.

But even if the discovery had been made outside California, it's doubtful that the technique would have been commercialized as quickly because, by the mid-1970s, the San Francisco Bay area had become the world's most favorable climate for entrepreneurship. By the time Swanson got the idea to create a biotechnology company, northern California had already given birth to Silicon Valley. By the mid-1970s, companies like Intel Corp. were California legends. It was part of the region's business lore how the first transistor company, Shockley Semiconductor, was founded in 1955 not far from Stanford University. And how that company's core group of engineers soon broke away, raised venture capital, and started a succession of other companies including Intel. In a 1999 interview with the *San Jose Mercury News,* Intel cofounder Gordon Moore looked back on how the silicon chip industry established a new business pattern. In Silicon Valley it was okay to break away from an established company, raise money, and take a risk on a new idea. When asked whether this start-up culture could have taken hold if William Shockley had stayed in New Jersey, where he coinvented the transistor at AT&T's Bell Laboratories, Moore replied: "I don't think so. There was just a different attitude out here. People were more adventurous.

There wasn't the fear of failure here that there was back east. Failure out here is like a rite of passage that you have to go through."

So in 1976, when Robert Swanson, then twenty-nine years old, became interested in the commercial potential of gene-splicing, he was following the example of financiers who had taken huge risks to start companies that, in turn, spawned industries. Swanson died tragically in 1999, felled by an untreatable brain cancer. But he recalled the trials and tribulations of founding Genentech in an oral history, available at the Bancroft Library at the University of California, Berkeley. In it, Swanson details how difficult it was for him to sell the idea of a gene-splicing company to the Kleiner Perkins venture capital firm, which was even then famous for having bankrolled a series of high-tech start-ups. In a 2001 interview in the *San Francisco Chronicle,* celebrating Genentech's twenty-fifth anniversary, firm cofounder Tom Perkins recalled that even after Swanson and Boyer convinced him that biotechnology had merit, he doled out money sparingly. "They wanted millions to start Genentech," Perkins recalled. "I remember telling them, 'It's not clear God will let us make a new form of life.'" Perkins initially allotted a few hundred thousand dollars, which Swanson used to hire contract researchers to prove that splicing genes into bacteria could indeed create human proteins. Only after this proof-of-principle experiment succeeded in 1977 did Perkins open the firm's purse and start funding Genentech in earnest. If Swanson had a tough time getting started in the most fertile venture capital environment of its day, think how much more difficult it would have been to found a company if gene-splicing had been discovered elsewhere.

Another early witness to the founding of Genentech thinks the Silicon Valley culture of risk and entrepreneurship favored the birth of biotechnology in California. Phillip Sharp was a young associate professor at the Massachusetts Institute of Technology in 1976 when a Boston-area venture capitalist asked him to evaluate a potential investment opportunity in California. It turned out to be Genentech. Sharp, who soon thereafter won a Nobel Prize for his own DNA discoveries, had been called in to evaluate the financial feasibility of Genentech's gene-splicing business model. Sharp not only pronounced the idea sound, but upon his return to Massachusetts began lining up scientific collaborators and venture funding for the company that became Biogen, one of the stalwarts of Boston biotechnology. "The idea was that Genentech had the West Coast and we were starting an organization that would involve the East Coast and Europe," says Sharp, who believes the Silicon Valley ethic gave California the jump in biotechnology. "The venture capitalists on the West Coast were a bit more aggressive," says Sharp. "Genentech started out as Swanson's looking for an opportunity."

Sharp is a legend in the Boston biotechnology, having once turned down the chance to serve as president of MIT. At the time he flew out to evaluate Genentech, Boston's Route 128 corridor was in the throes of a regional competition with Silicon Valley to see which area would be the dominant cluster of high-tech activity. By any measure, Silicon Valley ended up the winner of that high-tech competition. Its distinguishing asset was the concentration of venture capital firms on Sand Hill Road, located at the edge of the Stanford campus. The VCs of Sand Hill Road gave rise to the successive waves of the high-tech industry and later helped finance the biotech revolution as well.

This high-tech foundation helps explain why the San Francisco Bay area and Boston are the number one– and two–ranked clusters of biotech activity in the United States—and arguably in the entire world. In a recent survey the biotech consulting practice of Ernst & Young counted seventy-six public biotech firms in the San Francisco Bay area, followed by forty-eight in Boston.

Critical to their success as biotech clusters is the fact that San Francisco and Boston are situated close to some of the world's top academic research institutes. The University of California campuses at Berkeley, San Francisco, Santa Cruz, and Davis are supplemented by the research emanating from Stanford University. Boston enjoys an even greater density of academic talent with Harvard, MIT, Beth Israel Deaconess Medical Center, and the New England Medical Center, all located in a tight ring around the Boston suburb of Cambridge. *San Francisco and Boston exemplify the formula for creating a successful*

U.S. Biotech Clusters, 2000

In millions of dollars

Area	Number of public companies	Market capitalization	Number of employees	Revenue	Research & development	Net income
1. San Francisco Bay area	76	$92,168	26,464	$5,851	$2,956	($1,228)
2. New England	48	$53,575	20,641	$3,609	$2,105	($980)
3. San Diego	31	$23,272	7,976	$874	$555	($573)
4. New Jersey	21	$10,592	3,556	$550	$272	($176)
5. Mid-Atlantic	19	$22,240	3,871	$769	$591	($510)
6. Pacific Northwest	19	$17,190	3,258	$1,097	$1,122	($827)
7. New York State	16	$10,043	1,997	$242	$226	($136)
8. Southeast	16	$4,613	4,556	$784	$123	($60)
9. Los Angeles/ Orange counties	15	$70,794	25,051	$5,214	$1,049	$1,164
10. Midwest	15	$1,741	1,394	$182	$85.6	($86)
11. Texas	14	$4,083	1,463	$118	$168	($151)
12. Philadelphia/ Delaware Valley	13	$6,519	1,289	$164	$230	($269)
13. N. Carolina	13	$7,787	24,012	$2,205	$273	$223
14. Colorado	8	$1,259	999	$97	$80	($154)

Source: Ernst & Young

biotech cluster: Marry top-flight research institutes with strong venture capital networks.

Other U.S. regions have copied this formula with varying degrees of success. San Diego and Seattle have developed strong biotech clusters. San Diego has about thirty-one publicly traded biotech firms and many more private start-ups clustered around the University of California at San Diego, the Salk Institute, and the Scripps Research Institute. San Diego's current public bellwether company is IDEC Pharmaceuticals (IDPH), which collaborated with Genentech to get the first monoclonal antibody, Rituxan, on the market in 1997. The Seattle metropolitan area is home to about nineteen public biotech firms, the largest of which had been Immunex, before it was acquired by Amgen. Its leading research centers include the Fred Hutchinson Cancer Institute and the University of Washington. Seattle doesn't have quite the concentration of local venture capital as San Francisco,

Boston, or San Diego, but biotech entrepreneurs have gotten a boost from the wealth effect created by nearby Microsoft Corp. The effect starts at the source. Microsoft cofounders Bill Gates and Paul Allen have consciously encouraged biotech development in the Pacific Northwest. Gates endowed a chair at the University of Washington that brought noted gene scientist Leroy Hood to Seattle. Hood, in turn, has helped create several biotech firms and research institutes, including the Institute for Systems Biology. Allen has also had an abiding personal interest in medical technology since he won a battle with Hodgkin's disease in the 1980s. Through his Vulcan Venture investment firm, Allen has helped bankroll Seattle-area start-ups including Dendreon (DNDN), Seattle Genetics (SGEN), and Rosetta Inpharmatics, which was acquired by Merck in 2001 for more than $600 million.

Perhaps the most important new biotech cluster in the United States has arisen around suburban Washington, D.C., which is blessed by its proximity to the National Institutes of Health (NIH) and Johns Hopkins University. The NIH is a network of federal institutes that support research on every aspect of health from aging to heart disease to cancer to mental illness. It's worth a brief digression to focus on the role of federal funding in driving biotech developments. The NIH now spends about $27 billion a year to fund research, roughly double what it spent just five years ago. About 80 percent of all NIH funding is distributed through competitive research grants to scientists at major universities. For the last two decades, laws have encouraged academic researchers to file patents on their work through their universities. This NIH money, channeled through academic institutes, creates the steady flow of new compounds, experimental drugs, and tools that are licensed by biotech firms across the United States. That's why biotech companies cluster around top universities. (Investors can easily find out how much NIH money flows to different cities, states, and institutions. A visit to the NIH grants data page at http://grants2.nih.gov/grants/award/awardtr.htm reveals that Boston was the city that received the most NIH funding, California was the top state in terms of awards, and Johns Hopkins was the top university in 2001 awards.)

The Washington, D.C., metropolitan area enjoys a special benefit from increased NIH spending. In addition to feeding off the academic research done at nearby Johns Hopkins, the D.C. metropolitan area is home to the staff scientists employed directly by NIH. About 10 percent of the agency's budget is spent to support these federal scientists who work at NIH offices in suburban Maryland. This concentration of federal spending has proven a powerful stimulus for the establishment of biotech firms in and around Bethesda, Rockville, and other Maryland townships. The Human Genome Project is an example of an NIH program that has grown into an industry. The official government program is headquartered in Bethesda. Craig Venter used to be an NIH gene hunter until he quit the federal service in the early 1990s to found The Institute for Genomics Research (TIGR), a nonprofit gene research institute, and later, Celera Genomics, the company that prodded the government to speed up its gene-mapping effort with automated instruments. Today Celera, and its Rockville, Maryland, neighbor, Human Genome Sciences, are the leaders in a biotech cluster that has minted some twenty public firms in less than a decade's time. "We are the genomics capital of the world," says Human Genome Sciences chief executive William Haseltine. He believes Maryland's success as a biotech cluster is partly explained by local NIH spending that has created a network of skilled technicians that private start-ups can hire as they grow.

Other U.S. cities or regions are creating biotech clusters. North Carolina boasts thirteen public firms nestled around the Research Triangle area and Duke University. Austin, Texas, has a small but ambitious cluster of biotech firms. Colorado, Wisconsin, and other states are trying to encourage biotech centers around their leading medical institutes. Alan Walton, a venture capitalist with Oxford Bio-Science Partners in Boston, and the financier who helped found the Maryland biotech cluster, says luck plays a big role in transforming a group of biotech start-ups into a center of scientific and financial excellence. "I think what it takes is at least one hugely successful firm that creates spin-offs," says Walton. "A lot of regions have excellent science centers, but it takes that one commercial success to really ignite a local industry."

Despite certain regional differences, the companies in the various U.S. biotech clusters are more alike than dissimilar, as far as investors are concerned. That's because the U.S. companies are all listed on the same stock markets. Their venture capitalists, patent lawyers, scientists, and executives are all cut from the same cultural cloth and share the same professional and legal norms. Today, however, many nations are trying to create the sort of biotech ecosystems that began in San Francisco and Boston and have since spread throughout the United States. Other nations see biotech as more than the twenty-first-century sequel to high tech; in addition to creating jobs and economic growth, the industry could provide vital medicines that would otherwise have to be imported. Biotech is global. International financiers are already taking biomedical companies public on both U.S. and non-U.S. exchanges. The rate of company formation outside the United States will only increase over time.

The scientific acumen of these international biotech start-ups isn't in question. The United States has no monopoly on biological discovery. In some emerging areas, notably embryonic stem cell research, political controversy has slowed activity in the United States and created potential advantages for scientists in the United Kingdom, Israel, Sweden, and India, among other places. But early biotech history teaches us that success ultimately revolves around financial rather than scientific variables. It was the financial strength of West Coast venture capital that gave San Francisco the edge over Boston in biotech company formation more than two decades ago. The same financial factors are clearly at play in Europe today, where leading nations are finding that to succeed in biotechnology, they must overcome cultural, legal, and financial barriers and adopt U.S. capital formation techniques. In essence, Europe is trying to learn how to do business Silicon Valley–style. It is in Europe, where company formation is proceeding most aggressively, that investors need to pay the greatest attention to environmental variables when picking stocks.

European Biotech Renaissance

In the United States, biotech arose as an alternative, almost a rebellion, to the traditional way drug companies developed medicines. As noted earlier, the differences between drug and biotech research methods have been erased over time, until today the only real difference is that biotech firms are far smaller in sales and market capitalization than drug companies. But the U.S.-led biotech revolution had an unintended consequence on the global scene. To the extent that biotech has become the engine of drug discovery, Europe has found itself getting left behind as a source of new medicines. This trend runs contrary to history. European scientists and companies played a dominant role in medical research and drug development in the late nineteenth and early twentieth centuries. It was French scientist Louis Pasteur who in 1878 advanced the theory that germs cause disease. It was German scientist Theodor Escherich who in 1885 discovered that a particular bacterium causes infant diarrhea and gastroenteritis (to this day we call that microbe E-coli in his honor). The first scientific medicines were based on plant extracts and chemicals synthesized by European scientists and mass produced by European firms. In 1910, the Germany company Hoechst (since merged into Aventis) produced Salvarsan, a medicine that chemist Paul Ehrlich developed to treat syphilis, until then one of history's great scourges. (Edward G. Robinson stars in *Dr. Ehrlich's Magic Bullet,* a 1940 film that popularized the term that remains the goal of biotech researchers.) Canadian scientists working at the University of Toronto discovered insulin in 1921. For decades, non-U.S. scientists set the pace of pharmaceutical discovery, and European firms contributed more than their share of profitable drugs—a situation that persisted until the biotech revolution began to tip the scales decisively in favor of the United States.

One indicator of this imbalance is the comparative market capitalization of the top ten biotech firms in the United States and Europe. In the United States, institutional investors can choose many biotech stocks with market caps way above a billion dollars. Europe

Top Ten Biotech Firms
in the United States and Europe

*As ranked by millions of dollars in market capitalization**

U.S. company	Market cap	Europe company	Symbol on U.S. exchange	Market cap
Amgen (AMGN)	$58,117	Serono (SWX:SEO)	SRA	13,107
Genentech (DNA)	26,070	Elan (LSE:ELA)	ELN	9,761
Immunex (IMNX)	14,927	Shire Pharma (LSE:SHP)	SHPGY	5,788
MedImmune (MEDI)	10,487	Qiagen (Neuer Markt:QIA)	QGENF	2,974
Genzyme (GENZ)	9,470	Celltech (LSE:CCH)	CLL	2,947
IDEC Pharma (IDPH)	9,032	Actelion (SWX:ATLN)		847
Biogen (BGEN)	8,053	CAT (LSE:CAT)	CATG	834
Chiron (CHIR)	8,045	PowderJect (LSE:PJP)		719
Gilead (GILD)	6,228	SkyePharma (LSE:SKP)	SKYE	525
Millennium (MLNM)	4,176	Oxford Glyco (LSE:OGS)	OGSI	470

* Market cap as of January 31, 2002; euros converted to dollars at May 19, 2002, exchange rate.

Source: BioVenture View *newsletter*

has only a few companies in the billion-dollar range, evidence that there is far less public capital supporting biotech companies in Europe than in the United States. Why has Europe lagged in biotech company formation when it is certainly no slouch in the scientific department?

Paul Haycock, a venture capitalist in the London office of Apax Partners, said the root of the problem is the nimbleness and risk tolerance of U.S. financial markets as compared to their European competitors. One crucial example is the requirements for taking a company public, a prime concern to venture capitalists who invest millions in start-ups with the expectation that they'll be able to liquidate their investments at a profit through an IPO or merger. In the United States, says Haycock, the main requirement for going public is full disclosure of risks in the prospectus. By contrast, in 1992 he sat on a committee that finally persuaded the London Stock Exchange to liberalize its rules concerning biotech IPOs. The result was a reform that allowed British VCs to take a company public provided it had at least two experimental medicines in clinical trials and met other criteria for solid management. "In London there is still a degree of judgment and control; in the U.S. it's more caveat emptor," Haycock says. "Which is right and which is wrong? It's hard to say."

But there's no doubt that the U.S. laissez-faire approach has produced about three times the number of jobs, revenues, and public companies as European paternalism. As of 2000, Ernst & Young's biotech consulting practice calculated that U.S. biotech firms employed 174,000 persons as compared to about 61,000 biotech employees in Europe. The U.S. biotech industry rang up $25 billion in sales that year, versus roughly $8 billion (8.679 billion euros) in Europe. Ernst & Young tallied 339 public companies in the United States, compared to 105 in Europe. The report fixed the total market capitalization of U.S. biotech companies at $330 billion, compared to approximately $68.5 billion (75 billion euros) in Europe. (The discrepancies are even greater when looking at biotech in Japan. In 2001, the industry newsletter *BioCentury* counted only twenty biotech firms in Japan in 2001, and most of these were formed in the few years previous. Why weren't there more? Because Japanese scientists and managers simply weren't acculturated to take the risks associated with new company formation, say the newsletter's editors.)

European political and financial leaders are certainly aware of the U.S. lead in biotech, and whether inspired by national pride, economic self-interest, or a combination of the above, have taken steps in recent years to attempt to redress the biotech balance. But how do nations "fix" a problem that involves building a new business and investment culture? The answer varies from nation to nation, but the obvious answer is that it will take time, patience, and political will to graft the most desirable attributes of U.S. biotech culture— essentially Silicon Valley culture—onto European business communities that have their own traditions. And like all transplants, only time will tell if the host accepts or rejects the changes. The strongest biotech initiatives are being mounted in the United Kingdom, Germany, France, and Scandinavia.

- After the United States, biotech is strongest in the United Kingdom, where the first companies were formed in the early 1980s, not long after the industry was born in the United States. Despite the stricter rules of the London Stock Exchange, Britain now has about 270 biotech firms, employing more than eighteen thousand people; about 40 of these firms have made it onto the public stock exchanges. Leading British biotech firms include Celltech Group PLC (CLL), Cambridge Antibody Technology (CATG), Shire Pharmaceuticals (SHPGY), Bioglan Pharmaceuticals PLC (BGP.L), and Oxford GlycoSciences PLC (OGSI).

Biotech stocks have been listed on the London Stock Exchange long enough for British punters—their slang for retail investors—to experience the heartbreak of seeing a high-flying stock crash when a drug fails to get approval. The textbook disappointment is British Bio-Technology Group PLC, more commonly called British Biotech (BBIOY). In the late 1990s, shares of British Biotech collapsed after the company's lead compounds failed in clinical trials. The timing was unfortunate. British punters had only just discovered biotech in the mid-1990s and the prominent failure of a company so identified with the sector dragged down other biotech firms in the United Kingdom. "I've been around long enough to see these cycles come and go about every two or three years," says Paul Haycock, the British venture capitalist. "Our industry in the U.K. is mature enough so that the ups and downs are driven by product successes or failures." An investor from the United States will perceive little difference between British and American biotech firms.

- Until the mid-1990s, German politics made that nation relatively hostile to biotechnology. Germany was one of the world centers of the Green Party, whose blend of environmental and anticorporate political beliefs included, among other concerns, an aversion to genetically engineered foods. With a change of political climate around 1995, however, German leaders began to bemoan the fact that the United States, which had already soared past the rest of the world on the high-tech front, was also solidifying its lead in biotechnology. This was particularly galling given the important role German firms and chemists had played in twentieth-century drug development. In a few short years, the national emphasis on building a biotech industry spawned a series of initiatives backed by German local, state, and national officials. *The most important of these was the commitment to match every euro of venture capital invested in German biotech companies with varying levels of state funds.* Not surprisingly, the result was an enormous spurt of company creation. From being one of the lagging nations in biotech, Germany jumped into a leadership position, at least as measured by the numbers of companies in the industry. As of a 2000 count by the international consulting practice of Ernst & Young, Germany had something in excess of 330 biotech firms, of which more than 20 were publicly listed.

"Of course most of the German companies are young and the United Kingdom is still the leader in terms of the maturity of their companies and the number of products in clinical trials," says Michael Steinmetz, a former chemist for the Swiss drug firm Roche and now a venture capitalist for the transnational investment firm MPM Capital. For instance, when Ernst & Young tallied European clinical trials in 2000, the twelve nations in the survey listed 278 experimental medicines in development; German biotech firms accounted for just 6, while Swiss companies—with all deference to national borders, the economies of the two countries are closely entwined—had another 20 medicines in development. By contrast, the United Kingdom, with its smaller but better established biotech sector, tallied 128 experimental medicines in development. Many of the newly formed German companies have tended to focus in the areas of bioinformatics, tools, or other platform technologies whose products won't appear in clinical trial listings. Then again, the general sentiment of the investor community is that medicines, and not tools, are the products that will produce sustained earnings and growth, so German biotech will probably have a long, tough climb to get its product numbers up to levels consistent with its national ambition.

■ Despite having a strong biomedical research tradition, France has had trouble transferring science from its state-financed research institutes to biotech companies. "We are not famous for the entrepreneurial spirit," admits Jean-Pierre Loza, a biotech investment banker with Natexis Banques Populaires in Paris. Part of the problem in France has been the existence of laws that, until recently, prevented scientists from owning stock in companies that used their inventions. This is the exact opposite of the situation in the United States where, since the early 1980s, lawmakers have encouraged professors and universities to license their inventions to companies by letting both the inventor and the institution share in royalty income. So while Germany woke up in the mid-1990s and instituted subsidies and other reforms, and Great Britain started earlier and slowly built its domestic industry, France had gradually fallen farther behind in the number and maturity of its biotech companies. As of 2000, France had about 240 biotech firms, of which just 8 were publicly listed. "We used to be second behind Great Britain in biotech," Loza says. "Now we are third behind Germany."

Goaded into action by the German example, the French government has lately enacted several measures to allow scientists to benefit from licensing their inventions to biotech firms, and to make it easier for French biotech companies to distribute the stock options that are a key part of start-up compensation in the United States. The government has also approved an investment plan, more modest in scope than the German subsidy, to encourage private venture capital activity in France. These and other initiatives have already begun to have at least a psychological effect on the French biotech scene. "The mentality has changed tremendously over the last five years," says Laurent Ganem, a venture capitalist in the Paris office of Apax Partners. "The entrepreneurial spirit is fashionable and that, I would say, is a major cultural change."

■ One of the most remarkable clusters of European biotech activity is the cross-border region called Medicon Valley. Stretching from the University of Copenhagen in Denmark across the Baltic Sea to the University of Lund in southern Sweden, Medicon Valley has become a hotbed for the creation of biotech and medical device companies. According to Allan Reimann, who follows the Scandinavian biotech scene from the Copenhagen investment bank Gudme Raaschou, big drug companies are helping the process along.

"One of the things that is occurring here to speed up the biotech development is that large pharmaceutical companies are beginning to spin off research projects, and even research divisions, because they have seen that in order to be successful in biotech, scientists need to work in smaller teams," Reimann says. This spin-off trend stands in contrast to the pattern of early development in the United States, where biotech arose almost as a challenge to traditional drug discovery techniques. But after two decades, the European drug firms have seen the advantages of relying on small biotech companies for early-stage research, and have actively formed biotech partnerships and subsidiaries. In 2001, for instance, Pharmacia, a drug company with Swedish roots that is now headquartered in New Jersey, spun out its nine-hundred-person research division into a new Swedish company, Biovitrum AB. In Finland, which has about eighty-two biotech firms, the nation's leading drug company, Orion, has spun out dozens of research projects to form companies. "If you look at the new companies, nearly half of them come from Orion," Reimann said.

Scandinavia is not the only example of this spin-off

phenomenon. In 1998, the Swiss drug firm Roche allowed some of its scientists to leave the company and license some experimental heart drugs. The former Roche scientists raised the money to found Actelion, a Swiss biotech firm that has teamed up with Genentech to bring the medicines to market. Reimann says European drug companies have used the spin-off tactic to reduce their research expenses. If the spin-offs succeed in developing the medicine, the drug company sponsor gets a royalty or marketing right at low cost. If the spin-off fails, the drug company is insulated from the loss.

"Biotech started with the idea of people breaking away from Big Pharma," Reimann says. "Now, the pharma companies have more of an understanding of the role that biotech can play, and they are actively subcontracting out their R&D to these small teams of scientists backed by venture capital." Scandinavia is a prime but by no means exclusive example of this trend.

■ Finally, Canada occupies a special place between Europe and the United States, akin to nations on both sides of the Atlantic yet distinct from either of its cultural cousins. In recent years Canada has begun to develop a biotech industry on par with the European nations. Burrill & Co., a biotech investment bank in California, estimates that Canada had 339 biotech firms in 2001, including 83 that were publicly traded. Together these Canadian biotech companies employed about seven thousand people and created revenues of $1.5 billion in 2001, according to Burrill. The key centers of biotech activity were Toronto and Montreal, and the surrounding provinces of Ontario and Quebec, which together accounted for two-thirds of all Canadian biotech firms. But the western provinces of British Columbia and Alberta also boasted another 80 companies. Most Canadian biotech firms are small, early-stage companies. The few larger companies, with products on or close to the market, include QLT Therapeutics (QLTI, vision products), Cangene Corp. (CNJ.TO, protein products), and Hemosol Inc. (HMSL, red blood substitute). Canadian start-ups, such as MDS Proteomics, are attempting to crack new niches like protein discovery. But Canadian biotech suffers some of the same problems as Europe's fledgling efforts. Most of the companies are still small and experimental. The Toronto stock exchange is dwarfed by nearby Wall Street, and it's easy for Canadian companies to be listed on the larger U.S. exchanges. This has led to fears in Canada that the nation's domestic capital markets will be relegated to the role of minor league ball clubs, identifying the best players and sending them on to the U.S. exchanges. On the other hand, U.S. investors willing to investigate their northern neighbor could find some hardworking and undervalued companies.

Investor Tools: Lessons from Biotech Geography

For investors in the United States, learning about biotech clusters, whether in their own country or abroad, is merely another step in becoming a more sophisticated industry observer. You should understand everything you can about any company in which you invest, and that includes knowing why it planted itself where it did. In biotech the apple rarely falls far from the tree. Founding scientists and financiers generally plant companies close to wherever they happen to work. An innovation that spins out of MIT generally ends up forming a company in the Boston metropolitan area. If you are comparing two rival firms, one from Boston and the other from San Francisco, geography should not be the decisive factor in your investment decision. Either location provides access to the scientific and financial talent that companies need to survive. The calculus might be a little different if you're comparing two firms that seem otherwise equal, except that one is from a big cluster and the other is off the beaten track. Being in the thick of things generally makes it easier to recruit talent. On the other hand, salaries and other costs of doing business also tend to be higher in the congested areas, and start-ups in out-of-the-way places like to tout their "quality-of-life" advantage. My sense is that companies outside the main clusters face extra hurdles, so they have to be far ahead in other metrics to make up for the disadvantages of being outside the mainstream.

That being said, I'd like to devote the rest of this section to discussing whether investors in the United States ought to try dabbling in European biotech firms. With no disrespect to the quality of European offerings, the answer should generally be no. Sophisticated investors and high net-worth individuals may want the additional challenge posed by investing in overseas companies. But for most investors, there are so many options in the United States, it makes no sense to go abroad in order to find ways to increase the risk of biotech investing. This is particularly true since so many European firms are start-ups in the experimental stage where they trade on rumors instead of earnings. U.S. investors should hold European biotech firms up to the same standards by which the prudent investor would judge a U.S. biotech offering—specifically, does it have approved products on the market or is it late enough in the clinical trials process so that an earnings stream can be estimated? If the answer to these questions is no, then walk away and leave the field to risk-tolerant Europeans.

One reason for U.S. investors to be leery of investing in European biotech stocks is that the individual European exchanges are much smaller than U.S. equities markets. Biotech companies listed on European exchanges are far less liquid—that is, have smaller daily volumes—than biotech companies listed on the Nasdaq or other U.S. exchanges. Liquidity is of key importance to every investor, particularly the large institutional buyers whose judgments validate a stock's worth and give it stability. The less liquid a stock, the less likely it can be owned by these trendsetting fund managers. Many large funds simply won't invest in biotech firms below a certain market capitalization. That threshold varies depending on the size of the fund, but a market cap of $500 million to $1 billion is rapidly becoming the minimum for institutional investor interest, and as the chart on page 208 illustrates, there simply aren't enough of these larger companies in Europe yet.

The national stock markets in Europe are also going through a great deal of turbulence. There is a widespread realization in Europe that European growth industries operate at a distinct disadvantage relative to their U.S. competitors because the U.S. markets are so much larger and risk tolerant. The U.S. equity markets, particularly the Nasdaq, are aggressive instruments for capital formation. Sometimes they do run amok, as occurred during the dot.com bubble. Then U.S. investors might well have wished for some London-style judgment about which companies should have been deemed mature enough to go public. By and large, however, the U.S. markets have allowed new entrepreneurs to amass the capital to form a succession of new industries from silicon chips right through to broadband communications. Such capital formation has been absolutely critical to biotech firms, which are predestined to lose money for years. In order to compete with U.S. biotech, the European industry will have to revise its capital marketplace to achieve the size of the U.S. equity markets. "Setting up a pan-European market is an obvious requirement to attract with sufficient critical mass in one currency, the euro," says Paul Haycock, the British VC. "It is absolutely going to happen. It just hasn't happened yet."

While Europe slowly inches toward this next step in its economic integration, the creation of a pan-European stock exchange, various European nations have tried to cater to their own growth industries by creating exchanges modeled on the Nasdaq. In 1997, Germany launched the Neuer Markt as a vehicle that seemed ideal for high-tech and biotech start-ups. Unfortunately, the emergence of the Neuer Markt coincided with the rapid and unsustainable worldwide run-up in stock prices that accompanied the U.S. stock bubble of 2000. The prices of many Neuer Markt stocks collapsed in 2001, prompting calls for stricter regulation of insider trading, misleading statements, and other ills policed by the U.S. Securities and Exchange Commission. In September 2002, German stock governors said they would close the Neuer Markt.

The largest European biotech firms have also gone to the trouble of making their stocks available on one of the U.S. exchanges. As of May 2002, seven of the top ten European biotech firms, as ranked by market cap, had listings on either the Nasdaq or the NYSE (see page 208). These foreign companies want to build followings in the United States, and U.S. investors can buy them without having to deal with unfamiliar exchanges or encountering the currency conversion risks of buying abroad.

Eventually it may make sense for U.S. investors to own European biotech companies. Europe and the United States are roughly comparable in terms of demographics, standard of living, prescription drug consumption, and many other factors that make biotech investing sensible. Even if you never buy a European stock, however, chances are that some of your U.S. investments will have competitors in Europe. So whether you're simply keeping an eye on the competition, or seriously hunting for foreign stocks, here are two great resources to help you investigate biotech companies on the other side of the Atlantic:

- Corporate Information (www.corporateinformation.com) is a free site to help you research companies, develop industry profiles for a given country, or get capsule descriptions of the country's business climate and leading indicators.

- The *Financial Times* (www.ft.com) is a must-read for U.S. investors interested in European biotech. From its headquarters in London, the *FT* covers European business the way the *Wall Street Journal* covers business in the United States. In addition to news reports, its website provides free reports on stock markets, industry niches, and individual companies.

10

The Investment Frontier

We reach the final chapter of this investment guide, sobered by the realization that any such endpoint is necessarily artificial. Innovation continues relentlessly in every niche of the biotech industry as scientists and financiers devise new ways to apply the fundamental tools of gene splicing, molecular analysis, and protein synthesis. New companies and technologies creep toward commercialization. Some firms merge and grow, others disappear, and many players experience sudden disappointments or stunning successes that rewrite their fortunes overnight. Wall Street cycles through its fads. Biotech gets hot, then cool. Investments are also steered by more subtle trends. At one point, the prevailing wisdom might be to invest in companies that develop experimental medicines because, though they have longer time lines, they have the greatest profit potential. At other times, the investment winds shift and the "smart" money avoids drug developers, who take forever, and focuses instead on tool vendors, who can create markets without the need for regulatory approval. At still other times, a hybrid business model is in favor, a little bit of tool revenue to prime the pump, plus a pipeline of drugs in development for the bigger eventual payoff. And if such gyrations weren't enough to make an investor's head spin, greater market forces tug at biotech stocks the way the moon affects the tides. A bull market is almost a prerequisite for strong upward movement in biotech stocks. "The vast majority of (biotech) companies trade in sync with the Nasdaq," said Kris Jenner, manager of the T. Rowe Price Health Sciences Fund. "The reason has nothing to do with the biotech stocks. It has to do with the level of risk investors are willing to accept."

The Nasdaq is probably the best overall risk thermometer we have for biotech investing. When the Nasdaq is in decline, biotech usually slumps as well, and when the Nasdaq climbs, biotech also rises. Occasionally, the American Stock Exchange Biotech Index and the Nasdaq trade positions, and biotech stocks become more bullish. Investors are beginning to regard biotech firms, at least the large and profitable ones, as defensive and recession-proof investments, just like the drug companies—the theory being that sick people buy medicines even when consumers and corporations cut back on everything from cosmetics to computers. Thus, when high tech is particularly weak, biotech may perform better. For instance, biotech stocks bounced back faster after the September 11 terrorist attacks, on the strength of increased federal spending for bioterror countermeasures. For the most part, however, biotech stocks move in tandem with the high-tech sector, and the Nasdaq charts the pulse of technology.

In this chapter I want to remind you of the most important lessons that I've tried to communicate throughout the book and pull together the best tools and tips for identifying, evaluating, and investing in biotech companies. To do this, I'll study investment decisions from three different points of view. The first is to rely on the advice, suggestions, and rubrics of the money managers, analysts, and investment bankers who traffic in biotech shares on a daily basis and have the experience that is the hallmark of a professional. But I won't rely solely on such advice because there are vast differences between professional money managers and individual investors, beginning with the fact that managing biotech portfolios is the professional's full-time job. Professional biotech managers have other advantages. Most pros have advanced degrees in science, some are medical doctors, and virtually all of them have formal training as investment managers. They have access to infor-

Biotech Stock Index
Generally Mirrors the Nasdaq

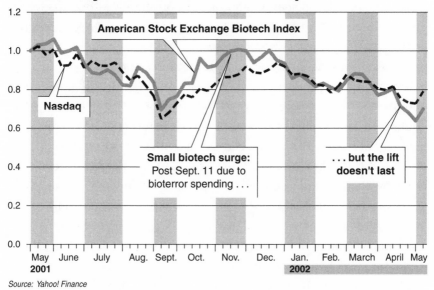

American Stock Exchange Biotech Index

Nasdaq

Small biotech surge:
Post Sept. 11 due to
bioterror spending . . .

. . . but the lift
doesn't last

May	June	July	Aug.	Sept.	Oct.	Nov.	Dec.	Jan.	Feb.	March	April	May

2001   2002

Source: Yahoo! Finance

---

mation you could never hope to approximate, including personal relationships or firsthand knowledge of many biotech executives. Before he started managing money for T. Rowe Price, for instance, Kris Jenner earned his M.D. from the Johns Hopkins School of Medicine and his Ph.D. in molecular biology from Oxford University. To tell you how Kris Jenner picks stocks and let it go at that would be like exhorting you to dunk like Michael Jordan.

For this reason, the second section of this chapter will focus on the tips, tricks, and hard-earned lessons of your peers—part-time investors, from a wide variety of backgrounds, who—like you, perhaps—have felt the lure of biotech's potential and learned to tolerate its risks. I'll tell you more about how I assembled this peer-group panel when I delve into their suggestions, but I think you'll find at least two significant rewards from this exercise. First, many of the experienced retail investors echo the same tips as the pros. It should make you feel better to realize that the advice I'll pass on in this chapter draws heavily from ordinary individuals who earned their degrees in biotech investing at the school of hard knocks. Second, and unsurprisingly, I got great suggestions for places to turn for cheap or low-cost research, and other guerrilla investing tips from folks who, like you, have limited time and budgets when it comes to investigating potential opportunities.

Finally, because every person's investment horizon is defined by their age and circumstances, I conclude this chapter with some recommendations for different types of investors. The retiree who is looking to inject a little excitement and yield into a portfolio has different goals than the middle-aged parent with one eye on the college fund and the other on Social Security. And neither of those viewpoints will make much sense to the young single person who may be fascinated with biotechnology, fearless when it comes to riding the investment roller coaster, and blessed with the prospect that, whatever may happen to biotech stocks or mutual funds in the short term, time will heal all wounds.

And that's the thought I want to leave you with as we begin this three-dimensional view of biotech investing, as seen by the pros, your peers, and personal circumstances. As you suffer the setbacks and disappointments that will be the inevitable side effects of biotech investing, take comfort from the knowledge that biotechnology is entering a long, steady boom, driven by two converging trends. The first is the aging of the population in the affluent, developed world, which creates a growing market for new medicines and diagnostic tests. The second trend is confidence that biotech companies, propelled by governmental investment in basic research and private backing for applied developments, are poised to deliver a steady stream of innovative products to address unmet medical needs. That is why biotech should be a core holding in any ambitious portfolio. Now that we've had our little pep talk, let's look at the particulars.

The Expert's Advice

I spoke to many professional money managers in the course of researching this book, but one episode exemplifies the pace, style, and stakes that influence the investment decisions of the pros. I had visited the offices of Kurt von Emster not long after he had taken over a $300 million biotech hedge fund. Prior to that, von Emster had spent eleven years managing life sciences mutual funds with peak assets in the neighborhood of $2 billion. Part of the reason von Emster decided to downsize the amount of money under his management was his belief that there is an inverse relationship between bigness and nimbleness (I'll have more to say about this later in the chapter when I discuss mutual funds). He's also convinced that biotech portfolios perform best when individual stocks are actively managed. That means, contrary to the standard advice that the best strategy is to buy and hold, von Emster argues—and not alone, mind you—that biotech is such a volatile field that you have to be ready to sell a stock you love when you think it's gotten overvalued, and then buy it back again when the herd of sellers seems to have trampled it to death. "Most investors think the only way to make money is to go long and hold, and that's just not so," he says, adding, "the trouble is the retail investor never sells." He jokingly suggests that a good biotech investment book would devote a whole chapter to selling. And while that might seem excessive, it's worth a good section to explain what he means.

In the purest sense stock prices are driven by information and perceptions. I'm not suggesting you need inside information to win, and neither is von Emster. That's not only illegal but, for the vast majority of investors, impractical. But it is possible, based upon good research and sound instincts, to have some insight before the rest of the market. For instance, when he and I spoke, von Emster had recently accumulated shares in a company that had a promising pipeline of experimental drugs in clinical trials. The stock had been beaten down because its lead medicine had experienced a setback with the FDA. But von Emster had decided—and this was a judgment and not a fact—that the setback would turn out to be a delay rather than a fatal flaw that would cause FDA disapproval. In the meantime, basic financial research showed that the firm in question was trading at something approaching its book value if it were liquidated. In other words, it had nearly as much in cash and cash equivalents on its balance sheet as its current market capitalization. To von Emster, this suggested two things: the company's stock was currently undervalued, and there was little downside risk in following his instincts on the FDA setback. The potential was virtually all on the upside.

In von Emster's opinion, this is the sort of insight that could occur to a retail investor who had taken the time to make him- or herself familiar with a company and its niche. But where the professionals and the amateurs part company, he says, is that the pros know that even when their insights are borne out, the market eventually corrects the undervaluation. At that point the value of the insight has been realized and the investment no longer makes sense. "Sometimes the opportunities are there and the retail investor can get access to good information and make good judgments," von Emster says. "But most retail investors don't realize that the value of that insight is transient. Once it's widely known, your advantage is gone." In short, the trick to successful biotech investing, in his view, is to set realistic expectations for what you expect to make when you buy a stock, and then have the discipline to sell and harvest the profit when you guess right. "It's relatively easy to make 10 percent," von Emster says. "It's difficult to make 50 percent."

The key is to realize the psychology behind his style of investing. Von Emster isn't falling in love with companies or technologies and deciding this is the next big thing. He is investing in situations where his analysis suggests there is an opportunity that the rest of the market hasn't yet realized, and setting firm benchmarks for selling based upon his estimates of the upside and downside potential. By the time the market has caught up—if, in fact, he has guessed correctly—he's ready to trim that holding and look around for another stock where his research suggests there is a similar combination of limited downside risk coupled with upside potential.

Obviously, such an approach involves a good deal of trading—more, perhaps, than is wise or practical for the average investor. When von Emster wants to sell, for instance, the trading specialist at his firm can execute the transaction faster than you can dial your broker or log on to your Internet account. And rather than seeing his profits get chewed up by commission charges, as is likely to happen to the retail investor who trades too frequently, von Emster does so much volume each year that he can often dicker over the price or terms of the trade, or get access to valuable research reports in exchange for his business. Nor do I mean to suggest that von Emster is continually on the prowl with every buck at his disposal. At the time we spoke, for instance, roughly 40 percent of his portfolio consisted of what he calls core holdings—companies that he has deemed have such solid prospects that he is comfortable with a buy-and-hold strategy for those issues. Of course that means up to 60 percent of his portfolio was being managed in short-term plays, where he hoped to pick up some incremental profit in a matter of weeks or months, based on some insight, instinct, or judgment.

We'll talk more about these aggressive strategies when we review what some of your peers have to say about their own experiences. But I can't emphasize enough that professionals truly *manage* the money under their control. I had some delightful lunches with Lissa Morgenthaler as she was finishing a successful stint at running the small but well-regarded Murphy New World Biotechnology Fund. Morgenthaler says she regularly parked money in cash accounts (the rules of her fund allowed this) when the biotech sector seemed to be in a tailspin. Making 2 percent on the money markets beat losing 10 or 15 percent in equities just because the Nasdaq was in a funk! Summer is her least favorite season for investing. Everything slows down. People delay surgeries. Regulators and investors take vacations. The market slips into the doldrums until the fall when there are more scientific conferences and the FDA tries to clear up its backlog of drug approvals. The resumption of normal activity in the fall tends to generate news, and the news generally rouses biotech stocks from their summer doldrums. This doesn't mean biotech stocks will always rise in the fall, or that a stock you buy after Labor Day will close higher by Christmas. Rather, other things being equal, market psychology generally favors a strong year-end finish for biotech. Professionals understand the market psychology and factor its vagaries into their decisions. As Morgenthaler puts it: "You're not just trying to pick the best biotech company, you're trying to predict what the herd will think is the best biotech company." In short, you want the herd to follow you.

You can begin to professionalize your own investment strategy by creating a system for evaluating new prospects. Analyst Winton Gibbons of Blair & Co. shared with me his partial checklist for assessing new investments. I modified it to incorporate advice from other quarters. Use this checklist as a starting point for your own research, and personalize it by creating your own system. If you're a paper person, designate a file folder for any new company of interest. Mark the date when you started tracking the stock, and what caught your attention in the first place. No system can guarantee success because investing is more art than science. You can follow all the steps in your checklist, and the stock market may still send you tumbling for a loss. But creating a system will help you avoid the errors that occur when you act impulsively, like jumping on a stock after the company has been puffed up in the media. That's herd investing. *You want to invest on the basis of some knowledge or insight that is ahead of the curve, not behind the headlines.*

With experience you'll start to see right through hype. When you read about some compound that "looks promising in preclinical [i.e., animal] studies," you will automatically translate this to mean "has not been tested on human beings and could be five to ten years from FDA approval." Seasoned investors generally don't put much stock in a novel therapy until after they've seen positive results from at least one Phase II trial. And they know that there's still plenty of downside risk even after a compound has gone through a successful Phase III trial and is being considered by an FDA advisory committee. Often, the safest and most sensible time to take a position in a company is *after* FDA approval, when the scientific and regulatory risks have been all but eliminated and you can make an investment based on firm, comparative metrics, including:

- Size of the market
- Nature of the competition
- Company's ability to make and sell the product
- Other developments in its pipeline, and their prospects for approval

226

Investment Checklist

Company/Ticker: _____ **Current Price:** _____ **Date:** _____

Reason for interest: _____

Financials
- Earnings: positive (or negative)
- Revenues (and revenue growth rate):
- Cash balance:
- Annual burn rate:
- Years of cash:

Products/Pipeline
- Marketed product(s):
  - Revenues, revenue growth, market share:
- Product(s) in development:
  - Status of clinical trials or FDA review for each:

Management
- Track record of key players:
- Team appropriate to stage of development (sales manager for marketed products, clinical director for trials):

Alliances and partnerships
- For each relationship note partner, goals, duration, revenue expectations:
- Past deal history:

Patents
- List key patents by number; read and evaluate strength of claims:
- Any litigation ongoing or likely:
- Any licensees (details of licenses):

Scientific variables
- Important publications:
- Key conferences, dates:
- Advisory board members:

Stock trends
- Market capitalization:
- 52-week high/low:
- Recent price trend (up, down, stalled):
- Analyst recommendations:
- Overall market (bullish/bearish):

Competition
- Key competitors (name/ticker):
- Market capitalization(s):
- Revenues/market share:
- Stock price(s) and direction:

Your thesis
- What you think will move the stock:
- Evidence to support premise:
- Target buy price:
- Investment expectation (are you buying to hold, and if so for how long?):
- Target sell price:

Action taken
- Buy, sell, or watch:
- Date:

Follow-up (lessons learned)
- 3 months:
- 6 months:
- 12 months:

The reason I've hammered home the point about selling and trading, and the transience of any good stock pick, is to help you understand how professionals view the market. Their investment style and goals fundamentally differ from yours. To the pros, stock picking is something of a game. That's not to mean they take their responsibility lightly. But pros try to remain emotionally detached from companies, technologies, even their own judgments. They try not to fall in love with their investments, because they may feel obliged to trim or liquidate a position in a great company in order to harvest profit, not because they've lost faith in the company, but because they think the herd has overvalued the stock and they see better places to put their money to work. Pros must have an aggressive stance toward money management because at the end of every year, their performance is rated and compared to similar funds. The name of the game is having the best yield. That forces the pros to keep one eye on that year-end tally when their wins and losses get locked in and their performance is judged. Individual investors shouldn't face the same year-end pressures, because their goals are presumably to grow income over time. But any investor interested in managing his or her money aggressively has to be willing to play the game the way the pros do. And even if you're not inclined to adopt an aggressive stance, those year-end reviews create swirls and eddies in the capital pond that can affect your investments.

The Veteran's (Peer's) Advice

Toward the end of the movie *Casablanca,* after Humphrey Bogart has shot the German officer and the gendarmes run up, seeking instructions, Claude Rains delivers one of cinema's most memorable lines. "Major Strasser has been shot," he says, and pauses before delivering the unforgettable kicker, "Round up the usual suspects." In writing this book, I didn't want to just round up the usual suspects, the professional, full-time investors. I wanted to round out your understanding of biotech investing by finding individual investors whose experiences might be relevant. Fortunately, I was able to round up such a group with the assistance of Biospace.com, a Web portal for a wide variety of biotech information and one of the sites featured in the resource guide in Appendix III. I created a brief survey form, which Biospace posted on its investor site for a few days, long enough for me to get 135 completed questionnaires—not a statistically valid sample by any stretch, but still a healthy helping of folks who were self-selected by what I considered to be the most desirable criteria—they were serious enough about their investments to make regular visits to a biotech portal. Here's what I found.

About two-thirds of the sample, or eighty-eight respondents in all, had been biotech investors for fewer than five years. Let's put that group of relative newcomers aside for a moment and focus on the other forty-seven respondents who turned out to have been biotech investors for a bit over eleven years on average. These were the folks I was most curious about, because they had survived at least a couple of bullish and bearish biotech markets. How had they managed their money? Well, most of these experienced investors (thirty-eight out of forty-seven) reported that they preferred to buy individual shares, while the remainder relied on mutual funds. For those who managed stocks the average portfolio consisted of fifteen separate issues. Of these forty-seven veteran investors, biotechnology represented about 40 percent of the average investment portfolio. And of course the key question is: How had these biotech investors done over time? The raw calculation showed an average return of 139 percent, but that number was inflated by a few respondents who claimed gains of between 500 and 2,000 percent. When I eliminated them from the mix, the average gain dropped to a more plausible, though still unreliable, 39 percent. The more solid, and still encouraging, figure was that after an average of eleven years, 87 percent of the sample, or forty-one of the forty-seven respondents, reported that they had positive yields. The other six persons in the sample reported an average loss of 24 percent.

It should come as no surprise that the vast majority of experienced investors reported strong gains. If biotech hadn't performed over time, they would have presumably moved on to some sector that did. Indeed, I found a much higher proportion of losing portfolios in the larger group of eighty-eight investors who averaged just over two years' biotech investing experience. Of this group, thirty-six persons, or roughly 41 percent of the sample, admitted that they were in the red—again it's a soft number, but the average loss was 25 percent. Despite the many losing portfolios, that still left nearly six out of ten novice investors ahead, with the overall gain averaging about 15 percent. New investors were far more likely than the veterans to rely on mutual funds. (About 30 percent of the new investors relied on mutuals versus 19 percent for the veterans.) Among those new investors who did pick individual stocks, the average portfolio held about twelve separate issues. Biotech represented 44 percent of all investments for the newcomer group, in line with how the veterans weighted biotech in their overall mix.

The survey asked each investor to share their top tips or lessons, advice they probably learned the hard way and would like to hand down to newcomers. I analyzed the two groups separately, beginning with the veterans, who had a lot more experience on which to base any opinions. The dominant theme among the veterans, expressed in a dozen different ways, boiled down to the same exhortation: Be patient. "Drugs take years to develop," wrote one seven-year veteran from Germantown, Pennsylvania. "Do your research, and understand the science and the people in the company." Another respondent from Vancouver, Canada, also with seven years' experience, wrote: "Nothing is fast in biotech. . . . Don't check the stock price every day, but every month look at the performance." One thirteen-year veteran from Valley Center, California, wrote: "Biotechs are long-term investments. Patience is the primary investor virtue." One person from San Francisco, California, added this practical research tip—if you're investing in a novel medicine, take the time to survey the physicians who would prescribe the medicine, even if that means cracking the phone book and cold calling doctors' offices. "Get as much information as you can from the end user [the decision maker] who will be purchasing or prescribing the company's product. What do they think? Is this a true breakthrough or hype? Are there any barriers to attaining market share? Would they invest?"

Patience was the most commonly urged virtue, but it wasn't the only one. Four other themes were each sounded by seven respondents:

- Harvest profits.
- Distrust analysts and brokers.
- Be a contrarian.
- Pick companies with experienced management and deep pipelines.

Several respondents seemed to have borrowed a page from the professional handbook—trim your holdings in successful stock picks and harvest the profits to offset the losses you're likely to experience elsewhere in your portfolio. "Set a price target at which you would be willing to sell at least half of your position and then stick to it," wrote one ten-year investor from Springfield, Ohio. An investor from Sarasota, Florida, wrote that his biggest mistake in twelve years of investing has been "not selling when the target price was met." A person from Brooklyn, New York, said eight years in biotech had taught him, "Sell when you profit, don't be greedy."

Although that sounds eerily like the experts' advice, these veteran retail investors seemed to distrust professionals. "Do not listen to brokers," wrote one eighteen-year veteran from Redwood City, California. "When it comes to biotech, they don't know their butt from a hot rock." Many veteran investors had apparently been misled more than once by rosy forecasts. "Wall Street does not know what it's talking about," said one investor from Wappinger's Falls in upstate New York. "Expect a lot of hype and volatility." One eighteen-year veteran from Felch, Michigan, said: "Do all of your own research. Never take any sell-side advice."

Other veterans suggested that the best biotech investing style was to be a contrarian, to buy when everyone else was selling and to sell when the herd was buying. "Look for the knee-jerk reaction either up or down, and go in the opposite direction," wrote an investor from San Diego, California, with eight years in the trenches. After investing in biotech for eighteen years, a writer from Arlington, Texas, said: "There are so many ups and downs in biotech, it almost always pays to wait until a down cycle or (negative) event" to buy shares in a company you believe is fundamentally sound.

The fourth strong theme running through the veteran suggestions was to focus on companies that had strong management and more than one product in development. "Ideally you want companies with a mix of Phase III and Phase II products," wrote an eight-year veteran from Empire, Michigan. Another investor, from Rancho Palos Verdes, California, wrote that after ten years he had decided only to buy the stocks of companies that have just had a new medicine approved by the FDA. He won't even consider early-stage companies in genomics or proteomics. One investor said that after fifteen years he had learned how to time his investments. "Follow a company that you think has a solid management and a good pipeline, wait for bad news in a down market, and then buy."

I noted two interesting differences when I analyzed the larger body of responses from the newer investors. The less experienced investors seemed more distrustful: of the media, the analysts, and even biotech companies. They were also disappointed they had not harvested some of the profits by trimming some holdings when biotech stocks were hot. The newer investors seemed less patient (only 17 percent of the sample), though I shouldn't overdramatize the differences between them and the veterans, because to some extent they're artificial. Having set up a series of categories to analyze the veteran responses, I forced the novice comments into the same groupings. Nevertheless, when I finished the tally, nearly half of the newcomers voiced one of two sentiments:

- Distrust of experts and the need to do independent research.
- Lament at their failure to sell off some of their winnings while the selling was good.

When you think about how the newer biotech investors received their baptism by fire, their relative lack of patience, their distrust of the so-called experts, and their second-guessing on their sell/hold decisions, all make perfect sense. Many of the newcomers were undoubtedly lured into biotech by the enormous publicity generated by the Human Genome Project and the stock bubble of 2000. When the inevitable correction occurred, there were a lot of unhappy campers who learned their lessons the hard way.

"Do not blindly invest in the hot companies that make nice stories in the media (i.e., stem cells, gene therapy)," wrote one biotech novice from St. Louis, Missouri. "Often these companies have an unproven technology, are years away from revenues, or have had their stocks run up to excessive levels." Another newcomer to biotech, who hailed from Indonesia, put it this way: "Don't trust anyone, especially start-up companies. Do your own due diligence, check and recheck that the company has the management that is capable of delivering the results. And don't fall in love with the company (wife is OK)."

Hand in hand with this distrust of analyst recommendations or media hype were comments like this comment from an investor hailing from Singapore: "Learn to be a disciplined seller. It's more important to tell yourself it's time to sell than to buy." An investor from Austin, Texas, said: "Set a sell price and stick to it in the event that the stock's value rises unreasonably high." A novice investor from Vienna, Virginia, elaborated on this theme. "When my stock was highly priced I was afraid to sell, worrying that it would [continue to] go up and I would be left out of further share price escalation. In nearly every case I should have sold at least part of my position at that point." A relatively new biotech investor from London offered this advice: "Don't be greedy. It's easy to make a moderate profit. But take [harvest] these profits because experience shows that you can buy the stock back at a lower price and probably do the same thing again."

Finally, although the newcomers evidenced less patience than the veterans, some were already learning that particular virtue. "Patience would seem to be the key," wrote an investor from Sydney, Australia. "Wait until the downside risk is very low on some rational basis (i.e., strong cash backing) and then purchase. Once you do purchase, be patient, very patient. If it doesn't get there, so be it."

The remaining themes, expressed in more or less equal weight by the remainder of the newcomers, included:

- High degree of risk involved in biotech investing
- Wisdom of following a contrarian strategy in timing sales and purchases
- Importance of picking companies with strong management and deep pipelines
- Need to diversify one's portfolio to diminish risk

Together these suggestions constitute a set of guiding principles that you'll have to apply according to your own circumstances, instincts, and inclinations. I'm not sure, for instance, how to reconcile the notion of being patient with the suggestion that you harvest profits. That balance will depend on how actively you choose to manage your money and how comfortable you are with trading. We'll talk more about some of these factors in the next section on personal investing styles.

I want to close this section on one point: What is the ideal size of the biotech stock portfolio? One thing we've all learned in life is not to put all our eggs in one basket. Given the average number of stocks people reported holding, it seems evident that most investors have taken this lesson to mean they should own a basket of stocks. But if you are just starting out, it would be foolish to go out and buy a basket of stocks, thinking that will spread out your risk. Your best overall risk reduction strategy is to know everything possible about the stocks you own, and there is a tension between having a large portfolio and having the time to study each holding. The stocks of small biotech companies are prone to sudden and catastrophic declines on bad news. A company that has a flop in a clinical trial or a rebuff by the FDA can lose 30 to 50 percent of its value overnight. Manage such risks by trying to avoid them. Small company stocks are always volatile, and they're especially so when a company is due to report clinical trial results, or when it's awaiting FDA action. If you own such a stock, and particularly if you've made money on it, consider harvesting profit and reducing your exposure in case the stock blows up. In fact, if you are risk averse, your best strategy could be to avoid early-stage companies entirely and invest only in profitable firms with multiple products on the market.

The bottom line is this: Never invest in more companies than you have time to exhaustively research. Let the size of your portfolio be determined by how much time you can devote to managing it.

Getting Personal

In the final analysis this book must be a guide to action, and that involves choosing which style of investing fits your inclinations and circumstances. Since I can't counsel you individually, let me do the next best thing, which is to take you through the chain of decisions that will help you begin your career in biotech investing or improve upon what you've already been doing.

The first decision, as I see it, is whether to invest in mutual funds, stocks, or some mix of the two. The most important variable in this decision must be an honest assessment of your ability and willingness to do the research essential to successful biotech stock ownership. Be honest. If you glossed over huge sections of this book and knotted your brows at my attempts to explain the science, you should probably invest in a mutual fund. Even if you grasped most of the concepts, but you're intimidated by the prospect of doing your own research, mutual funds are a perfectly respectable option. Remember, many of the new investors who responded to my survey, and a fair number of the biotech veterans, invest primarily or exclusively through mutual funds.

If you are considering mutual funds, here are some points to consider:

- A three- to five-year commitment should be a minimum. Even that is a short horizon because with a mutual fund, what you're buying is the ebb and flow of the industry.

When biotech is up, all the funds tend to be up, and when the sector is down, the reverse is true because all the managers are picking stocks from the same universe.

- Timing matters. The difference in performance between any two funds will probably be less important over the long run than when you put your money into the fund. So assess the general market conditions before you invest. The biotech cycle generally peaks every three to five years. The best time to buy into a fund is when biotech is out of favor. The worst time is when the sector is hot.

- Make whatever initial investment makes sense given your circumstances, and the market conditions at the time. Plan to add to your position on a regular basis, as if you were making a 401(k) contribution. If you get started when the sector is weak, don't lose faith if the fund sinks. The sector has always cycled back for those with the patience to wait. If you get in when biotech is hot, keep your contributions small until the prices collapse, then boost your regular contributions. This is supposed to be money you're not counting on for three to five years, or better yet, for ten to twenty years. Let the cycles work for you.

- As it approaches the time to redeem your investment, try to turn the tables and sell when biotech is hot and your fund has been fattened up by all those novices following the herd.

When it comes to picking funds, it's hard to beat the fund selector at Morningstar.com. Biotechnology funds are a subset of Morningstar's "Health" category. Some health funds—the term *Life Sciences* is also popular—also invest in large drug companies, HMOs, and hospital chains, in addition to biotech. The fund selector allows you to rate these funds on the basis of performance, annual costs, how long their managers have been on the job, the minimum initial investment, and whether they are load or no-load. Since you're making a minimum time commitment to the fund, don't be deterred from investing in a load-bearing fund just because it takes an initial bite. Sometimes the no-load funds have higher management fees and things tend to even out over a few years. The only other point worth mentioning is to think about whether you want to be part of a big fund that perhaps promises greater management stability, or a smaller fund that may be able to react more nimbly. But don't obsess about details. Pick a fund. Make a monthly investment plan and stick to it. Given enough time, you should do well.

If, on the other hand, you've been hankering to pick biotech stocks, let me suggest that your investment strategy should depend on a frank assessment of the following factors, taken together:

- Your age
- Your experience at buying and selling stocks
- Your familiarity with science or your willingness to learn it
- Your personality and objectives

Your age is the most important variable when it comes to managing money. Young people, or folks in the prime income-earning years, would seem well suited to becoming biotech investors because time is on their side. But I believe retirees could make good biotech investors because they have the time and motivation to study drugs and diseases. However, picking biotech stocks is risky at any age, so here's the prime directive to guide your investing. I'll call it Bernstein's Rule, because I heard it from Karen Bernstein, editor of *BioCentury,* the influential industry newsletter. The first time we met, several years ago, I asked her what advice she would give to prospective investors. She thought for a moment before she said: Don't invest any more money then you are prepared to lose.

So whether you're in your sixties or your forties or your twenties, realize that biotech stocks could be the riskiest part of your portfolio. Start cautiously. If you're just beginning, allocate no more than 5 to 10 percent of your total investments to biotech stocks, and don't go out and commit that money in a hurry. Remember, you don't buy *anything* until you've done your own research. If you enjoy the research process and do well at your initial investments, biotech should grow as a percentage of your portfolio over time. Ultimately a portfolio that is 20 percent biotech should be the upper limit. Although many of the veteran investors reported having a higher percentage of their overall holdings in biotech, at that level it seems to me that picking biotech stocks must have become their hobby. So unless you become an exceedingly good stock picker, or you just like the process, I don't think you want to be overexposed to the sector at any age.

Your experience at stock trading is important to anyone who wants to pick their own biotech portfolio. It isn't a prerequisite. But how much do you want to try learning at once? If you're a novice at buying and selling shares, and you're trying to crack one of the world's riskiest industries, you've compounded your challenges. You'll have to learn the tricks of the market at the same time as you're mastering the intricacies of biotechnology. If you are naïve to the ways of Wall Street, start with a mutual fund to become more familiar with biotech while you gradually learn your way around. You may also want to join an investment club (start your search at www.better-investing.org). On the other hand, you didn't learn to ride a bicycle by reading a book. You have to try it. So if you've never invested before, but you're drawn to biotech, don't let me squelch your enthusiasm. Just remember that when you learned to ride a bike, you started on training wheels. Make sure you heed Bernstein's Rule and invest only what you can afford to lose at first, and then gradually expand. You might start by picking one or two stocks a year. Over time your portfolio will grow, but never own more stocks than you have time to research. Investors who are already experienced at buying stocks should heed what the pros and your peers have said: Make sure you learn how to sell. If you've been a buy-and-hold investor, perhaps you want to become a buy, harvest, and hold investor. Anything you can do to improve your trading skills is going to give you an edge.

Your familiarity with science is a key variable for the biotech investor, and if you don't have a science background, you face a steep learning curve. Many of the people who responded to my survey had advanced degrees in biology, chemistry, or medicine. If you don't have a science background, do remedial education. Start by picking a specialty, whether it's a disease area or a tool market. Make it something that interests so that you won't mind reading about the topic in your spare time. Always start with what the company says about its technology. But don't stop there. Use your favorite Internet search engine to learn more. The Web is full of information about health and disease. We all know people who've contracted a disease, or have had a family member become ill, and suddenly they learn enough to converse with specialists and weigh treatment options. Investors should bring the same intensity to their biotech research as people trying to understand their own disease. If you already have a good science background, don't be lulled into a false sense of assurance. Biotech scientists are pretty smart folks, but they don't know in advance which experiments will succeed. Don't become so enamored with your logic that you lose sight of the risk. Buying on disappointing news may be the best way to use your scientific smarts. Uninformed investors tend to overreact to any bad news. If your research suggests a company has an approach that is based on sound science, and it's getting unfairly pounded in the market, that may be the time to take an informed risk and jump in. Buying stocks near the bottom of their fifty-two-week range helps minimize your downside.

Your personality and goals should be the most important variables in setting your investment strategy. Over the years I've heard many biotech investors—amateurs and pros alike—admit that one of the reasons they pick stocks is because they enjoy the process. The science is fascinating, the investment process is challenging, and there is a potential payoff in terms of profit as well as the satisfaction of helping to create new medical treatments. Professional money manager Lissa Morgenthaler put it this way: "The companies are fun and fascinating. It's an intellectual challenge. And you get to make money. It's an addictive combination." One retail investor from California who answered my survey admitted that she "collects biotech [stocks] as the amateur's way to stay current in this phase of science. It's a hobby for me and financial goals are secondary." This person reported that after thirteen years, the nine biotech stocks she owns make up about 60 percent of all her investments, and she reckons she's ahead about 25 percent. So biotech investing need not be an expensive form of bungee-cord jumping. There is a certain tension between becoming infatuated with biotechnology and being disciplined enough to regard individual stocks dispassionately. You need both the passion and the discipline. Let excitement and curiosity guide your research, and trust your logic and training in making decisions. The key to success in biotech investing is striking a balance between these two seemingly contradictory inclinations.

Afterword

It's time to put the lessons in this book to work in creating your own biotech investing program. Start by deciding whether you are a stock picker or a mutual fund investor, and determine how much you can afford to invest in money and time. To start out, be stingy with your money and generous with your time. Decide which niche or niches within the biotech industry seem most interesting and profitable to you. Specializing by disease is a strategy I've pushed because history shows that novel medicines are a good business, and because specialization by disease helps focus your research. Catalog your strengths and weaknesses as a potential investor. A science background and stock-picking experience are pluses. If you are not experienced in science or finance, create a plan to get up to speed, perhaps by taking night-school classes. Make a list of any friends or relatives who work in the medical profession, or at biotech firms, or who do academic research. They could serve as advisers or sounding boards to validate your investment ideas. Make a list of publications you should monitor and scientific gatherings you should track. Set aside time to come up with ideas and do research. Invest only when you feel as if you've done your homework.

To make money as a stock investor, you must anticipate where the market is going and get there first. You need ideas that are ahead of the curve. Having spent much of the book stressing the complexity and risks of biotech investing, you may need a confidence booster. And you deserve one. You are already ahead of the pack because you understand that biotech investing is a marathon and not a sprint, and you'll pace yourself accordingly. You will beat the herd simply by avoiding obvious pitfalls, like buying overhyped early-stage companies. You'll make fewer mistakes, and that's no small advantage in itself.

But you have also learned how to make good calls, by using the FDA regulatory process to screen out the wildly experimental compounds and focus instead on the companies that are about to cross the finish line with Phase III data, or an advisory panel endorsement, or, better yet, an FDA approval. You also understand the natural volatility of biotech stocks, and how to harvest profits when your good picks go up, instead of simply gripping the handrails and cursing when they enter the downside of their roller-coaster ride. And if your interests extend beyond medicine, you know how to explore biotech developments in agriculture, industrial processes, instrumentation, or software.

In becoming a biotech investor, you have tapped into a rich vein of need and innovation. The need arises from the expectation that the health care market will expand as the societies of the developed world grow older. The innovation flows from the confluence of government-sponsored academic research and private investment in product development. These are secular trends that show no sign of slackening. Success isn't guaranteed. Indeed, recent history shows just how violently and rapidly Wall Street can cycle from boom to bust. Stock prices sagged across the board in 2002 as investor confidence was undermined by allegations of corporate fraud at Enron, WorldCom, Arthur Andersen, and other firms. The biotech sector had its own scandal, as insider trading charges were leveled against former ImClone Systems chief executive Sam Waksal. The involvement of Martha Stewart in that affair guaranteed widespread media coverage of biotech's black eye.

The good news–bad news message of the market downturn is

that stock prices should eventually rebound, as they have in the past. But beware: simply because the market has corrected itself once doesn't mean it won't overheat and collapse again, at some point. Prosecutors may set a few examples, regulators may close a few loopholes, but some people—executives and investors alike—will be carried away by their own greed, duplicity, or wishful thinking.

It takes patience, research, and level-headed thinking to succeed as a biotech investor. By heeding the lessons and adopting the systems I've outlined here, you greatly improve your chances of profiting from the surge of biomedical invention that has been building for more than two decades, and which appears to have many decades more before it runs its course. So take a deep breath. The terrain is challenging, but time is on your side. Good luck in meeting your investment goals!

Appendix I

Public Biotechnology Firms

Company Name
TICKER – Mkt. Cap. 5-24-02
website

A

Aastrom Biosciences Inc.
ASTM—$22.7 million
www.aastrom.com

Abgenix Inc.
ABGX—$1.164 billion
www.abgenix.com

Able Laboratories Inc.
ABRX.OB—$65.4 million
www.ablelabs.com

Acambis plc
ACAM—$367.5 million
www.acambis.com

Access Pharmaceuticals
Inc.
AKC—$40.5 million
www.accesspharma.com

Aclara Biosciences Inc.
ACLA—$81.0 million
www.aclara.com

Actelion Ltd.
ALIOF.PK—n/a
www.actelion.com

Active Biotech
ACTBF.PK—n/a
www.activebiotech.com

Adherex Technologies
Inc.
ARXT.PK—n/a
www.adherex.com

Adolor Corp.
ADLR—$421.7 million
www.adolor.com

Advanced Magnetics Inc.
AVM—$26.0 million
www.advancedmagnetics.
com

Advanced Medical Solu-
tions
AMSJF.PK—n/a
Website n/a

Advanced Tissue Sciences
Inc.
ATIS—$157.3 million
www.advancedtissue.com

AeroGen Inc.
AEGN—$27.4 million
www.aerogen.com

AEterna Laboratories Inc.
AELA—$166.8 million
www.aeterna.com

Affymetrix Inc.
AFFX—$1.490 billion
www.affymetrix.com

Albany Molecular
Research Inc.
AMRI—$697.4 million
www.albmolecular.com

Alexion Pharmaceuticals
Inc.
ALXN – $295.7 million
www.alexionpharm.com

Alkermes Inc.
ALKS—$1.283 billion
www.alkermes.com

Alliance Pharmaceutical
ALLP—$31.7 million
www.allp.com

Allos Therapeutics Inc.
ALTH—$205.3 million
www.allos.com

Alltracel Pharmaceuticals
plc
APL—n/a
www.alltracel.com

AltaRex Corp.
ALXFF.PK—n/a
www.altarex.com

Alteon Inc.
ALT—$89.1 million
www.alteonpharma.com

Amarillo Biosciences Inc.
AMAR.OB—$4.0 million
www.amarbio.com

Amarin Corp. plc
AMRN—$59.0 million
www.amarincorp.com

American Biogenetic
Sciences Inc.
MABAA.OB—$4.0 million
www.mabxa.com

Amgen Inc.
AMGN—$52.687 billion
www.amgen.com

Amylin Pharmaceuticals
Inc.
AMLN—$723.7 million
www.amylin.com

Andrx Corp.
ADRX—$349.8 million
www.andrx.com

Angiotech Pharmaceuti-
cals Inc.
ANPI—$680.4 million
www.angiotech.com

Anika Therapeutics Inc.
ANIK—$10.9 million
www.anikatherapeutics.
com

AnorMED Inc.
AORMF.PK—n/a
www.anormed.com

Antares Pharma Inc.
ANTR—$31.1 million
www.antarespharma.com

Antex Biologics Inc.
ANX—$16.0 million
www.antexbiolgics.com

Antigenics Inc.
AGEN—$330.7 million
www.antigenics.com

Antisoma plc
ASM.L, AIOAF.PK—n/a
www.antisoma.com

AP Pharma Inc.
APPA—$46.2 million
www.appharma.com

Aphton Corp.
APHT—$175.9 million
www.aphton.com

Applied Biosystems
Group
ABI—$3.908 billion
www.appliedbiosystems.
com

Applied Molecular Evolu-
tion Inc.
AMEV—$143.5 million
www.amevolution.com

Aradigm Corp.
ARDM—$106.4 million
www.aradigm.com

Arena Pharmaceuticals
Inc.
ARNA—$204.4 million
www.arenapharm.com

Argonaut Technologies
Inc.
AGNT—$30.1 million
www.argotech.com

Ariad Pharmaceuticals
Inc.
ARIA—$142.6 million
www.ariad.com

Arius Research Inc.
YAR.V—n/a
www.ariusresearch.com

ArQule Inc.
ARQL—$172.9 million
www.arqule.com

Array BioPharma Inc.
ARRY—$283.8 million
www.arraybiopharma.com

AtheroGenics Inc.
AGIX—$195.6 million
www.atherogenics.com

Atlantic Technology
Ventures Inc.
ATLC.OB—$2.9 million
www.atlan.com

Atrix Laboratories Inc.
ATRX—$485.0 million
www.atrixlabs.com

AutoImmune Inc.
AIMM—$14.9 million
www.autoimmuneinc.com

Avanir Pharmaceuticals
AVN—$107.8 million
www.avanir.com

AVANT Immunotherapeu-
tics Inc.
AVAN—$76.2 million
www.avantimmune.com

AVAX Technologies Inc.
AVXT—$7.3 million
www.avax-tech.com

AVI BioPharma Inc.
AVII—$137.2 million
www.antivirals.com

Avigen Inc.
AVGN—$179.6 million
www.avigen.com

Axcan Pharma Inc.
AXCA—$575.4 million
www.axcan.com

Axis-Shield plc
ASD.L—n/a
www.axis-shield.com

Axonyx Inc.
AXYX—$53.5 million
www.axonyx.com

B

Bavarian Nordic A/S
BBVNKF.PK—n/a
www.bavarian-nordic.com

Biacore International AB
BCOR—$235.9 million
www.biacore.com

Biocompatibles Interna-
tional plc
BCTBF.PK—n/a
www.biocompatibles.com

BioCryst Pharmaceuticals
Inc.
BCRX—$60.8 million
www.biocryst.com

BioFocus plc
BIO.L—n/a
www.biofocus.com

BioGaia AB
BIOGb.ST—n/a
www.biogaia.com

Biogen Inc.
BGEN—$7.347 billion
www.biogen.com

Bioglan Pharmaceuticals
plc
BGPHF.PK—n/a
www.bioglan.com

BioInvent
BINV.ST—n/a
www.bioinvent.com

Bioject Medical Technolo-
gies Inc.
BJCT—$46.3 million
www.bioject.com

BioMarin Pharmaceutical
Inc.
BMRN—$329.9 million
www.biomarinpharm.com

Biomerica Inc.
BMRAC—$3.3 million
www.biomerica.com

Biomira Inc.
BIOM—$152.4 million
www.biomira.com

Bioniche Life Sciences
Inc.
BNHLF.PK—n/a
www.bioniche.com

Bionova Holding Corp.
BVA—$12.0 million
www.bionovaholding.com

BioPhausia AB
BIOPa.ST—n/a
www.biophausia.com

Biopure Corp.
BPUR—$211.5 million
www.biopure.com

Biora AB (Sweden)
BIORY.PK—n/a
www.biora.com

Biosearch Italia
BOSHF.PK—n/a
www.biosearch.it

Biosite Inc.
BSTE—$468.0 million
www.biosite.com

BioSource International
BIOI—$58.8 million
www.biosource.com

BioSpecifics
BSTC—$9.1 million
www.biospecifics.com

Biota Holdings Ltd.
BTAHY.PK—n/a
www.biota.com.au

Bio-Technology General
Corp.
BTGC—$303.3 million
www.btgc.com

BioTie Therapies Corp.
BTT1V, BORPF.PK—n/a
www.biotie.com

BioTime Inc.
BTX—$33.7 million
www.biotimeinc.com

Biotissue Inc.
BTSUF.PK—n/a
www.biotissue.com

Biotrace International plc
BEIOF.PK—n/a
www.biotrace.com

BioTransplant Inc.
BTRN—$67.7 million
www.biotransplant.com

Biovail Corp.
BVF—$5.312 billion
www.biovailpharm.com

Boston Life Sciences Inc.
BLSI—$32.4 million
www.bostonlifesciences.
com

British Biotech plc
BBIOY—$106.6 million
www.britbio.co.uk

C

Caliper Technologies
Corp.
CALP—$185.1 million
www.calipertech.com

Calypte Biomedical Corp.
CALY.OB—$5.0 million
www.calypte.com

Cambridge Antibody
Technology Group plc
CATG—$582.8 million
www.cambridgeantibody.
com

Cangene Corp.
CGNOF.PK—n/a
www.cangene.com

Carrington Laboratories
Inc.
CARN—$16.8 million
www.carringtonlabs.com

Celera Genomics
CRA—$965.4 million
www.celera.com

Celgene Corp.
CELG—$1.433 billion
www.celgene.com

Cell Genesys Inc.
CEGE—$499.0 million
www.cellgenesys.com

Cell Pathways Inc.
CLPA—$66.4 million
www.cellpathways.com

Cell Therapeutics Inc.
CTIC—$288.5 million
www.cticseattle.com

Cellegy Pharmaceuticals
Inc.
CLGY—$40.2 million
www.cellegy.com

Celltech Group plc
CLL—$5.454 billion
www.celltech.co.uk

Cel-Sci Corp.
CVM—$8.4 million
www.cel-sci.com

Celsis International plc
CEITF.PK—n/a
www.celsis.com

CeNeS Pharmaceuticals
plc
CPHAF.PK—n/a
www.cenes.com

Cephalon Inc.
CEPH—$3.052 billion
www.cephalon.com

Cepheid Inc.
CPHD—$130.9 million
www.cepheid.com

Cerep
CERF.LN—n/a
www.cerep.com

Cerus Corp.
CERS—$700.8 million
www.ceruscorp.com

Charles River Laborato-
ries International Inc.
CRL—$1.670 billion
www.criver.com

Chiron Corp.
CHIR—$7.068 billion
www.chiron.com

Cholestech Corp.
CTEC—$236.2 million
www.cholestech.com

Chromos Molecular Sys-
tems Inc.
CMLUF.PK—n/a
www.chromos.com

Cima Labs Inc.
CIMA—$393.5 million
www.cimalabs.com

Ciphergen Biosystems Inc.
CIPH—$123.7 million
www.ciphergen.com

Cohesion Technologies
Inc.
CSON—$21.8 million
www.cohesiontech.com

CollaGenex Pharmaceuti-
cals Inc.
CGPI—$105.6 million
www.collagenex.com

Collateral Therapeutics
Inc.
CLTX—$142.6 million
www.collateralthx.com

Columbia Laboratories
Inc.
COB—$152.8 million
www.columbialabs.com

Compugen Ltd.
CGEN—$62.4 million
www.cgen.com

ConjuChem Inc. (Canada)
CJHMF.PKCor—n/a
www.conjuchem.com

Connetics Corp.
CNCT—$383.7 million
www.connetics.com

Corixa Corp.
CRXA—$269.2 million
www.corixa.com

Cortech Inc.
CRTQ—$13.0 million
website—n/a

Cortex Pharmaceuticals
Inc.
COR—$36.7 million
www.cortexpharm.com

Corvas International Inc.
CVAS—$66.0 million
www.corvas.com

Crucell NV
CRXL—$164.6 million
www.crucell.com

Cubist Pharmaceuticals
Inc.
CBST—$420.6 million
www.cubist.com

CuraGen Corp.
CRGN—$401.8 million
www.curagen.com

Curasan AG
CURG.DE—n/a
www.curasan.com

Curative Health Services Inc.
CURE—$150.7 million
www.curative.com

Curis Inc.
CRIS—$48.8 million
www.curis.com

CV Therapeutics Inc.
CVTX—$581.4 million
www.cvt.com

Cyanotech Corp.
CYAN—$14.8 million
www.cyanotech.com

CyBio
CQJG.DE—n/a
website—n/a

Cygnus Inc.
CYGN—$126.4 million
www.cygn.com

Cypress Bioscience Inc.
CYPB—$14.0 million
www.cypressbio.com

Cytogen Corp.
CYTO—$104.8 million
www.cytogen.com

Cytomyx Holdings plc
CYX.L—n/a
www.cytomyx.com

Cytovax Biotechnologies Inc.
CXB.TO—n/a
www.cytovax.com

CytRx Corp.
CYTR—$9.9 million
www.cytrx.com

D

deCODE Genetics Inc.
DCGN—$226.5 million
www.decode.com

Deltagen Inc.
DGEN—$154.8 million
www.deltagen.com

Demegen Inc.
DBOT.OB—$3.1 million
www.demegen.com

Dendreon Corp.
DNDN—$87.4 million
www.dendreon.com

DepoMed Inc.
DMI—$60.1 million
www.depomedinc.com

Diacrin Inc.
DCRN—$30.9 million
www.diacrin.com

DiagnoCure Inc.
DGCR.PK—n/a
www.diagnocure.com

DIANON Systems Inc.
DIAN—$744.2 million
www.dianon.com

Digene Corp.
DIGE—$407.9 million
www.digene.com

Discovery Laboratories Inc.
DSCO—$46.9 million
www.discoverylabs.com

Discovery Partners International Inc.
DPII—$141.9 million
www.discoverypartners.com

Diversa Corp.
DVSA—$384.5 million
www.diversa.com

DOR BioPharma Inc.
DOR—$14.4 million
www.dorbiopharma.com

Draxis Health Inc.
DRAX—$115.3 million
www.draxis.com

Drew Scientific Group plc
DRW.L—n/a
website n/a

Drug Royalty
DGRYF.PK—n/a
www.drugroyalty.com

DURECT Corp.
DRRX—$373.0 million
www.durect.com

DUSA Pharmaceuticals Inc.
DUSA—$34.6 million
www.dusapharma.com

Dyax Corp.
DYAX—$82.7 million
www.dyax.com

E

Ecogen Biologia Molecular
EECN.PK—n/a
www.ecogen.com

Ecopia BioSciences Inc.
ECBI.PK—n/a
www.ecopiabio.com

EDEN Bioscience Corp.
EDEN—$55.9 million
www.edenbio.com

Elan Corp. plc
ELN—$3.277 billion
www.elan.ie

Elite Pharmaceuticals Inc.
ELI—$58.7 million
www.elitepharma.com

Embrex Inc.
EMBX—$186.5 million
www.embrex.com

Emisphere Technologies
Inc.
EMIS—$80.4 million
www.emisphere.com

Enchira Biotechnology
Corp.
ENBC—$872,000
www.enchira.com

EntreMed Inc.
ENMD—$135.7 million
www.entremed.com

Envirogen Inc.
ENVG—$4.0 million
www.envirogen.com

Enzo Biochem Inc.
ENZ—$528.9 million
www.enzo.com

Enzon Inc.
ENZN—$1.290 billion
www.enzon.com

Epimmune Inc.
EPMN—$28.0 million
www.epimmune.com

EPIX Medical Inc.
EPIX—$152.8 million
www.epixmed.com

Epoch Biosciences Inc.
EBIO—$45.2 million
www.epochpharm.com

Esperion Therapeutics
Inc.
ESPR—$143.3 million
www.esperion.com

Essential Therapeutics
Inc.
ETRX—$53.7 million
www.microcide.com

Evotec OAI
EVOT.PK—n/a
www.evotecoai.com

EXACT Sciences Corp.
EXAS—$260.7 million
www.exactlabs.com

eXegenics Inc.
EXEG—$16.0 million
www.exegenicsinc.com

Exelixis Inc.
EXEL—$434.9 million
www.exelixis.com

F

Flamel Technologies S.A.
FLML—$29.6 million
www.flamel-
technologies.fr

Forbes Medi-Tech Inc.
FMTI—$10.6 million
www.forbesmedi.com

Fulcrum Pharma plc
FUL.L—n/a
www.fulcrumpharma.com

G

GalaGen Inc.
GGENE.OB—$37,000
www.galagen.com

Galen Holdings plc
GALN—$1.421 billion
www.galenplc.com

Genaera Corp.
GENR—$81.9 million
www.genaera.com

Genaissance Pharmaceuticals Inc.
GNSC—$40.1 million
www.genaissance.com

Gene Logic Inc.
GLGC—$363.3 million
www.genelogic.com

Genelabs Technologies Inc.
GNLB—$34.9 million
www.genelabs.com

Genencor International Inc.
GCOR—$688.6 million
www.genencor.com

Genentech Inc.
DNA—$19.735 billion
www.gene.com

Generex Biotechnology Corp.
GNBT—$101.4 million
www.generex.com

Genescan Europe AG
GEPG.BE—n/a
www.genescan.com

Genetix Ltd.
GTX.L—n/a
www.genetix.com

Genetronics Biomedical Corp.
GEB—$19.2 million
www.genetronics.com

Genmab A/S (Denmark)
GEN.CO—n/a
www.genmab.com

Genome Therapeutics Corp.
GENE—$71.0 million
www.genomecorp.com

Genomic Solutions Inc.
GNSL—$24.3 million
www.genomicsolutions.com

Genomics One Corp. (Canada)
GNX.V—n/a
www.genomicsone.com

GenSci Regeneration Sciences Inc.
GNS.TO—n/a
website—n/a

Genset SA
GENXY—$24.8 million
www.genxy.com

Genstar Therapeutics Corp.
GNT—$15.4 million
www.genstartherapeutics.com

Genta Inc.
GNTA—$615.1 million
www.genta.com

GenVec Inc.
GNVC—$65.5 million
www.genvec.com

Genzyme Biosurgery
GZBX—$175.6 million
www.genzymebiosurgery.com

Genzyme General Division
GENZ—$7.108 billion
www.genzyme.com

Genzyme Molecular Oncology
GZMO—$46.2 million
www.genzyme.com/molecularoncology

Geron Corp.
GERN—$144.8 million
www.geron.com

Gilead Sciences Inc.
GILD—$7.219 billion
www.gilead.com

Gliatech Inc.
GLIA.OB—$387,000
www.gliatech.com

GLYCODesign Inc.
GD.TO—n/a
www.glycodesign.com

GlycoGenesys Inc.
GLGS—$43.4 million
www.glycogenesys.com

GPC Biotech AG
GPCG.DE—n/a
website—n/a

GTC Biotherapeutics
GZTC—$49.7 million
www.transgenics.com

Guilford Pharmaceuticals Inc.
GLFD—$188.8 million
www.guilfordpharm.com

GW Pharmaceuticals plc
GWPL—n/a
www.gwpharm.com

H

Haemacure Corp.
HAE.TO—n/a
www.haemacure.com

Harvard Bioscience Inc.
HBIO—$183.6 million
www.harvardbioscience.com

Helix Biopharma Corp.
HBP.TO—n/a
www.helixbiopharma.com

Hemagen Diagnostics Inc.
HMGN—$8.4 million
www.hemagen.com

Hemosol Inc.
HMSL—$107.4 million
www.hemosol.com

Heska Corp.
HSKA—$32.5 million
www.heska.com

Hollis-Eden Pharmaceuticals Inc.
HEPH—$79.9 million
www.holliseden.com

Human Genome Sciences Inc.
HGSI—$2.183 billion
www.hgsi.com

Hybridon Inc.
HYBN.OB—$52.6 million
www.hybridon.com

Hycor Biomedical Inc.
HYBD—$28.7 million
www.hycorbiomedical.com

Hyseq Inc.
HYSQ—$70.9 million
www.hyseq.com

I

Ibex Technologies Inc.
IBT.TO—n/a
website—n/a

ICOS Corp.
ICOS—$1.403 billion
www.icos.com

ID Biomedical Corp.
IDBE—$149.7 million
www.idbiomed.com

Idec Pharmaceuticals Corp.
IDPH—$6.765 billion
www.idecpharm.com

IDEXX Laboratories Inc.
IDXX—$1.056 billion
www.idexx.com

IGEN International Inc.
IGEN—$851.8 million
www.igen.com

ILEX Oncology Inc.
ILXO—$519.8 million
www.ilexonc.com

Illumina Inc.
ILMN—$205.3 million
www.illumina.com

ImClone Systems Inc.
IMCL—$781.3 million
www.imclone.com

Immtech International Inc.
IMMT—$33.0 million
www.immtech-international.com

ImmuCell Corp.
ICCC—$7.7 million
www.immucell.com

ImmuLogic Pharmaceutical Corp.
IMUL.OB—$652,000
website—n/a

Immune Response Corp.
IMNR—$14.2 million
www.imnr.com

Immunex Corp.
IMNX—$14.581 billion
www.immunex.com

ImmunoGen Inc.
IMGN—$185.9 million
www.immunogen.com

Immunomedics Inc.
IMMU—$626.7 million
www.immunomedics.com

Incara Pharmaceuticals
Corp.
INCR—$5.2 million
www.intercardia.com

Incyte Genomics Inc.
INCY—$518.2 million
www.incyte.com

Indevus Pharmaceuticals
Inc.
IDEV—$293.6 million
www.indevus.com

Inex Pharmaceuticals
Corp.
IEX.TO—n/a
www.inexpharm.com

Inflazyme Pharmaceuti-
cals Ltd.
IZP.TO—n/a
www.inflazyme.com

InforMax Inc.
INMX—$29.0 million
www.informaxinc.com

Inhale Therapeutic Sys-
tems Inc.
INHL—$406.3 million
www.inhale.com

InKine Pharmaceutical
Co. Inc.
INKP—$41.2 million
www.inkine.com

Innogenetics (Belgium)
INNX.BE—n/a
www.innogenetics.com

InSite Vision Inc.
ISV—$38.4 million
www.insitevision.com

Insmed Inc.
INSM—$62.7 million
www.insmed.com

Inspire Pharmaceuticals
Inc.
ISPH—$68.9 million
www.inspirepharm.com

Integra Life Sciences
Holdings Corp.
IART—$498.8 million
www.integra-ls.com

Interferon Sciences Inc.
IFSC.OB—$2.1 million
www.interferonsciences.
com

Interleukin Genetics Inc.
ILGN—$19.7 million
www.ilgenetics.com

InterMune Inc.
ITMN—$870.2 million
www.intermune.com

Intrabiotics Pharmaceuti-
cals Inc.
IBPI—$62.6 million
www.intrabiotics.com

Introgen Therapeutics
Inc.
INGN—$83.0 million
www.introgen.com

Invitrogen Corp.
IVGN—$1.866 billion
www.invitrogen.com

IOMED Inc.
IOX—$8.5 million
www.iomed.com

ISIS Pharmaceuticals Inc.
ISIS—$514.6 million
www.isip.com

IsoTis Tissue Engineers
(The Netherlands)
ISOT.AS—n/a
www.isotis.com

ISTA Pharmaceuticals Inc.
ISTA—$15.9 million
website—n/a

K

Karo Bio
KARO.ST—n/a
website—n/a

Keryx Biopharmaceuti-
cals
KERX—$53.1 million
www.keryx.com

KOS Pharmaceuticals Inc.
KOSP—$434.0 million
www.kospharm.com

Kosan Biosciences Inc.
KOSN—$221.4 million
www.kosan.com

KS Biomedix
LSB.L—n/a
www.ksbiomedix.com

L

La Jolla Pharmaceutical
Co.
LJPC—$240.0 million
www.ljpc.com

Labopharm Inc.
DDS.TO—n/a
www.labopharm.com

Large Scale Biology Corp.
LSBC—$40.7 million
www.lsbc.com

Lexicon Genetics Inc.
LEXG—$341.2 million
www.lexgen.com

Life Medical Sciences Inc.
CHAI.OB—$2.0 million
website—n/a

LifeCell Corp.
LIFC—$54.1 million
www.lifecell.com

Lifecore Biomedical Inc.
LCBM—$142.0 million
www.lifecore3.com

Ligand Pharmaceuticals
Inc.

LGND—$1.215 billion
www.ligand.com

LION Bioscience AG
LEON—$114.4 million
www.lionbioscience.com

Lorus Therapeutics Inc.
LORFF.OB—$67.4 million
www.lorusthera.com

Luminex Corp.
LMNX—$178.7 million
www.luminexcorp.com

Lynx Therapeutics Inc.
LYNX—$18.2 million
www.lynxgen.com

M

MacroChem Corp.
MCHM—$74.6 million
www.machrochem.com

Martek Biosciences Corp.
MATK—$532.1 million
www.martekbio.com

Matritech Inc.
NMPS—$90.8 million
www.matritech.com

Maxim Pharmaceuticals
Inc.
MAXM—$102.0 million
www.maxim.com

Maxygen Inc.
MAXY—$341.7 million
www.maxygen.com

Medarex Inc.
MEDX—$702.3 million
www.medarex.com

The Medicines Co.
MDCO—$297.3 million
www.themedecines
company.com

Medicis Pharmaceutical
Corp.
MRX—$1.497 billion
www.medicis.com

MediGene AG
MDGGn.DE—n/a
www.medigene.com

MedImmune Inc.
MEDI—$7.948 billion
www.medimmune.com

Medivir AB
MVIRb.ST—n/a
www.medivir.com

Meridian Bioscience Inc.
VIVO—$106.7 million
www.meridianbioscience.
com

MGI Pharma Inc.
MOGN—$175.6 million
www.mgipharma.com

Micrologix
MBI.TO—n/a
website—n/a

Millennium Pharmaceuti-
cals Inc.
MLNM—$4.688 billion
www.mlnm.com

Miravant Medical Tech-
nologies
MRVT—$15.1 million
www.miravant.com

ML Laboratories plc
MLB.L—n/a
www.mllabs.com

Modex
MODX.BE—n/a
website—n/a

Mologen Holding AG
(Germany)
MGNG.BE—n/a
www.mologen.com

MorphoSys AG (Germany)
MORG.DE—n/a
www.morphosys.com

MWG
NWUG.DE—n/a
website—n/a

Myriad Genetics Inc.
MYGN—$568.4 million
www.myriad.com

N

Nabi Biopharmaceuticals
NABI—$224.0 million
www.nabi.com

Nanogen Inc.
NGEN—$66.5 million
www.nanogen.com

NaPro BioTherapeutics
Inc.
NPRO—$211.1 million
www.naprobio.com

Nastech Pharmaceutical
Co. Inc.
NSTK—$160.9 million
www.nastech.com

Neogen Corp.
NEOG—$95.5 million
www.neogen.com

NeoPharm Inc.
NEOL—$206.6 million
website—n/a

Neoprobe Corp.
NEOPOB—$10.6 million
www.neoprobe.com

NeoRx Corp.
NERX—$65.2 million
www.neorx.com

Neose Technologies Inc.
NTEC—$165.7 million
www.neose.com

NeoTherapeutics Inc.
NEOT—$8.1 million
www.neotherapeutics.com

Neurobiological Technolo-
gies Inc.
NTII—$54.5 million
www.ntii.com

Neurochem Inc.
NRM.TO—n/a
www.neurochem.com

Neurocrine Biosciences
Inc.
NBIX—$1.069 billion
www.neurocrine.com

Neurogen Corp.
NRGN—$209.9 million
www.neurogen.com

NeuroSearch A/S
NEUS.CO—n/a
www.neurosearch.com

Nexell Therapeutics Inc.
NEXL—$1.3 million
www.nexellinc.com

NexMed Inc.
NEXM—$76.6 million
www.nexmed.com

NicOx S.A. (France)
NCOX.LN—n/a
www.nicox.com

Northfield Laboratories
Inc.
NFLD—$73.8 million
www.northfieldlabs.com

Northwest Biotherapeu-
tics
NWBT—$64.1 million
www.nwbio.com

Novavax Inc.
NVAX—$117.1 million
www.novavax.com

Noven Pharmaceuticals
Inc.
NOVN—$548.7 million
www.noven.com

Novogen Ltd.
NVGN—$147.2 million
www.novogen.com

Novuspharma SpA (Italy)
NVUSF.PK—n/a
www.novuspharma.com

NPS Pharmaceuticals Inc.
NPSP—$618.9 million
www.npsp.com

Nymox Pharmaceutical
Corp.
NYMX—$83.2 million
www.nymox.com

O

Oncolytics Biotech Inc.
ONCY—$30.9 million
www.oncolyticsbiotech.
com

Onyx Pharmaceuticals
Inc.
ONXX—$133.5 million
www.onyx-pharm.com

Ophidian Pharmaceuti-
cals Inc.
OPHD—$7.45 million
(2-1-02)
www.ophidian.com

OraPharma Inc.
OPHM—$48.3 million
www.orapharma.com

OraSure Technologies Inc.
OSUR – $250.3 million
www.orasure.com

Orchid Biosciences Inc.
ORCH—$97.6 million
www.orchid.com

Organogenesis Inc.
ORG—$25.7 million
www.organogenesis.com

Orphan Medical Inc.
ORPH—$111.2 million
www.orphan.com

Ortec International Inc.
ORTC—$28.9 million
www.ortecinternational.
com

OSI Pharmaceuticals Inc.
OSIP—$1.151 billion
www.osip.com

Ostex International Inc.
OSTX—$27.0 million
www.ostex.com

Oxford BioMedica
OXB.L—n/a
website—n/a

Oxford GlycoSciences plc
OGSI—$299.9 million
www.ogs.com

OXiGENE Inc.
OXGN—$24.3 million
www.oxigene.com

OXIS International Inc.
OXIS.OB—$2.5 million
www.oxis.com

P

Pain Therapeutics Inc.
PTIE—$241.3 million
www.paintrials.com

Paladin Labs Inc.
PLB.TO—n/a
www.paladinlabs.com

Palatin Technologies Inc.
PTN—$46.1 million
www.palatin.com

Paracelsian Inc.
PRLN.OB—$3.8 million
www.paracelsian.com

Paradigm Genetics Inc.
PDGM—$41.8 million
www.paragen.com

PAREXEL International
Corp.
PRXL—$333.8 million
www.parexel.com

Penwest Pharmaceuticals
Co.
PPCO—$288.3 million
www.penw.com

Peregrine Pharmaceuti-
cals Inc.
PPHM—$192.4 million
www.peregrineinc.com

PerkinElmer Inc.
PKI—$1.770 billion
www.perkinelmer.com

Pharmacopeia Inc.
PCOP—$249.9 million
www.pcop.com

Pharmacyclics Inc.
PCYC—$78.6 million
www.pcyc.com

Pharmagene plc (UK)
PGN.L—n/a
www.pharmagene.com

PharmaNetics Inc.
PHAR—$71.5 million
www.pharmanetics.com

PharmaPrint Inc.
PPRT.PK—n/a
website—n/a

Pharmexa A/S (Denmark)
PHARMX.CO—n/a
www.pharmexa.com

Pharming Group, NV (The
Netherlands)
PHGUF.PK—n/a
www.pharming.com

Pharmos Corp.
PARS—$64.5 million
www.pharmoscorp.com

Pharsight Corp.
PHST—$25.6 million
www.pharsight.com

PhotoCure ASA
PHCUF.PK—n/a
www.photocure.com

Phytopharm plc (UK)
PYM.L—n/a
www.phytopharm.com

PlasmaSelect AG (Ger-
many)
PSTG.BE—n/a
www.plasmaselect.com

Polydex Pharmaceuticals
Ltd.
POLXF—$9.1 million
www.polydex.com

PowderJect Pharmaceuti-
cals plc (UK)
PJP.L—n/a
www.powderject.com

POZEN Inc.
POZN—$151.9 million
www.pozen.com

PPL Therapeutics plc
PTH.L—n/a
website—n/a

Praecis Pharmaceuticals
Inc.
PRCS—$167.1 million
www.praecis.com

Prescient Neuropharma
Inc. (Canada)
PRE.V—n/a
www.prescientneurophar
ma.com

Procyon Biopharma Inc.
PBP.TO—n/a
www.proyonbiopharma.
com

ProCyte Corp.
PRCY.OB—$25.4 million
www.procyte.com

Profile Therapeutics plc
PTP.L—n/a
www.profiletherapeutics.
com

Progenics Pharmaceuti-
cals Inc.
PGNX—$176.0 million
www.progenics.com

Protein Design Labs Inc.
PDLI—$1.070 billion
www.pdl.com

Protein Polymer Tech-
nologies Inc.
PPTI.OB—$13.7 million
www.ppti.com

Protherics plc (UK)
PTI.L—n/a
www.protherics.com

Provalis plc
PVLS—$29.5 million
www.provalis.co.uk

Pyrosequencing AB (Sweden)
PYROa.ST—n/a
www.pyrosequencing.com

Q

Qiagen NV
QGENF—$2.168 billion
www.qiagen.com

QLT Inc.
QLTI—$811.1 million
www.qltinc.com

Questcor Pharmaceuticals Inc.
QSC—$62.3 million
www.questcor.com

Quidel Corp.
QDEL—$174.2 million
www.quidel.com

Quintiles Transnational Corp.
QTRN—$1.677 billion
www.quintiles.com

R

ReGen Therapeutics
pGT.L
RGT.L—n/a

Regeneron Pharmaceuticals Inc.
REGN—$755.2 million
www.regeneron.com

ReNeuron
REN.L—n/a

Repligen Corp.
RGEN—$75.2 million
www.repligen.com

Rhein
RNBT.DE—n/a

Ribozyme Pharmaceuticals Inc.
RZYM—$21.2 million
www.rpi.com

Rigel Pharmaceuticals Inc.
RIGL—$150.0 million
www.rigel.com

S

Salix Pharmaceuticals Ltd.
SLXP—$324.0 million
www.salixpharm.com

Sangamo Biosciences Inc.
SGMO—$147.0 million
www.sangamo.com

SangStat Medical Corp.
SANG—$571.1 million
www.sangstat.com

Sanochemia Pharmazeutica AG
SCPH.DE—n/a
www.sanochemia.com

SciClone Pharmaceuticals Inc.
SCLN—$129.1 million
www.sciclone.com

Scios Inc.
SCIO—$1.223 billion
www.sciosinc.com

Seattle Genetics Inc.
SGEN—$151.3 million
www.seattlegenetics.com

Select Therapeutics Inc.
XZL—$2.9 million
website—n/a

Senetek plc
SNTK—$53.1 million
www.senetekplc.com

Sepracor Inc.
SEPR—$1.066 billion
www.sepracor.com

Sepragen Corp.
SPGNA.OB—$3.4 million
www.sepragen.com

Sequenom Inc.
SQNM—$190.6 million
www.sequenom.com

Serologicals Corp.
SERO—$469.8 million
www.serologicals.com

Serono S.A. (Switzerland)
SRA—$35.550 billion
www.serono.com

Shaman Pharmaceuticals Inc.
SHPH.PK—n/a
website—n/a

Sheffield Pharmaceuticals
Inc.
SHM—$47.7 million
www.sheffieldpharm.com

Shire Pharmaceuticals
Group plc
SHPGY—$4.628 billion
www.shire.com

SignalGene Inc. (Canada)
SGI.TO—n/a
www.signalgene.com

SkyePharma plc
SKYE—$576.9 million
www.skyepharma.com

Sonus Pharmaceuticals
Inc.
SNUS—$46.3 million
www.sonuspharma.com

Spectral Diagnostics Inc.
DIAGF.PK—$20.4 million
www.spectraldiagnostics.
com

SpectRx Inc.
SPRX—$57.7 million
www.spectrx.com

SR Pharma plc
SPA.L—n/a
www.srpharma.com

StemCells Inc.
STEM—$43.9 million
www.stemcellsinc.com

Stressgen Biotechnologies
Corp.
SSB.TO—n/a
www.stressgen.com

SuperGen Inc.
SUPG—$166.3 million
www.supergen.com

Symyx Technologies Inc.
SMMX—$512.9 million
www.symyx.com

SYN-X Pharma Inc.
(Canada)
SYY.TO—n/a
www.synxpharma.com

Synaptic Pharmaceutical
Corp.
SNAP—$66.5 million
website—n/a

Synsorb Biotech Inc.
SYBBD—$4.0 million
www.synsorb.com

T

Tanox Inc.
TNOX—$532.3 million
www.tanox.com

Targeted Genetics Corp.
TGEN—$61.8 million
www.targen.com

TCPI Inc.
TCPI.PK—n/a
website—n/a

Tecan Group AG
TECZn.S—n/a
www.tecan.com

Techne Corp.
TECH—$1.300 billion
www.rndsystems.com

Telik Inc.
TELK—$345.2 million
www.telik.com

Tepnel Life Sciences plc
(UK)
TED.L—n/a
www.tepnel.com

Teva Pharmaceutical
Industries Ltd.
TEVA—$8.556 billion
www.tevapharm.com

Texas Biotechnology
Corp.
TXBI—$205.6 million
www.tbc.com

Theratase plc (UK)
THE.L—n/a
www.theratase.com

Theratechnologies Inc.
(Canada)
TH.TO—n/a
www.theratech.com

Third Wave Technologies
Inc.
TWTI—$113.1 million
www.twt.com

3-Dimensional Pharma-
ceuticals Inc.
DDDP—$128.6 million
www.3dp.com

Titan Pharmaceuticals
Inc.
TTP—$119.1 million
www.titanpharm.com

TM Bioscience Corp.
(Canada)
TMC.V—n/a
www.tmbioscience.com

Transgene SA (France)
TRGNY—$37.2 million
www.transgene.fr

Transgenomic Inc.
TBIO—$118.5 million
www.transgenomic.com

Transition Therapeutics
Inc. (Canada)
TTH.V—n/a
www.transitiontherapeutics.
com

Transkaryotic Therapies
Inc.
TKTX—$1.369 billion
www.tktx.com

TranXenoGen Inc.
TXN.L—n/a
www.tranxenogen.com

Triangle Pharmaceuticals
Inc.
VIRS—$244.4 million
www.tripharm.com

Trimeris Inc.
TRMS—$896.2 million
www.trimeris.com

Trinity Biotech plc
TRIB—$58.1 million
www.trinitybiotech.ie

Tripos Inc.
TRPS—$172.3 million
www.tripos.com

Tularik Inc.
TLRK—$474.2 million
www.tularik.com

U

Unigene Laboratories Inc.
UGNE.OB—$22.3 million
www.unigene.com

United Therapeutic Corp.
UTHR—$296.3 million
www.unither.com

V

V.I. Technologies Inc.
VITX—$79.6 million
www.vitechnologies.com

Valentis Inc.
VLTS—$66.2 million
www.valentis.com

Variagenics Inc.
VGNX—$35.4 million
www.variagenics.com

Vasogen Inc. (Canada)
MEW—$146.9 million
www.vasogen.com

VaxGen Inc.
VXGN—$116.6 million
www.vaxgen.com

Vernalis Group plc
VER.L—n/a
www.vernalis.com

Versicor Inc.
VERS—$338.9 million
www.versicor.com

Vertex Pharmaceuticals
Inc.
VRTX—$1.479 billion
www.vpharm.com

Vical Inc.
VICL—$146.8 million
www.vical.com

Vion Pharmaceuticals Inc.
VION—$54.0 million
www.vionpharm.com

Viragen Inc.
VRA—$79.0 million
www.viragen.com

ViroLogic Inc.
VLGC—$67.6 million
www.virologic.com

ViroPharma Inc.
VPHM—$48.4 million
www.viropharma.com

Visible Genetics Inc.
VGIN—$64.8 million
www.visgen.com

Viventia Biotech Inc.
VBI.TO—n/a
www.viventia.com

VIVUS Inc.
VVUS—$234.2 million
www.vivus.com

Vyrex Corp.
VYRX.OB—$2.6 million
www.vyrex.com

W

Weston Medical Group plc
WMG.L—n/a
www.weston-medical.com

Whatman plc
WHM.L—n/a
www.whatman.com

X

Xenova Group plc (UK)
XNVA—$118.6 million
www.senova.co.uk

XOMA Ltd.
XOMA—$340.4 million
www.xoma.com

XTL Biopharmaceuticals
Ltd. (Israel)
XTL.L—n/a
www.xtlbio.com

Xtrana Inc.
XTRN.OB—$5.0 million
www.xtrana.com

Z

Zonagen Inc.
ZONA—$19.3 million
www.zonagen.com

ZymoGenetics Inc.
ZGEN—$480.6 million
www.zymogenetics.com

ZymeTx Inc.
ZMTX.OB—$688,000
www.zymetx.com

Appendix II

Biotechnology Firms by Niche

ADMET

ArQule
Harvard Bioscience
Pharmagene

Agbio/Veterinary/ Environmental

Bionova Holding
Bioscan
Draxis Health
Ecogen Biologia Molecular
EcoScience
Eden Bioscience
Embrex
Envirogen
GlycoGenesys
Heska
IDEXX Labs
ImmuCell
Paradigm Genetics
Polydex Pharmaceuticals

Antibodies

Abgenix
BioInvent
Cambridge Antibody Technology
Crucelll
Dyax
Genmab
Medarex
MorphoSys
Protherics

Autoimmune/ Inflammation

Abgenix
Acambis
Access Pharmaceuticals
Active Biotech
Aeterna Labs
Alexion Pharmaceuticals
Angiotech Pharmaceuticals
Anika Therapeutics
AnorMED
Antigenics

AtheroGenics
AutoImmune
Avanir Pharmaceuticals
AVANT Immunotherapeutics
BioMarin Pharmaceutical
BioTie Therapies
BioTransplant
Boston Life Sciences
Cambridge Antibody Technology
Celltech
Connetics
Corixa
Cortech
Cypress Bioscience
Galen Holdings
Genelabs Technologies
Genmab
GLYCODesign
GPC Biotech
Hollis-Eden Pharmaceuticals
Human Genome Sciences
ICOS
Idec Pharmaceuticals

ImmuLogic Pharmaceutical
Immune Response
Inflazyme Pharmaceuticals
InKine Pharmaceutical
ISIS Pharmaceuticals
KS Biomedix
La Jolla Pharmaceutical
MGI Pharma
Millennium Pharmaceuticals
Nabi Pharmaceuticals
NicOx
Ophidian Pharmaceuticals
OXIS International
Paladin Labs
Pharmexa
Phytopharm
Protein Design Labs
Regeneron Pharmaceuticals
Salix Pharmaceuticals
Sepracor
SR Pharma
Tanox
Teva Pharmaceutical Industries
Texas Biotechnology
Transition Therapeutics
Tularik
Vasogen
Vertex Pharmaceuticals
Viragen
Xoma
XTL Biopharmaceuticals

Bioinformatics

Cerep
CyBio

deCODE
Discovery Partners
Gene Logic
Genomica
Incyte Genomics
InforMax
LION Bioscience
Mologen Holding
Pharmacopeia
Pharsight
Tripos

Biomanufacturing

GTC Therapeutics
Modex
Neose Technologies
Pharming Group
PPL Therapeutics
TranXenoGen

Biomaterial/Skin/ Wound

Advanced Medical Solutions
Advanced Tissue Sciences
Alltracel Pharmaceuticals
Anika Therapeutics
Biocompatibles International
Bioniche Life Sciences
BioPhausia AB
BioSpecifics
Biotissue
Carrington Labs
Co.don
Cohesion Technologies
Curasan
Curative Health Services
Curis
GenSci Regeneration Sciences

Genzyme Biosurgery
Gliatech
Haemacure
Human Genome Sciences
Ibex Technologies
Innogenetics
Integra Life Sciences Holdings
IsoTis Tissue Engineers
Life Medical Sciences
LifeCell
Lifecore Biomedical
Modex
Organogenesis
Ortec International
Procyon Biopharma
Procyte
Protein Polymer Technologies
Theratechnologies
V.I. Technologies

Biopharmaceuticals

Amgen
Biogen
Chiron
Genentech
Genzyme General
Immunex
Serono

Blood products/ substitutes

Alliance Pharmaceutical
Biopure
BioTime
Cerus
HemaCare
Hemasol
Northfield Labs
PlasmaSelect

Sonus Pharmaceuticals
V.I. Technologies
Whatman

Cancer

Abgenix
Access Pharmaceuticals
Adherex
Aeterna Labs
Allos Therapeutics
Alltracel Pharmaceuticals
AltaRex
Amarillo Biosciences
AnorMED
Antigenics
Antisoma
Aphton
Ariad Pharmaceuticals
Arius Research
AtheroGenics
AVAX Technologies
AVI BioPharma
BioCryst Pharmaceuticals
Biomira
BioTie Therapies
BioTransplant
Boston Life Sciences
British Biotech
Cel-Sci
Celgene
Cell Genesys
Cell Pathways
Cell Therapeutics
Celltech
Chiron
Corixa
Crucelll
Cytogen
Demegen
Dendreon
DiagnoCure

DOR BioPharma
DUSA Pharmaceuticals
EntreMed
Enzon
Epimmune
EXACT
eXegenics
Exelixis
Genaera
Genstar Therapeutics
Genta
GenVec
Genzyme Molecular
  Oncology
Geron
GLYCODesign
GlycoGenesys
GPC Biotech
Human Genome Sciences
Idec Pharmaceuticals
ILEX Oncology
ImClone Systems
ImmunoGen
Immunomedics
Inex Pharmaceuticals
InKine Pharmaceutical
Introgen Therapeutics
ISIS Pharmaceuticals
Keryx Biopharmaceuti-
  cals
Kosan Biosciences
KS Biomedix
Large Scale Biology
Ligand Pharmaceuticals
Lorus Therapeutics
Maxim Pharmaceuticals
Medarex
MediGene
MGI Pharma
Micrologix
Millennium Pharmaceuti-
  cals

Miravant Medical Tech-
  nologies
NaPro BioTherapeutics
NeoPharm
Neoprobe
NeoRx
Nexell Therapeutics
Novuspharma
Oncolytics Biotech
Onyx Pharmaceuticals
Orphan Medical
OSI Pharmaceuticals
Oxford BioMedica
Oxford GlycoSciences
OXiGENE
Peregrine Pharmaceuti-
  cals
Pharmacyclics
Pharmexa
PhotoCure
Phytopharm
Praecis Pharmaceuticals
Prescient Neuropharma
Procyon Biopharma
Progenics Pharmaceuti-
  cals
QLT
Repligen
Ribozyme Pharmaceuti-
  cals
SciClone Pharmaceuticals
Seattle Genetics
Select Therapeutics
Shire Pharmaceuticals
  Group
Stressgen Biotechnologies
SuperGen
Synsorb Biotech
Telik
Theratechnologies
Titan Pharmaceuticals
Valentis

Vertex Pharmaceuticals
Vical
Vion Pharmaceuticals
ViroLogic
Viventia Biotech
Xenova Group
XTL Biopharmaceuticals

Cardiovascular

Actelion
Alexion Pharmaceuticals
Allos Therapeutics
Alteon
American Biogenetic
  Sciences
AtheroGenics
Atlantic Technology
  Ventures
AVANT Immunotherapeu-
  tics
AVI BioPharma
BioCryst Pharmaceuticals
BioTie Therapies
Collateral Therapeutics
Corvas International
CV Therapeutics
Esperion Therapeutics
Forbes Medi-Tech
Galen Holdings
GenVec
GTC Therapeutics
Ibex Technologies
ICOS
Incara Pharmaceuticals
Indevus Pharmaceuticals
KOS Pharmaceuticals
The Medicines Co.
MediGene
NeoRx
Novogen
Pharmacyclics

Pharming Group
Protherics
Questcor Pharmaceuti-
  cals
Sangamo Biosciences
Scios
Texas Biotechnology
United Therapeutic
Valentis
Vasogen
Xenova Group

Chemistry

Albany Molecular
  Research
Argonaut Technologies
ArQule
Array BioPharma
BioFocus
Cerep
deCODE
Discovery Partners
Epoch Biosciences
Pharmacopeia
Symyx Technologies
3-Dimensional Pharma-
  ceuticals
Tripos

Combinatorial
biology

Applied Molecular Evolu-
  tion
Diversa
Maxygen

Computational
chemistry/biology

ArQule
Array BioPharma

Compugen
deCODE
Maxygen
Pharmacopeia
Protherics
3-Dimensional Pharma-
  ceuticals

Dental

Atrix Labs
Biora AB
CollaGenex Pharmaceuti-
  cals
OraPharma

Dermatology

Bioglan Pharmaceuticals
Cellegy Pharmaceuticals
Connetics
DUSA Pharmaceuticals
Medicis Pharmaeutical
OSI Pharmaceuticals
Paladin Labs
PhotoCure
Procyte
QLT

Diagnostics/Imaging

Advanced Magnetics
American Biogenetic
  Sciences
Axis-Shield
Biomerical
Biosite
BioSource International
Biotrace International
Calypte Biomedical
Celsis International
Cepheid
Cholestech

Cygnus
Cytogen
DiagnoCure
DIANON Systems
Digene
Draxis Health
Drew Scientific Group
Dyax
Enzo Biochem
EPIX Medical
EXACT Sciences
Genstar Therapeutics
Hemagen Diagnostics
Hycor Biomedical
ID Biomedical
IGEN International
Immunomedics
Innogenetics
Interleukin Genetics
Martek Biosciences
Matritech
Meridian Bioscience
Myriad Genetics
Neogen
Neoprobe
OraSure Technologies
Ostex International
Palatin Technologies
Paracelsian
PharmaNetics
Quidel
Spectral Diagnostics
SpectRx
SYN-X
TCPI
Tepnel Life Sciences
TM Bioscience
Trinity Biotech
ViroLogic
Xtrana

Drug delivery

Access Pharmaceuticals
Adherex
AeroGen
Alkermes
Alltracel Pharmaceuticals
Amarin
Andrx
Antares Pharma
AP Pharma
Aradigm
Atrix Labs
Bioject Medical Technolo-
  gies
BioSante
Cellegy Pharmaceuticals
Cima Labs
ConjuChem
Cygnus
DepoMed
DOR BioPharma
DURECT
Elan
Elite Pharmaceuticals
Emisphere Technologies
Enzon
Flamel Technologies
Galen Holdings
Generex Biotechnology
Genetronics Biomedical
Helix Biopharma
Inhale Therapeutic Sys-
  tems
IOMED
Labopharm
MacroChem
ML Labs
Nastech Pharmaceutical
NexMed
Novavax
november

Noven Pharmaceuticals
Penwest Pharmaceuticals
PowderJect Pharmaceuti-
  cals
Profile Therapeutics
Senetek
Sheffield Pharmaceuticals
SkyePharma
Sonus Pharmaceuticals
StemCells
Weston Medical Group

Functional genomics

Arena Pharmaceuticals
Cambridge Antibody
  Technology
CuraGen
Deltagen
Exelixis
Genencor International
Lexicon Genetics
Nanogen
Paradigm Genetics
Pharmagene
Rigel Pharmaceuticals
Sangamo Biosciences
SignalGene

Gene/Cell therapy

Aastrom
Atlantic Technology
  Ventures
AVI BioPharma
Avigen
Bavarian Nordic
Cell Genesys
Chromos Molecular Sys-
  tems
Collateral Therapeutics
Diacrin
Genstar Therapeutics

GenVec
Geron
Introgen Therapeutics
MediGene
Modex
Mologen Holding
Nexell Therapeutics
november
Oxford BioMedica
Targeted Genetics
Transgene
Transkaryotic Therapies
Valentis
Vical

Generics

Able Labs
Biovail
SuperGen
Teva Pharmaceutical
 Industries

Genomics

Arena Pharmaceuticals
Celera Genomics
CuraGen
Cytomyx Holdings
deCODE
Deltagen
Diversa
Ecopia BioSciences
Epoch Biosciences
Exelixis
Gene Logic
Genencor International
Genetix
Genome Therapeutics
Genomic Solutions
Genomica
Incyte Genomics
Karo Bio

Large Scale Biology
Lynx Therapeutics
Myriad Genetics
Sangamo Biosciences
SignalGene
TM Bioscience

Hematology

Ariad Pharmaceuticals
CytRx
Questcor Pharmaceuti-
 cals
Transkaryotic Therapies

High throughput screening

Array BioPharma
Cerep
CyBio
Cytomyx Holdings
Discovery Partners
Diversa
Ecopia BioSciences
Enchira Biotechnology
Maxygen
Sequenom
Symyx Technologies
3-Dimensional Pharma-
 ceuticals

Infectious diseases

Acambis
Active Biotech
Amarillo Biosciences
American Biogenetic
 Sciences
AnorMED
Antex Biologics
Antigenics
Avanir Pharmaceuticals

AVANT Immunotherapeu-
 tics
BioCryst Pharmaceuticals
BioSante
Biosearch Italia
Biota Holdings
Cangene
Cel-Sci
Cell Genesys
Corixa
Corvas International
Crucelll
Cubist Pharmaceuticals
Cytovax Biotechnologies
Demegen
Dendreon
Enzo Biochem
Enzon
Epimmune
Essential Therapeutics
eXegenics
Genaera
Gilead Sciences
GLYCODesign
GlycoGenesys
GPC Biotech
Hollis-Eden Pharmaceuti-
 cals
Hybridon
ID Biomedical
Immtech International
Immune Response
Immunomedics
Interferon Sciences
InterMune
Intrabiotics Pharmaceuti-
 cals
ISIS Pharmaceuticals
Kosan Biosciences
Maxim Pharmaceuticals
MedImmune
Medivir

Micrologix
Nabi Pharmaceuticals
NexMed
Ophidian Pharmaceuti-
 cals
Praecis Pharmaceuticals
Progenics Pharmaceuti-
 cals
Protein Design Labs
Provalis
Questcor Pharmaceuti-
 cals
Ribozyme Pharmaceuti-
 cals
Salix Pharmaceuticals
SciClone Pharmaceuticals
Stressgen Biotechnologies
Synsorb Biotech
Triangle Pharmaceuticals
Trimeris
Tularik
Unigene Labs
VaxGen
Versicor
Vertex Pharmaceuticals
Vical
Vion
Viragen
ViroLogic
ViroPharma
Viventia Biotech
Xoma
XTL Biopharmaceuticals
ZymeTx

Metabolic

Alteon
Amylin Pharmaceuticals
Axcan Pharma
Bio-Technology General
BioMarin Pharmaceutical

Cellegy Pharmaceuticals
Genset
Insmed
Karo Bio
Keryx Biopharmaceuti-
 cals
Ligand Pharmaceuticals
Neurocrine Biosciences
Neurogen
Noven Pharmaceuticals
NPS Pharmaceuticals
Orphan Medical
OSI Pharmaceuticals
Oxford Glycosciences
Pharming Group
Phytopharm
Provalis
Regeneron Pharmaceuti-
 cals
Synaptic Pharmaceutical
Telik
Transition Therapeutics
Transkaryotic Therapies
Tularik
Unigene Labs
Waratah

Microarrays

Affymetrix
Ciphergen Biosystems
Genomic Solutions
Hyseq
Illumina
Incyte Genomics
Nanogen
TM Bioscience

Microfluidics

Aclara Biosciences
Caliper Technologies
Cepheid

Evotec OAI

Musculoskeletal

Anika Therapeutics
Ariad Pharmaceuticals
Bioniche Life Sciences
GenSci Regeneration
 Sciences
InterMune
IsoTis Tissue Engineers

Neurological

Adolor
Arena Pharmaceuticals
Avanir Pharmaceuticals
Axonyx
Boston Life Sciences
Celgene
Celltech
CeNeS Pharmaceuticals
Cephalon
Cortex Pharmaceuticals
Curis
Diacrin
Elan
Genset
Guilford Pharmaceuticals
GW Pharmaceuticals
Indevus Pharmaceuticals
The Medicines Co.
NeoTherapeutics
Neurobiological Technolo-
 gies
Neurochem
Neurocrine Biosciences
Neurogen
NeuroSearch
NPS Pharmaceuticals
Nymox Pharmaceutical
OXIS International
Pain Therapeutics

Pharmos
POZEN
Praecis Pharmaceuticals
Prescient Neuropharma
ReGen Therapeutics
ReNeuron
Repligen
Scios
Sepracor
Shire Pharmaceuticals
  Group
StemCells
Synaptic Pharmaceutical
Titan Pharmaceuticals
Vernalis Group
Vyrex

Nutraceuticals

Carrington Labs
Cyanotech
Forbes Medi-Tech
GalaGen
Martek Biosciences
NutriPharma
Paradigm Genetics
PharmaPrint
Shaman Pharmaceuticals
Vyrex

Ophthalmic

Atlantic Technology
  Ventures
Bio-Technology General
InSite Vision
ISTA Pharmaceuticals
Miravant Medical Tech-
  nologies
Pharmacyclics
Pharmos
QLT

Pharmacogenetics

Cepheid
deCODE
Epoch Biosciences
Genaissance Pharmaceuti-
  cals
Genomica
Hyseq
Illumina
Orchid Biosciences
Sequenom
SignalGene
Third Wave Technologies
Variagenics

Proteomics

Celera Genomics
Ciphergen Biosystems
CuraGen
Cytogen
Cytomyx Holdings
deCODE
Enchira Biotechnology
Evotec OAI
Genencor International
Genetix
Incyte Genomics
Large Scale Biology
Lynx Therapeutics
Myriad Genetics
Oxford GlycoSciences

Pulmonary

Alliance Pharmaceutical
CytRx
Discovery Labs
Genaera
Inflazyme Pharmaceuti-
  cals

Inhale Therapeutic Sys-
  tems
Inspire Pharmaceuticals
InterMune
KOS Pharmaceuticals
PPL Therapeutics
SciClone Pharmaceuticals
Tanox
Targeted Genetics
Texas Biotechnology
Vyrex

Reproductive

Columbia Labs
ICOS
Ligand Pharmaceuticals
MacroChem
NexMed
Polydex Pharmaceuticals
VIVUS

Supply/Service

Albany Molecular
  Research
Applied Biosystems
Biacore
BioGaia AB
Charles River Labs Inter-
  national
Cyanotech
Fulcrum Pharma
Genescan Europe
Genetix
Genomic Solutions
Genomics One
Harvard Bioscience
Invitrogen
Luminex
Martek Biosciences
ML Labs
MWG

Parexel International
PerkinElmer
Pyrosequencing
Qiagen
Quintiles Transnational
Rhein
Sepragen
Serologicals
Tecan Group
Techne
Theratase
Transgenomic

Visible Genetics
Whatman

Transplant

Alexion Pharmaceuticals
BioTransplant
MedImmune
Protein Design Labs
Repligen
SangStat Medical
TranXenoGen

Urological

Bioniche Life Sciences
Curis
Paladin Labs
Senetek
Sepracor
Unigene Labs
VIVUS
Zonagen

Appendix III

Research Resources

FREE SERVICES

Many websites offer financial or biotech industry information, and they are a great way to become familiar with the sector. Some of the free sites may move to paid basis over time, or put certain services on a subscription footing.

Biotech Industry Research

BIO.COM: Offers news, analysis, stock information, and other services including a list of helpful links to scientific journals (a great way to scan for titles that might be unique to companies or niches of interest). (www.bio.com)

BIOSPACE: An excellent portal site that provides summaries of press releases, clinical trials info, investor chat rooms, job postings, and a wealth of other information. Bookmark it. (www.biospace.com)

BIOTECHNOLOGY INDUSTRY ORGANIZATION: As the trade organization of the industry, BIO provides education, advocacy, investor information, and legislative updates affecting biotech firms. (www.bio.org)

PHARMACEUTICAL RESEARCH AND MANUFACTURERS OF AMERICA: PhRMA represents the large drug companies. It provides lobbying and public information services similar to those described for BIO. In addition, PhRMA puts out periodic reviews of different disease niches that are very helpful to investors (click on "Search for Cures" on the home page). (www.phrma.org)

SIGNALS MAGAZINE: A web-based publication that does in-depth features about industry trends. The searchable archive is a great way to get insightful overviews on topics of interest. The magazine is an offshoot of Recombinant Capital. (www.signalsmag.com)

Financial and Stock Market Research

BIGCHARTS.COM: Offers free financial tracking and charting information. (www.bigcharts.com)

MARKETWATCH.COM: A general-interest financial website with strong biotech coverage. Use it for news, stock quotes, and a general sense of market direction. (www.marketwatch.com)

WHISPERNUMBER.COM AND EARNINGSWHISPERS.COM: Focus on events that will move stocks. Track earnings reports, news, rumors, and IPOs. A variety of free and paid services. (www.whispernumber.com or www.earningswhispers.com)

YAHOO! FINANCE: A mainstay research tool that provides quotes, news, research, and some analysis. (http://finance.yahoo.com)

Government and Regulatory Research

NATIONAL INSTITUTES OF HEALTH: The NIH is a network of twenty-seven separate institutes that fund an enormous array of medical research. Use it to find experts and technology overviews on research niches. (www.nih.gov)

SECURITIES & EXCHANGE COMMISSION: The SEC regulates publicly held firms. The most useful ongoing service of the SEC is the EDGAR database, which provides free access to annual and quarterly reports and other filings. (www.sec.gov)

U.S. FOOD & DRUG ADMINISTRATION: The sections on drugs and biologics will be of greatest interest to investors. Check the FDA website for details of advisory panel meetings, and for the full presentations made by company scientists and FDA staffers. FDA also offers free e-mail alerts on a variety of topics. (www.fda.gov)

U.S. PATENT & TRADEMARK OFFICE: Provides online access to patents and patent application. (www.uspto.gov)

PAID SERVICES

There are several excellent newsletters that track industry happenings, including the progress of clinical trials. Annual subscription fees exceed $1,000, so if these are too much for your budget, perhaps you can find a business library that subscribes.

BIOCENTURY: A weekly report supplemented by daily headlines of developments in the United States and Europe. Limited free services include a list of links to other resources.(www.biocentury.com)

BIOWORLD: A daily biotech news report supplemented by various financial and clinical-trials databases. (www.bioworld.com)

RECOMBINANT CAPITAL: Tracks deals, alliances, clinical trials, revenues, and other factors affecting biotech and drug companies. Some free services. (www.recap.com)

WINDHOVER INFORMATION: Publishes a variety of newsletters on health care industry deals and financings, mostly on a subscription basis, but there is a good deal of free information as well. (www.windhover.com)

Acknowledgments

A great many people contributed to the completion of this book, many of whom I have already named in the text. Some people, however, asked not to be quoted or supported my work in other ways that deserve recognition. First of all thanks to agent Robert Shepard and editors David Sobel and Robin Dennis of Henry Holt & Co., who brought me this project. Artist Joe Shoulak turned my scribbles into graphics. My editors at the *San Francisco Chronicle,* notably Marcus Chan and Ken Howe, tolerated my hectic schedule as the book neared deadline. My family was similarly forgiving of the many hours I spent glued to my desk, and helped in various ways: Aeneas made me take play breaks; Julius maintained our home network; and Mia, well, she's long been my toughest editor and biggest fan.

In my earliest research, Brook Byers of the venture capital firm Kleiner, Perkins, Caufield & Byers, sketched out a history of the different biotech clusters and introduced me to many of the key players across the nation. Bill Rastetter, chief executive of IDEC Pharmaceuticals, and Howard Birndorf, chairman of Nanogen Inc., painted a portrait of biotech in San Diego. Fred Cutler, director of UCSD Connect, San Diego's well-regarded economic development organization, was also helpful in understanding what made his and other clusters click.

Ruth Gordon, president of the Washington Biotechnology & Biomedical Association, played a similar role in explaining Seattle's biotech industry. Ed Fritzky, former chief executive of Immunex, and Steve Gillis, chief executive of Corixa Corp., provided the industry perspective.

Mark Skaletsky, chairman of Essential Therapeutics; Henri Termeer, chief executive of Genzyme; and Peter Feinstein of BioVentures Investors, all helped bring me into the Massachusetts biotech scene. Tony Evnin of Venrock Associates provided background from his many years as a biotech venture capitalist.

Steve Burrill of Burrill & Company was enormously helpful, not just by introducing me to biotech leaders in Europe but also by giving me a key insight into how to organize this book. Chad Floe of Lehman Brothers in London and Anders Hove of the Bellevue Group in Zurich both provided background on European biotech, as did Joern Aldag, chief executive of Evotec OAI in Hamburg.

Michael Sterns, formerly of Biospace, put together a worldwide panel of biotech investors. Photographer Gary Fong tried to make me look like an author.

There is a much larger universe of people who have been regular sources in my daily coverage of the biotech industry, and it is only through their patient instruction that I have had the background to complete this book. I cannot hope to name them all, but a few demand special recognition.

David Flores, publisher of *BioCentury,* and Don Johnston, publisher of *BioWorld,* have long given me free access to their publications, which continue to be the bedrock of my understanding of the industry. In addition, Flores allowed me to use, in Appendix II, *BioCentury*'s lists of public biotech firms and their niches. Scott Morrison at Ernst & Young has always helped me see the big picture. On the financial front, Tom Dietz at Pacific Growth Equities, Franklin Berger at J.P. Morgan H&Q, Rod Ferguson at J.P. Morgan Partners, and Jim McCamant of the Medical Technology Stock Letter have always been ready to take my frantic phone calls. Thanks as well to Cindy Robbins-Roth, who has taken me and many other biotech reporters under her wing over her many years as an industry observer.

Finally, I am sure that between the time of my writing and your reading, many things will probably have changed. Companies will merge or disappear, executives will change jobs, drugs in development will get approved or fail. The biotech industry is not a static target. For all the shortcomings of this work I take full responsibility. My hope is that the lessons of caution and the guidelines for research that I have tried to get across will enable you to write your own successful chapter in biotech investing.

Index

GMOs (genetically modified organisms)
(*cont.*)
safety of, 122–23, 125–27
techniques, 123–29
GNSC (Genaissance Pharmaceuticals Inc.), 66
GNVC (GenVec Inc.), 185
goals, investment strategy and, 239–40
Golden rice technology, 128
Gottlieb, Scott, 189
government research resources, 272–73
GRAS (generally recognized as safe)
principle, 126
"green shoe" allotment, defined, 95–96
GTC Biotherapeutics (GTCB), 161–62
Gyros AB, 109

Harvard Bioscience Inc. (HBIO), 59–60
Haseltine, Dr. William, 53–54, 167, 205
Haycock, Paul, 208–10
HBIO (Harvard Bioscience Inc.), 59–60
health funds, 236–37
hematology niche, biotech firms, 266
hemophilia research, 182, 184
hepatitis B vaccine, 13
Herceptin
development of, 21
FDA approval of, 29
herd investing, defined, 226
hGC (human chorionic gonadotropin), 33
HGSI. *See* Human Genome Sciences (HGSI)
high throughput screening niche, biotech
firms, 266
Hoechst, 207
Hood, Leroy, 204
human antibodies, 30
human chorionic gonadotropin (hGC), 33
human genome, 8
Human Genome Project
human proteome compared to, 84–85
launching of, 8
propelling biotech boom, 47
understanding, 50–53
Human Genome Sciences (HGSI)
alliance of, 167
Maryland biotech cluster and, 205
overview of, 53–54
human proteome, defining, 84–85
Hunkapiller, Mike, 56
Hybrigenics, 89
Hyseq Inc. (HYSQ)
microarrays and, 102–3
overview of, 57–58

ICAAC (Interscience Conference on
Antimicrobial Agents and
Chemotherapy), 190–91
ICOS Corp. (ICOS), 57
IDEC Pharmaceuticals (IDPH)
anticancer antibodies, 29–30
biotech clusters and, 203
Illumina Inc. (ILMN)
overview of, 103
pharmacognetic technology, 66
imaging niche, biotech firms, 264–65

ImClone Systems
alliance of, 167
anticancer antibodies, 31–32
Immerge BioTherapeutics, 187–88
immune system rejection research, 180
Immunex, 118, 203
income, tracking genomic companies, 70
Incyte Genomics (INCY)
microarrays and, 102
overview of, 56–57
industrial biotechnology, 147–68
analyzing alliances, 163–68
giants of, 149–56
overview of, 147–49
start-ups, 156–59
from transgenic animals/plants, 159–63
infectious diseases
biotech firms, 266–67
overview of, 189–91
inflammation niche, biotech firms,
261–62
INGN (Introgen Therapeutics), 185
Inhale Therapeutic Systems (INHL), 44
initial public offerings. *See* IPOs (initial
public offerings)
Innovase LLC, 158
insect resistance, 132–33
The Institute for Genomics Research
(TIGR), 56, 205
instrument makers, proteomics, 78–83
insulin, bioengineered
discovering, 7
Genentech producing, 10
Integrilin, 55, 118
Intel network, 20
InterMune (ITMN), 157
International Service for the Acquisition of
Agri-Biotech Applications (ISAAA),
131–32
Interscience Conference on Antimicrobial
Agents and Chemotherapy (ICAAC),
190–91
Introgen Therapeutics (INGN), 185
investment advice, from professionals,
222–28
creating checklists, 226–27
money management, 225–26, 228
overview of, 220–21
selling and trading, 223–25, 228
veteran investors' distrust of, 231–33
investment advice, from veterans, 228–35
be a contrarian, 231–32, 234
distrust professionals, 231–33
how to diminish risk, 234–35
invest in strong management companies,
232
overview of, 221
portfolios, 229–30, 234–35
researching end user information, 230
selling and trading, 231–33
virtue of patience, 230, 232–33
investment fundamentals
clinical trials process, 13–17
DNA structure discovery, 1–2

About the Author

Award-winning journalist Tom Abate is one of the nation's most influential observers of the biotechnology industry. Technology, biotechnology, and health care reporter for the *San Francisco Chronicle* since 1997, Tom writes the widely quoted "BioScope" column from the biotech industry's home city of San Francisco. Prior to covering biotechnology, Abate was a reporter and columnist covering the high-tech industries of Silicon Valley. Previously a science and technology writer for the *San Francisco Examiner,* he has also written for *The Scientist, BioScience, The Oregonian,* the *Detroit News,* the *Christian Science Monitor,* and others. Originally a New Yorker, he and his wife live in the San Francisco Bay area.